PHILOSOPHICAL MEDICAL ETHICS:
ITS NATURE AND SIGNIFICANCE

PHILOSOPHY AND MEDICINE

Editors:

H. TRISTRAM ENGELHARDT, JR.
University of Texas Medical Branch, Galveston, Tex., U.S.A.

STUART F. SPICKER
University of Connecticut Health Center, Farmington, Conn., U.S.A.

VOLUME 3

PHILOSOPHICAL MEDICAL ETHICS: ITS NATURE AND SIGNIFICANCE

PROCEEDINGS OF THE THIRD TRANS-DISCIPLINARY SYMPOSIUM
ON PHILOSOPHY AND MEDICINE
HELD AT FARMINGTON, CONNECTICUT, DECEMBER 11–13, 1975

Edited by

STUART F. SPICKER

University of Connecticut Health Center, Farmington, Conn., U.S.A.

and

H. TRISTRAM ENGELHARDT, JR.

University of Texas Medical Branch, Galveston, Tex., U.S.A.

D. REIDEL PUBLISHING COMPANY

DORDRECHT-HOLLAND / BOSTON-U.S.A.

Library of Congress Cataloging in Publication Data

Trans-disciplinary Symposium on Philosophy and Medicine,
    3d, Farmington, Conn., 1975.
    Philosophical medical ethics, its nature and significance.

    (Philosophy and medicine ; v. 3)
    Includes bibliographical references and index.
    1.   Medical ethics — Congresses.   I.   Spicker,
Stuart F., 1937—   II.   Engelhardt, Hugo Tristram,
1941—   III.   Title.
R724.T65   1975   174'.2   76—57992
ISBN 90—277—0772—3

Published by D. Reidel Publishing Company,
P.O.Box 17, Dordrecht, Holland

Sold and distributed in the U.S.A., Canada, and Mexico
by D. Reidel Publishing Company, Inc.
Lincoln Building, 160 Old Derby Street, Hingham,
Mass. 02043, U.S.A.

Printed in The Netherlands

TABLE OF CONTENTS

TABLE OF CONTENTS

SECTION IV / CHANGING HUMAN NATURE: MEDICINE IN THE SERVICE OF VIRTUE

SECTION V / METAPHYSICS AND MEDICAL ETHICS

SECTION VI / MORAL AGENTS IN MEDICINE

SECTION VII / THE PHYSICIAN AS MORAL AGENT

PROLOGUE

It is a pleasure and honor for me to welcome this distinguished group to the Third Trans-Disciplinary Symposium on Philosophy and Medicine held at the University of Connecticut Health Center.

The title of the symposium is an important one: 'Philosophical Medical Ethics: Its Nature and Significance.' We are all increasingly aware of the ethical component in medical care, of how ethical decisions must be made at every step, not only in clinical work, but also in medical education. Our critics tell us that medicine, as it has moved from empiricism to science, has become somehow less humane. Philosophy, the liberal arts, should have much to say to us about this; this conference will hopefully be another strand in the links being forged between the two cultures.

I wish you well in your deliberations here and success in all your good efforts to help philosophy and medicine to understand that both are parts of the unity of human knowledge, and that they will continue to profit, as they have in the past, from each other's insights. Both come together easily if our overriding concern is always the good of the individual human being.

ROBERT U. MASSEY
Dean, School of Medicine
The University of Connecticut
Health Center
Farmington, Connecticut

S. F. Spicker and H. T. Engelhardt, Jr. (eds.), Philosophical Medical Ethics: Its Nature and Significance, 1. *All Rights Reserved. Copyright © 1977 by D. Reidel Publishing Company, Dordrecht-Holland.*

INTRODUCTION TO MEDICAL ETHICS

> Medicina autem in philosophia non fundata, res infirmata est.
>
> Francis Bacon ([5])

The last two decades have seen an explosion of interest transforming the field of medical ethics. The term itself is, as readers in the field know, an ambiguous one. Medical ethics arises in part from concerns by physicians with etiquette. In this regard, American thought has a heavy indebtedness to Thomas Percival's *Medical Ethics* [27] as well as to codes such as the first adopted by the American Medical Association in May 1847 [1]. Such concerns with etiquette can be traced to the very beginnings of Western medicine in the Corpus Hippocraticum in such works as *On Decorum* and *The Physician*. The roots arise as well from the soil of theological and religious concerns about the practices of sterilization, contraception, abortion, euthanasia, etc. And discussions of a legal and political nature can be traced from the Code of Hammurabi [21] to modern medical licensure and medicare legislation [33].

In the presence of impassioned discussion reflecting the concerns of religion, law, and etiquette, the contributions to be made by philosophy are often obscured. One may forget that philosophy's concerns with medicine are nearly as old as philosophy itself. Both Plato and Aristotle often used examples bearing on the practice of medicine and the character of the physician. Plato, in fact, spoke as clearly as any contemporary writer to the question of the proper conduct of physicians in the practice of medicine in a lovely description of those physicians who treat their patients as free men, as persons, by supporting free and informed consent, and those physicians who treat their patients as slaves, as objects.

Athenian: ... You agree that there are those two types of so-called physicians?
Clinias: Certainly I do.
Athenian: Now have you observed that, as there are slaves as well as free men among the patients of your community, the slaves, to speak generally, are treated by slaves, who pay them a hurried visit, or receive them in dispensaries? A physician of this kind never gives a servant any account of his complaint, nor asks him for any; he gives him some empirical injunction with an air of finished knowledge, in the brusque fashion of a dictator, and then is off in hot haste to the next ailing servant — that is how he lightens his master's medical labors for him. The free practitioner, who, for the most part, attends free men, treats their disease by going into things thoroughly from the beginning

S. F. Spicker and H. T. Engelhardt, Jr. (eds.), Philosophical Medical Ethics: Its Nature and Significance, 3–17. All Rights Reserved. Copyright © 1977 by D. Reidel Publishing Company, Dordrecht-Holland.

in a scientific way, and takes the patient and his family into his confidence. Thus he learns something from the sufferer, and at the same time instructs the invalid to the best of his power. He does not give his prescriptions until he has won the patient's support, and when he has done so, he steadily aims at producing complete restoration to health by persuading the sufferer into compliance (*Laws* 4.720 b—e, [28]).

This passage shows the perennial nature of the problems of treating the patient as a person. It shows as well the historical depth of philosophical interest in medicine.

The history of philosophy includes more reflections upon medical ethics than the casual reader might suspect. Many of these reflections are pertinent to contemporary issues such as abortion and population control. Plato, for example, recommends abortion in cases of incest (*Republic* 5.461c); and Aristotle argues for letting seriously deformed children die, while forbidding infanticide as a means of population control, suggesting instead the use of early abortions. 'As to the exposure in rearing of children, let there be a law that no *deformed* child shall live, but that on the ground of an *excess* in the number of children . . . let abortion be procured before sense and life have begun; what may or may not be lawfully done in these cases depends on the question of life and sensation' (*Politics VII*, 16,335 b20—26, [4]). It is worth noting that this passage not only reflects an age-old concern over the ethics of the treatment of deformed children and the morality of abortion; the passage on abortion also influenced subsequent thought concerning abortion, including that of St. Thomas Aquinas. St. Thomas, like most medieval thinkers, distinguished between the morality of early and late abortions [2], finding the former to be a lesser sin than the latter which was considered to be murder — a distinction borrowed in part from Aristotle ([3]).

Thus, philosophers have since the time of the Greeks addressed issues in medical ethics. Some, such as St. Thomas Aquinas in his reflections concerning contraception, have had a continued major impact on the character of medical care. Others, such as Seneca and Hume who wrote on suicide [32, 16] or Hegel who reflected on death and disease [7], have been less influential. In any event, it has not been until recently that a wide range of issues has been drawn together under the rubric of medical ethics, and has become as such a concern for philosophers. A sustained focus on philosophical issues in patient care, experimentation, abortion, the definition of death, or a sustained analysis of the language of rights to health care is of very recent origin. This is not to deny the existence of an important and large body of literature in the natural law tradition bearing on the issues of sterilization, contraception, and abortion [25, 26]. Such discussions, though often developed in a language theoretically neutral to religious appeals, were usually set in the framework of particular religious communities [18, 19]. In fact, the major modern focus upon medical ethics has been drawn from religious communities and from the works of theologians such as Joseph Fletcher [11], James Gustafson [14], Paul Ramsey [30, 31], Harmon Smith [34], and Kenneth Vaux [36], to name only a few.

Medical ethics as a focus of philosophical concern in part reflects the increasingly secular character of our society and the recognition that the discussion of such important issues in a pluralistic society requires an appeal beyond the claims of any particular religious community to basic conceptual and ethical issues. Indeed, one of philosophy's signal contributions is that of providing the logic and method for an ethical pluralism. By engaging in an analysis of the meaning and significance of the claims which can be made concerning the rightness or wrongness, value or disvalue of particular kinds of medical practice, philosophy appeals to general conceptual considerations. It involves a commitment to reasoning in terms of rules of inference and by means of advancing truth claims open to general examination and agreement. As a result, around the public discussion of policies of health care and medical practice there has developed a philosophical literature examining conceptual and operational definitions of death [17, 23], the meaning of the concept of person and its bearing on the morality of abortion [35], analyses of the extent to which there is a moral difference between active and passive euthanasia [29], and inquiries concerning the status of claims to a right of free and informed consent in human experimentation and treatment [13].

These discussions have proceeded at various levels. Some have been very immediately concerned with issues of policy [24]. Others have provided analyses concerning the nature and structure of arguments in the debate concerning particular medical ethical issues [8, 9]. Many of these discussions have led to the refinement of distinctions important for ethics in general [6]. These have included assessments of the validity of natural law arguments (which have implications beyond the issues of sterilization and contraception) [10], and analyses of the ways one should balance interests in goals such as scientific progress with responsibility to respect persons (e.g., rights to free and informed consent) [12]. The latter have included discussions of the right of citizens to be secure from the general hazards of scientific investigation (e.g., research with recombinant D.N.A.) [20]. That is, broader appreciation of the risks involved in certain lines of scientific research and questions of public accountability of scientists have also been explored, leading to expanded concepts of responsibility.

In many respects, the analysis addressed to the character and validity of arguments in medical ethics is more important than the consideration of immediate policy issues. It lays the foundations in terms of which issues of policy can be discussed and resolved. Questions of policy presuppose basic ethical premises concerning the nature and relative merit of human values, the claims of persons to be respected independently of their value for others, the ways in which arguments about the morality of actions can be decided by appeals to facts or norms in nature, and the validity of criteria to identify the presence or absence of persons (e.g., criteria for death), to name only a few issues. Such basic concerns about the nature of values, the status of rights and duties, and the nature of persons are required if anything more than superficial answers are to be given to the pressing policy questions that medicine and the biomedical sciences raise.

The selection of papers in this volume is meant to offer analyses of ethical issues basic to medicine and the biomedical sciences. These papers represent the edited versions of presentations given as a part of the Third Disciplinary Symposium on Philosophy and Medicine, 'Medical Ethics: Its Nature and Significance,' which was held at the University of Connecticut Health Center, December 11, 12, and 13, 1975. This symposium, like the previous ones in the series, brought together physicians, philosophers, and other humanists to address conceptual issues in medicine. The result is a series of explorations ranging from the history of medical ethics to the role of the physician as a moral agent.

The 'Opening Remarks' by Chester R. Burns indicate some of the historical and conceptual roots of the current ambiguity in our use of the term 'medical ethics'. As he shows, a part of the ambiguity is rooted in the wide scope of the terms 'moral,' 'morality,' or 'ethics.' For the American physician of the nineteenth century, medical ethics was in great part identified with the Christian religion or the canons of deportment associated with 'better breeding' — a sensitivity inspired by ideals of education in the classics. These sentiments were not, as the material cited by Burns indicates, easily reconciled. Though individuals spoke of the importance of a good general, indeed classical education, such renowned physicians as Benjamin Rush warned against education in moral philosophy because of its origin in pagan schools likely to erode the proper moral sensitivities of the Christian physician. In this sense, Benjamin Rush was at least in part correct — philosophy has as one of its central aims a search for rational grounds and appeals for action beyond the ethos of any particular religious or cultural group. As a consequence, one is forced to distinguish at least five different senses of medical ethics — medical ethics as [1] a body of professional etiquette, (2) a reflection of the generally accepted ethos or mores of the community, (3) particular religious commitments or sentiments, (4) canons of conduct incorporated into law, and (5) philosophical medical ethics which has its focus on appeals to general reasons for and against particular lines of conduct. It is this last sense which is our concern here.

Albert R. Jonsen, for example, examines the maxim *primum non nocere* as a point of departure for considering how to balance the goods and evils to which medicine may expose patients. He begins by tracing the maxim from its origin in the Hippocratic text *Epidemics* through Galen to the present, and then he proceeds to the construction of four types of usages to which the maxim might be put. In terms of those types, moral action in medicine can be seen, so he argues, as (1) a moral enterprise, an attempt to alleviate the distress and debilities in the lives of fellow humans out of concern for the good of those humans (i.e., out of concern to avoid harm to them), (2) a commitment to giving due care as (avoiding harm through) the maintenance and improvement of medical knowledge and skills in diagnosis and treatment, (3) a judicious appeal to risk—benefit ratios in choices by physicians of those procedures with the best chance of success and the lowest risk of harm in terms of the risk—budget which fits the life-style of the patient involved, and (4) the development of a benefit—detriment equation, where 'do no harm' comes to mean inflict no harm not associated with a compensating benefit (i.e., always assess treatment in terms of its effect upon the quality of the patient involved). Using this four-theme analysis of 'do no harm,' Jonsen turns to considerations of those occasions when doing no harm would lead one to allowing the death of a patient for the good of the patient.

In commentary upon Jonsen's paper, Louis Lasagna takes the meaning of the maxim 'do no harm' to enjoin optimizing treatment. In addition he argues that thinking of medicine as a moral enterprise over-dramatizes the function of the physician. Moreover, he questions how avoiding harm is to be reconciled with the extensive federal regulations concerning the testing of drugs — rules which may delay for American patients the benefits of drugs already approved in other countries. Or how is the physician to balance a paternalistic concern not to harm the patient with the knowledge that fully informed consent may frighten patients away from treatment they need? For all these issues, he finds answers within a clearly recognized context of pluralism and fallibilism.

Richard M. Hare brings the sobering warning that these pressing issues are to be resolved only through careful analysis of the arguments involved. Philosophers can help individuals concerned with the problems of medical ethics by making them attend more carefully to their reasoning. For example, terms such as 'human being,' 'kill,' and so forth must be subjected to an analysis that displays their various meanings in different arguments. Philosophers can, in short, offer canons for valid argument that can lead to greater clarity in the resolution of problems. Hare illustrates this with a comparison of absolutist and utilitarian approaches to exception-making in considerations of euthanasia and of the different work done by moral principles in circumstances in which one is deciding on the general rules which physicians should follow. In these explorations Hare follows a predominantly utilitarian mode of analysis.

In contrast, James Rachels, commenting on Hare's paper, raises a series of objections against purely utilitarian analyses of medical ethical issues, holding that Hare's universal prescriptivism (deciding that an action is not moral if it fails to pass the test of being universalized) is a better test of the morality of actions than is an appeal to a utilitarian calculus, Rachels focuses as well on the rules one should have concerning euthanasia, the slippery slope argument, and the practice of exception-making. Rachels distinguishes between those slippery slope arguments which (1) hold that once one accepts acts of a certain type as moral, one is then logically committed to accepting others as moral (which one would not in fact want to accept as moral), and (2) those slippery slope arguments that contend that accepting one type of action as moral will in fact lead people to engage in actions which are immoral, though not at all logically connected with the first type of action. Against the background of these distinctions Rachels argues that we can indeed properly recognize certain forms of euthanasia as justified. Further preserving life or honoring the sanctity of life has its proper moral sense, so Rachels argues, in terms of preserving the life of an entity that is still a subject (capable of some level of sentience). Moreover, in dealing with human subjects, he holds that the central issue should be consent.

The issue of euthanasia is further examined in the papers by Marvin Kohl and John Troyer. Kohl argues forthrightly for voluntary beneficent euthanasia, including the use of 'living wills' and the death of comatose individuals and infants under this rubric. His argument is that persons lack good grounds for constraining individuals faced with pain and suffering in a terminal state from receiving assistance in ending their lives as quickly and as painlessly as possible. Kohl argues to this conclusion from a general consideration of rights, and in particular claims to a right to life. Kohl concludes that 'the right to life' identifies an entitlement: (1) to the bare minimum one needs for continued life (provided this does not violate anyone else's similar rights, and that resources are available towards this end, and that proper consideration is given to those cases where those in need of care are so due to their own fault or are in some special sense enemies); (2) to be protected against unjust assault, or interference with one's vital interests as long as such protection involves no more than the minimally necessary force. Kohl sees this notion of a right to life as fully compatible with the provision of voluntary beneficent euthanasia. It is interesting to note that his argument for voluntary beneficent euthanasia includes as well an argument for a general right to health care.

Troyer argues that Kohl's contentions concerning euthanasia all hinge upon the moral permissibility of suicide, and that since Kohl does not attend to this issue, his principal claims concerning euthanasia fail. In his paper, John Troyer analyzes difficulties attendant to talking about rights, while defending the concept of rights against a more rhetorical interpretation by Kohl. In fact, Troyer argues that we do indeed have natural rights, but that these are at best *prima facie* rights. With respect to euthanasia, Troyer holds that it is best to begin by considering the right to commit suicide and then to proceed to an argument for a limited right to euthanasia as an extension of the right to suicide. In this regard, John Troyer is much more sanguine about the first step of the argument than about the second. Although Troyer feels less sure of the moral permissibility of euthanasia than he does of the moral permissibility of suicide, he argues that it is perhaps best not to have laws forbidding voluntary beneficent euthanasia. But one must be clear as to what one will include within the term 'voluntary beneficent euthanasia.' As John Troyer indicates, Marvin Kohl's concept of voluntary beneficent euthanasia includes cases where proxy consent is required and actual (direct) permission of the patient involved is not possible, as well as individuals in coma concerning whom it is difficult to understand how continued existence is an injury (except perhaps to their estate, etc.). Whatever arguments there might be for killing such individuals, Troyer concludes that in the first case they are not voluntary, and in the second case they are not clearly kind or merciful. Thus, we are pressed to engage in a careful balancing of various goods and values, as well as reconciling such calculi of goods and values with our respect of the freedom of others. Moreover, our interests in achieving goals, as well as respecting persons, must be achieved in terms of the very practical need to develop general rules for conduct.

Considerations similar to those raised with respect to euthanasia arise with regard to moral problems in the use of human subjects for purposes of research. And, as Sidney Morgenbesser indicates, such issues cannot be

adequately explored without addressing the broad issues in political philosophy — what he refers to as the macro aspects of medical experimentation.
These are basic issues concerning the institutional arrangement of state
interests and the interests of the medical profession, drug companies,
patients, and citizens in general. In the main, though, Morgenbesser addresses
the micro issues. In particular he accents the issue of consent which he takes
to be central in a way that obviates many of the problems of drawing lines
between treatment and research — both require the informed permission of
the patient or subject.

He further argues that special safeguards in research should be maintained
and in fact enlarged — for example, so that new forms of surgery, like new
drugs, should require formal review and assessment of their risks versus their
benefits. Further, the general function and possible benefit of review
committees is considered, with the conclusion that they play modest but
important roles in the construction of useful consent forms, the protection of
patient's rights, and the determination of the actual nature and extent of risks
to which subjects will likely be exposed. The prime focus, though, remains
upon informed consent and the right to autonomy of the patient or
experimental subject. Morgenbesser clearly ranks the pursuit of knowledge
below considerations either of patient autonomy or patient care. The right to
refuse to consent to risk extends logically to social constraint upon the
latitude open for scientific investigation (e.g., recombinant D.N.A. research).
In such circumstances, society may either directly or through delegated
authority, circumscribe freedom of inquiry if there is danger of direct
physical harm to society as a result of the research. Finally, there are many
other important but untouched issues which cluster about human experimentation, including the morality of using animals, the amount of pain to
which animals may be legitimately subjected, the use of volunteers in
experiments from which the volunteers will not benefit, moral concerns
about compensating experimental subjects for their injuries, and the
propriety of using prison volunteers.

Natalie Abrams examines in considerable detail the problem of consent to
human experimentation by prisoners and children. Her point of departure is
the concept of informed consent and the fact that it requires not only the
provision of the relevant information, but the capacity to choose freely. The
second element introduces yet another consideration: what counts as
coercion sufficient to overbear free choice. Abrams examines the circumstances under which threats or offers to prisoners would make consent
invalid. Such considerations require distinguishing those forms of coercion

which a person could have reasonably resisted from those which he or she could not have. In attempting to resolve these issues, one faces the risk of restricting or eliminating the options or freedom open to prisoners (e.g., volunteering for human research) under the guise of protecting prisoners from coercion. Moreover, one is confronted with the question of whether one can distinguish between threats and coercions by appealing to whether the prisoners concerned would, under the circumstances of their confinement, want the option to participate in an experiment, and must also consider whether the consent situation occurs in circumstances where the prisoners are properly treated from a moral point of view (and the associated question of whether prisoners should be given the opportunity to move to a more proper state of treatment through participation in research). As Abrams indicates, many of these issues turn on one's theory of punishment and thus on what one would hold to be due to prisoners. After all, part of the issue of what counts as moral treatment of prisoners turns on whether or not placing prisoners in various states of wretched existence is just.

Finally, Abrams argues that proxy consent is not consent at all in the usual sense of respecting the freedom of another to choose. Proxy consent in the case of children is an alternative to consent where parents are usually the best judges of the well-being of the child involved. But since what is being appealed to is not respect for freedom but the quality of judgements concerning another's well-being, it can be appropriate for courts to intervene when the judgement of parents with respect to their children is suspect.

Questions of freedom and the role of medicine in molding human activities ranges from contemporary questions concerning behavior control and psychosurgery back to the ruminations of Aristotle. Joseph Owens gives a very suggestive analysis of Aristotle's treatment of the role of physiology, and by implication medicine, in the formation of virtue. Aristotle held that a proper means for restoring morality in weak-willed individuals is to be found through physiology. Medicine bears upon the physiological disposition that underlies moral behavior and thus complements moral education. Owens finds in Aristotle a justification for the use of tranquilizers and other therapeutic aids to constrain human impulses to moral goals. As Stuart F. Spicker indicates, Owens through Aristotle turns Hare's question of 'how can the moral philosopher help the physician?' to 'how can the physician help the moral philosopher?' In this view, the goal of medicine is not only health, but the improvement of individual moral conduct through the improvement of moral judgement — not only to make persons healthier, but better.

Towers, Chisholm, and Engelhardt address in different ways the question of how humans come into being and pass away. Bernard Towers focuses on the implications that evolutionary concepts of reality and of man's origin have for the ways in which ethics in general and medical ethics in particular should be conceived. For this he draws in part upon the reflections of Teilhard de Chardin. His contention is that medical ethics must be seen in terms of biological evolution so that we recognize ourselves as part of a process; we must frame discussions about medical ethics in terms of the information about our evolutionary origins. Roderick Chisholm picks up the theme of coming to be and passing away not in terms of the evolution of the human species, phylogeny, but rather in terms of the development of the individual, ontogeny. With issues such as the definition of death, the discontinuation of life-sustaining equipment, and abortion in the background, Chisholm analyzes what it means to say that a person comes into being or passes out of being. His conclusions are that we do not have good grounds for holding when it is that persons come into existence or when they pass out of existence, and that therefore one has to choose with regard to the definition of death and the justification of abortion on grounds other than whether the taking of a person's life is involved.

In commenting upon the papers of Towers and Chisholm, Tristram Engelhardt indicates that the concept of person is central to both essays. For Towers the question is whether values are in evolutionary processes themselves or whether the values concerning evolution depend on the purposes of persons. If it is the second, evolution becomes less likely to reveal moral principles directly and more likely to be relevant to knowing the character of the world in order to succeed better in one's moral activities. As to the concept of person in human ontogeny, Engelhardt argues that one must distinguish with care between the concepts 'human' and 'person,' and attend to the fact that the concept person itself is ambiguous and that in fact we operate with more than one concept — one which is a strict sense of person as a self-conscious moral agent, and another which is used to identify those instances of human life to which we impute the rights of moral agents. These distinctions are crucial for understanding the coming to be and the passing away of persons, especially with regard to the definition of death and the morality of abortion. Moreover, he argues, there are good reasons for holding that one can identify when persons come into existence and when they pass away so as to judge when taking human life does not involve the life of a person.

The closing papers by MacIntyre and Pellegrino explore the extent to which disputes concerning medical ethics can be resolved in a pluralistic society. The essay by Alasdair MacIntyre, 'Patients as Agents,' represents a development of a theme presented in an earlier paper. 'How Virtues Become Vices: Values, Medicine, and Social Context,' published in the first volume of this series. The problem is how to function in a society without a tradition or the acknowledgement of moral authority. MacIntyre contends that we are in such a situation when we attempt to arbitrate many moral problems, including medical ethical problems. The arbitration is impossible, since we lack an overriding criterion to appeal to in our moral arguments. 'If two reasonable parties to such a moral debate cannot discover criteria to appeal to which will settle the matter impersonally for both, then neither party can be basing its own conviction on such an appeal' ([22], pp. 198–199). There is no common moral footing, and as a result the positions held by different disputants in medical ethical discussions become incommensurable. In MacIntyre's view, then, pluralism marks the end of rational discourse, for such discourse requires a tradition within which it can occur, and authorities to nurture it and sustain its conduct. Pluralism thus also marks the end of the physician's function within a tradition endowing him or her with special authority.

MacIntyre is contending that one of the reasons we have failed to solve the problems of medical ethics is that we have failed to understand whose problems they are. They are not, so he contends, problems of physicians, surgeons, and nurses, but rather they are problems of patients bereft of the structure afforded by tradition and authority. As a consequence, the problems of euthanasia or abortion, the duties of physicians with their patients, etc., cannot be viewed as problems internal to medicine. They are disputes that can be understood only in terms of the broader social context. As MacIntyre indicates, the usual recourse in such difficulties is bureaucratic regulations – rules for the guidance of medicine which were in the past unnecessary because of the force of tradition, as well as the fact that physicians did not confront their patients as strangers, but as individuals whom they knew personally. The relative anonymity of the modern physician–patient interchange compounded by a pluralism of beliefs, has elicited regulations which structure medical care in order to protect patients from physicians who are strangers to their patients and their patients' norms. The solution through regulations is destined to failure, so MacIntyre argues, because it presupposes a uniform context of interpretation which is never available. The remedy is not to attempt a return to tradition and authority, for such are not available. Instead, the patient must assume responsibility for himself, and the physician can no longer assume that they are bound by a common moral code; thus it becomes the prerogative, if not the obligation, of the patient to make his or her own decisions concerning abortion, euthanasia, etc. 'We have to invite patients to become active moral agents in an area where they have been passive' ([22], p. 211).

In commentary, Edmund Pellegrino expands upon MacIntyre's position. He suggests that the future will bring further challenges not only to physician's moral authority, but to his technological authority as well. Responsible choices on the part of the patient presuppose that the patient is informed and able to assess technical issues involved in medical decisions. This implies providing laymen with skills enabling them to question critically and to assess the judgements of medical experts – an ability which would need to be nurtured through education and a greater interest in self-reliance by patients. This suggests a new foundation for professional medical ethics and has a person—centered focus on the meaning of healing – it is the patient's values and goals which determine what counts as healing. A code of professional ethics in our present circumstances must make respect of the patient's autonomy a central value.

The volume ends with four brief notes which summarize a round table discussion on the complementary issue – The Physician as Moral Agent. André Hellegers warns of the danger of eroding the physician's proper moral responsibilities to treat medical not social complaints through a conflation of four quite different models of disease: (1) the somatic view of disease, (2) the epidemiological or biostatistical view of disease, (3) the functional or social model of disease, and (4) the model of disease as the absence of health defined as total physical, mental, and social well-being. The third and fourth are, according to Hellegers, not only misguided but potentially pernicious in that they call upon the physician to make judgements with respect to social values concerning which he has no special expertise. Moreover, the combination of all four gives the physician the preposterous task of providing the patient with 'infinite life and infinite happiness without harm to others or to the cosmos, with "the patient" defining whether he or she is diseased rather than the physician' ([15], p. 227). Hellegers contends that the third and fourth images are already widely used in the provision of non-therapeutic abortions, in the prescription of drugs for mood control, in some forms of plastic surgery, and in the developing debate on euthanasia. Under these last two models, not only does the physician no longer operate as a moral agent, but he or she also runs the risk of losing the freedom to dissent from practices enjoyed by the patient or society. Hellegers takes the position that the physician's concern for the particular patient should take precedence over general social considerations.

In contrast, Sissela Bok contends that because our resources are finite and because of the social costs of certain forms of treatment we must reassess our notion that the physician should act primarily as an agent of the patient's interests. Bok has in mind issues such as whether the use of antibiotics to combat mild infections will increase resistance against these drugs and thus endanger future sufferers, or how much of our scarce resources should be invested in the cure of any particular patient. Acknowledging that lines are difficult to draw, she suggests that we begin with those cases where the values at stake are relatively easy to identify — for example, we should not press the maintenance of the lives of hopelessly unconscious individuals, not treat individuals against their will, and recognize the legitimacy of living wills. As medical treatment becomes more expensive, the physician is confronted with the duty to act not only as an agent on behalf of the patient's well-being but also as a trustee of our scarce resources.

Robert Daly questions the extent to which physicians can be regarded as moral agents by confronting us with three decisions concerning the range of the physician's moral authority. (1) One must decide what the content of medical ethical issues are and the scope of the particular duties assigned to the role 'physician' in order to assess the physician as a moral agent. (2) One must arbitrate contests of will between physicians and other agents — especially as we toy with Utopian visions of health and well-being. (3) One must decide how to relate moral practice and moral theory in medicine so as to judge when physicians are to be held to blame for wrong conduct. In short, we need to determine the geography of the physician's moral responsibilities.

These considerations are closed by Daniel Callahan who, through examining the circumstances under which physicians may for the good of their patients violate laws, explores the status of the physician as a moral agent bound by usual social restraints. Callahan has in mind here cases such as a physician not providing a patient with fully informed consent on the grounds that such information would dissuade the patient from a hazardous procedure which in the physician's judgement is the best choice for the patient. Callahan also raises questions concerning the supposed moral rule that the welfare of a physician's individual patient takes moral precedence over other moral obligations the physician may have to his or her profession and society. An assessment of the physician's duty as a moral agent is complete only if it includes an acknowledgement of the rights and duties of moral agents generally.

We are left then with a series of starting points for the further exploration of issues in medical ethics. Philosophy is, after all, an ongoing dialogue of persons interested in giving reasons concerning their beliefs. Properly construed, it is a modest endeavor which settles for better answers rather than best answers, realizing that we can at most hope to become clearer about worse or better choices, even if we cannot in the end come to absolute and final answers. The absence of final answers should be neither discouraging nor unexpected, but rather remind us that the business of being a responsible, rational person includes participation with other persons in an examination of the judgements that guide our lives. It involves a commitment to clarifying the goods and goals we wish to achieve and to understanding the nature of the respect we owe to each other. In short, the project of a philosophical medical ethics reaches into the future.

The Symposium which was the parent of this volume was made possible through the support of The Franklin J. Matchette Foundation, The Society for Health and Human Values, The University of Connecticut Research Foundation, and The School of Medicine of The University of Connecticut Health Center. Our debt to these agencies is gratefully acknowledged. We also wish to express our gratitude to Carolyn C. Brinzey, K. Danner Clouser, Robert U. Massey, James E. C. Walker, and Richard M. Zaner, who among many others contributed time, energy, and moral support to this Symposium. Special thanks are due to Mary Beth Krafcik whose labors in the organization of the third Symposium were indispensable.

H. TRISTRAM ENGELHARDT, Jr.
STUART F. SPICKER

May, 1976

BIBLIOGRAPHY

1. American Medical Association and New York Academy of Medicine: 1848, *Code of Medical Ethics Adopted by the American Medical Association of Philadelphia in May 1847 and by the New York Academy of Medicine in October 1847*, Academy of Medicine, New York.
2. Aquinas, St. Thomas, *Summa Theologica*, I, 118 art. 2.
3. Aquinas, St. Thomas: *Opera Omnia XXVI, In Aristoteles Stagiritae, Politicorum seu de Rebus Civilibus*, Paris, 1975, Vives, Book VII, Lectio XII, p. 484.
4. Aristotle, *Politics VII*, in R. McKeon (ed.), *The Basic Works of Aristotle*, Random House, New York, 1941, 1302.
5. Bacon, F.: 1664, *Opera Omnia, de dignitate et augmentis scientiarum*, Frankfort, p. 104.
6. Bennett, J.: 1971, 'Whatever the Consequences', *Analysis* 26, 83–102.
7. Bole, T.: 1974, 'John Brown, Hegel and Speculative Concepts in Medicine', *Texas Reports on Biology and Medicine* 32, [1], 287–297.

8. Brody, B. A.: 1971, 'Abortion and the Law', *Journal of Philosophy* **68**, 357–369.
9. Brody, B. A.: 1973, 'Abortion and the Sanctity of Human Life', *American Philosophical Quarterly* **10**, 133–140.
10. Cohen, C.: 1969, 'Sex, Birth Control, and Human Life', *Ethics* **79**, 251–262.
11. Fletcher, J.: 1954, *Morals and Medicine*, Beacon Press, Boston.
12. Freund, P. A. (ed.): 1969, *Experimentation with Human Subjects*, George Braziller, New York.
13. Fried, C.: 1974, *Medical Experimentation: Personal Integrity and Social Policy*, North-Holland/American Elsevier, Amsterdam and New York.
14. Gustafson, J.: 1973, 'Mongolism, Parental Desires, and the Right to Life', *Perspectives in Biology and Medicine* **16**, 529–557.
15. Hellegers, A.: 1976, Round Table Discussion, this volume, pp. 225–230.
16. Hume, D.: 1777, 'Of Suicide', in T. H. Green and T. H. Grose (eds.), *David Hume: The Philosophical Works*, 4 vols., reprint of the new edition London 1882, Scientia Verlag Aalen, Aslen, Germany, 1964, IV, 406–414.
17. Kass, L. R.: 1971, 'Death as an Event: A Commentary on Robert Morrison', *Science* **173**, 698–702.
18. Kelly, G.: 1958, *Medico-Moral Problems*, Catholic Hospital Association, St. Louis, Missouri.
19. Kenny, J. P.: 1962, *Principles of Medical Ethics*, 2nd ed., Newman Press, Westminster, Maryland.
20. Lappé, M.: 1976, 'The Non-Neutrality of Hypothesis Formulation', in H. Tristram Engelhardt, Jr. and Daniel Callahan (eds.), *Science, Ethics and Medicine*, Hastings Center, Hastings-on-Hudson, N.Y., 1976.
21. Leake, C. D.: 1969, 'Theories of Ethics and Medical Practice', *Journal of the American Medical Association* **208**, 842–847.
22. MacIntyre, A.: 1976, 'Patients as Agents', this volume, pp. 197–212.
23. Morison, R. S.: 1971, 'Death: Process or Event?', *Science* **173**, 694–698.
24. National Commission for the Protection of Human Subjects of Biomedical and Behavioral Research: 1976, *Appendix: Research on the Fetus*, U.S. Department of Health, Education, and Welfare, Washington, D.C.
25. Noonan, J. T., Jr.: 1966, *Contraception*, Harvard University Press, Cambridge.
26. Noonan, J. T., Jr.: 1970, 'An Almost Absolute Value in History', in J. T. Noonan, Jr. (ed.), *The Morality of Abortion*, Harvard University Press, Cambridge, 1970, pp. 1–59.
27. Percival, T.: 1803, *Medical Ethics*, Johnson and Bickerstaff, Manchester.
28. Plato, *Laws*, in E. Hamilton and H. Cairns (eds.), *The Collected Dialogues of Plato*, Princeton University Press, Princeton, 1961.
29. Rachels, J.: 1975, 'Active and Passive Euthanasia', *New England Journal of Medicine* **292**, 78–80.
30. Ramsey, P.: 1970, *Fabricated Man*, Yale University Press, New Haven and London.
31. Ramsey, P.: 1970, *The Patient as Person*, Yale University Press, New Haven and London.
32. Seneca, 'Letter 70: Suicide', in M. Hadas (trans.), *The Stoic Philosophy of Seneca*, W. W. Norton, New York, 1958, pp. 202–207.
33. Shryock, R. H.: 1967, *Medical Licensing in America, 1650–1965*, Johns Hopkins Press, Baltimore.
34. Smith, H. L.: 1970, *Ethics and the New Medicine*, Abingdon Press, Nashville and New York.
35. Tooley, M.: 1972, 'Abortion and Infanticide', *Philosophy and Public Affairs* **2**, 37–65.
36. Vaux, K.: 1974, *Biomedical Ethics*, Harper and Row, New York.

SECTION I

FROM PAST PERSPECTIVES
TO PRESENT PERPLEXITIES

CHESTER R. BURNS

AMERICAN MEDICAL ETHICS:
SOME HISTORICAL ROOTS

OPENING REMARKS

If the nature and significance of philosophical medical ethics were well known and thoroughly understood, we would not be assembled here today. As significant as this meeting is, though, we must be cautious in applying the language of historical assessment. It is easy to be rhetorical — to say that all physicians of the past were philosophical imbeciles, or that all physicians of the past were interested in etiquette, not ethics. I wish to deal with a few of the inaccuracies and anxieties which undergird such statements.

For most Americans before 1900, 'moral' connoted certain religious, psychological, and social components of human endeavor. 'Moral' was used to refer to the religious convictions of individuals, their beliefs about right and wrong behavior, opinions about other attributes of human behavior, especially mental phenomena, and judgements concerning the particular conditions of a given community. The lines separating these components were blurred indeed. A physician could be moral if religiously devout or possessed of gentlemanly virtues; or a physician could study moral philosophy; or he could alter the morality of a particular patient; or he could influence the morality of a community in a special way. Let us look briefly at some of these meanings.

Christianity was the basis for the ethos of most American physicians prior to 1900. In a rather extraordinary parade of speeches and essays, many physicians of that time asserted that the ideal doctor was a Christian. Benjamin Rush ([10], pp. 439–40) declared that all physicians should profess the Christian religion. Ebenezer Alden ([1], p. 14) exhorted each member of the Dartmouth Medical Society to hold a 'firm and unwavering belief in the truths of divine revelation.' Thomas Sewall charged the medical graduates of Columbian College to observe the Sabbath, guard against infidel sentiments, and recognize that 'all the most eminent physicians of our country openly espouse the Christian religion' ([13], pp. 7–8). So it went throughout the 19th century, especially on commencement days and at

S. F. Spicker and H. T. Engelhardt, Jr. (eds.), Philosophical Medical Ethics: Its Nature and Significance, 21–26. All Rights Reserved. Copyright © 1977 by D. Reidel Publishing Company, Dordrecht-Holland.

meetings of medical societies. Christian ethics were the predominant ideals of personal morality among American physicians.

The ideal American doctor was also expected to be a gentleman. A physician should cultivate a 'pure and elevated style of conversation, urbanity and gentleness of manners, and kindness of heart,' said Sewall to the graduating students ([13], p. 6). Some of the important codes of ethics adopted by state medical societies included discussions of the need for a doctor's personal character to be that of a perfect gentleman. The doctor must not acquire habits of swearing, drunkenness, gambling, or debauchery. He must not be guilty of criminal acts nor engage in disreputable business practices. And, to be a gentleman, he must be educated.'There will be but little hazard in advancing as a truth, that colloquial ease, and grace, and extent of knowledge, and polish of sentiment, are found, almost exclusively, with men of classical and original education,' asserted John Beale Davidge ([4], p. 9) to his Maryland colleagues. A gentleman, physician or otherwise, was not uneducated. Well known, however, is the fact that the majority of 18th and 19th century American medical practitioners were not educated, in a formal sense — which brings us to a brief consideration of the extent to which these practitioners might have studied moral philosophy.

The senior year of a collegiate experience was the usual time for studies of moral philosophy [14]. But since very few American physicians prior to 1900 had earned a bachelor's degree, very few had formally studied moral philosophy. By 1900, only The Johns Hopkins University School of Medicine required college studies [6]. Yet, the number of medical students going beyond the minimal requirements was steadily increasing. For example, 1500 of 10,709 students attending 76 medical schools in 1897 had received a bachelor's degree and, presumably, had studied either moral philosophy or some of the social sciences and humanities that were beginning to compete with the old moral philosophy ([8], p. 10).

Probably more significant, though, than this growing interest in formal education, was an attitude about the study of moral philosophy offered by Benjamin Rush at the turn of the 19th century, and sustained throughout the century by many of his disciples. Rush recommended the study of Christian ideals and of metaphysics, but he had little use for moral philosophy. 'I object to its (moral philosophy) being made a part of academical education. It was originally introduced into Christian colleges from pagan schools, and has constantly tended to impress a belief of the independence of morals upon religion. A course of lectures upon the evidences, doctrines, and precepts, of Christianity, will not only supply its place, by legitimating its objects, but will expand the mind of our pupil by fixing it upon the most elevated subjects of human contemplation' ([12], pp. 174–175). Christian ideals were paramount; moral philosophy was suspect.

Metaphysics was strongly recommended as part of premedical and medical education. Metaphysics, though, was neither classical philosophy nor modern moral philosophy. Rush defined metaphysics as 'a simple history of the faculties and operations of the mind, unconnected with the ancient nomenclature of words and phrases, which once constituted the science of metaphysics' ([12], p. 142). Later he designated this science of the mind as 'phrenology' (not to be confused with the phrenology of Spurzheim and Gall) and mentioned the writings of Locke, Condillac, Hartley, and Reid ([12], p. 271).

Although Rush objected to the study of moral philosophy, he did not reject the moral faculties that were studied by moral and mental philosophers [11]. These moral faculties included a sense of deity, conscience, and a moral faculty *per se*. It was the duty of a physician to study these moral faculties, healthy and diseased. These studies would provide the doctor with knowledge useful in the care of patients and knowledge helpful in rendering advice to the community. Hence, Rush objected to those beliefs of moral philosophers that were anti-Christian, but he did not reject investigations of the moral faculties as components of the human mind.

As is well known, though, distinctions between the philosophy of mind and moral philosophy were not precise during the 18th and 19th centuries. Several American physicians recommended the study of metaphysics for many of the same reasons as those given by Rush, but insistence on a distinction between moral philosophy and metaphysics was not so important to many of Rush's successors. In their recommendations, metaphysics and moral philosophy were used interchangeably, and, during the last half of the 19th century, psychology, not ethics, began to appear as a substitute for either or both [7].

This latter substitute confirmed the emphasis of most physicians: a study of metaphysics and moral philosophy would provide physicians with an understanding of the feelings of the sick, and of the mentally ill especially. American doctors were interested in the rudiments of the behavioral sciences contained in the mental and moral philosophy of the 19th century. These same physicians had little or no interest in the legacies of speculative metaphysics and philosophical ethics residing in this mental and moral philosophy. They did not believe that doctors should study moral philosophy as preparation for constructing a system of medical ethics.

Solution of ethical problems required allegiance to the ethical rules codified by local and state medical societies, and, nationally, by the American Medical Association in 1847, not arm-chair speculation about the nature of goodness and badness. Almost every analysis of a problem in medical ethics included, in one way or another, some discussion of a code. Additionally, those physicians after Rush who wrote about medical ethics (and there were many) did not usually recommend a course of lectures on Christianity instead of a course on modern moral philosophy. But they did, with persistence, relate the morality of a physician to Christian ideals *and* the normative characteristics of being a gentleman.

The process of creating medical ethics within a framework of such personal values provided a source of continuing paradoxes and conflicts. Assertions that physicians should be Christians often camouflaged the different implications that Catholic and Protestant beliefs could have for medical ethics. Moreover, Christian practitioners usually ignored Jewish norms. Even if the implications of various religious beliefs had been analyzed, the following question persisted: were physicians *good* physicians because they were faithful Jews or Catholics or Protestants? Similarly, were physicians *good* physicians because they were gentlemen or ladies? Finally, were physicians *good* physicians because they had studied moral philosophy and understood philosophical theories of ethics?

Most 19th century American physicians who dealt with problems of medical ethics would have said 'No' to this last question, even though many appreciated the moral import of their professional roles. Whether they knew Kant, Bentham, or Aristotle was unimportant compared to the issue of whether or not they altered or ought to alter the moral predicament of an individual patient.

Some physicians, including Rush, believed that they were obligated to attend to the morals of their patients. One doctor noted that 'the influence of medical practitioners is capable of becoming as great and extensive, in a moral point of view, as that of even the clergy. Their intimacy with the people in all situations and circumstances affords them an advantageous opportunity, both by example and precept, to inculcate, most forcibly, the lessons of morality and virtue' ([2], p. 14). For American doctors before 1900, these were mostly lessons of Christian virtue, readily identifiable in the writings of Worthington Hooker [5], a Connecticut physician who, in 1849, published the only significant monograph on medical ethics to be written by an American practitioner during the 19th century. Commenting on the moral influences which physicians exerted during their daily rounds, Hooker believed that a physician should exhibit Christian faith, hope, and charity at the bedside of the sick, even persuading his patients to adopt Christian beliefs. Hooker did not wish to separate professional ethics from Christian ethics, even though his monograph on medical ethics was an elaborate commentary on the code adopted by the American Medical Association in 1847.

In attempting to codify rules about the extent of their moral responsibility towards patients, contradictions were the order of the day for most pre-1900 physicians. An injunction in the code of ethics adopted by the New York State Medical Society in 1823 declared that professionally conscientious physicians were not responsible for the moral conditions of their patients, whereas a section of the code of ethics adopted by the College of Physicians of Philadelphia in 1843 stated just the opposite: physicians ought to attend to the moral predicaments of their patients ([15], p. 15; [3], p. 182). The latter injunction was the one included in the code adopted by the American Medical Association, even though John Bell, in introducing that code, urged physicians to fulfill their public health obligations 'without assuming the office of moral and religious teaching' ([9], p. 86). Moral neutrality versus moral suasion was as much a dilemma for conscientious 19th century practitioners as for practitioners today.

It would appear that moral philosophers of the 18th and 19th centuries did not help most American physicians caught on the horns of this dilemma. Whether or not 20th century moral philosophers can help today's medical practitioners remains to be seen; but this comment, perhaps to the relief of some, brings us back to this week's symposium, even though it may stimulate attitudes of defensiveness from some philosophers and physicians.

Let us be reassured. Only within the past two decades have American philosophers and physicians demonstrated commitment to the purposes signified by this conference. Moreover, our symposium may be the first of its kind in the history of philosophy and medicine: a public, group effort to dissect the conceptual relationships between moral philosophy *qua* moral philosophy, and the ethical dilemmas of medical professionals. We are trying to respond to the vigorous turmoils of conscience affecting us all, as persons and professionals. We believe that our responses may lead to a better understanding of the nature and significance not only of philosophical medical ethics, but also of man himself.

The University of Texas Medical Branch,
Galveston, Texas

NOTE

[1] This allegiance to the AMA Code extended well into the 20th century. For an early example, see Gouley, J. W. S.: 1906, *Conferences on the Moral Philosophy of Medicine,* Rebman, New York.

BIBLIOGRAPHY

1. Alden, E.: 1820, *An Address Delivered in Hanover, New Hampshire Before the Dartmouth Medical Society, on their First Anniversary, December 28, 1819,* Boston.
2. Brooks, J.: 1820, *An Address, Delivered Before the Second Medical Society of the State of Vermont, at Their Annual Meeting in Dummerston, January 12, 1820,* Brattleborough.
3. College of Physicians of Philadelphia: 1841–46, 'Rules of Professional Conduct', *Transactions of the College of Physicians of Philadelphia,* vol. 1.
4. Davidge, J. B.: 1805, *An Oration Delivered Before, and Published by the Request of the Medical Faculty of Maryland, at Their Last Biennial Congress in the City of Baltimore on the Sixth Day of June, 1805,* Baltimore.
5. Hooker, W.: 1849, *Physician and Patient; or a Practical View of the Mutual Duties, Relations, and Interests of the Medical Profession and the Community,* Baker and Scribner, New York.
6. Hudson, R. P.: 1972, 'Abraham Flexner in Perspective: American Medical Education, 1865–1910', *Bulletin of the History of Medicine,* 46, 545–61.
7. Logan, T.: 1844, *The Ethics of Medicine: An Anniversary Address, Delivered 3rd April, 1844, Before the Medico-Chirurgical Society of Louisiana,* New Orleans.
8. Parsons, J. R., Jr.: 1904, 'Professional Education', in N. M. Butler (ed.), *Monographs on Education in the United States,* J. B. Lyon Co., Albany.
9. *Proceedings of the National Medical Conventions, Held in New York, May, 1846, and in Philadelphia, May, 1847,* 1847, Philadelphia.
10. Rush, B.: 1809, *Medical Inquiries and Observations,* 3rd ed., vol. 1, Philadelphia.
11. Rush, B.: 1812, *Medical Inquiries and Observations Upon the Diseases of the Mind,* Philadelphia.
12. Rush, B.: 1811, *Sixteen Introductory Lectures Upon the Institutes and the Practice of Medicine, With a Syllabus of the Latter,* Bradford and Innskeep, Philadelphia.
13. Sewall, T.: 1828, *A Charge Delivered to the Graduating Class of the Columbian College, D.C. at the Medical Commencement, March 22, 1827,* Washington.
14. Smith, W.: 1956, *Professors and Public Ethics Studies of Northern Moral Philosophers Before the Civil War,* Cornell University Press, Ithaca, New York.
15. *A System of Medical Ethics Published by Order of the State Medical Society of New York,* 1823, New York.

ALBERT R. JONSEN

DO NO HARM: AXIOM OF MEDICAL ETHICS

When the maxim 'do no harm' is invoked in discussions about medical ethics, it is identified as the primary principle of the ethics of the medical profession. A book on malpractice begins: 'What is needed . . . is a return to basics, to the first principle of medicine, *primum non nocere*; therein lies the answer to the malpractice crisis' ([18], p. 17). Henry Beecher writes, 'If doctors were certain of the benefit of penicillin, for example, yet did not use it, their decision could be construed as running counter to the basic rule of the physician, *primum non nocere*' ([2], p. 94).

Although those who quote the maxim often attribute it to the Hippocratic Oath, it is found in another work of the Hippocratic Corpus, Book I, Chapter 11 of the *Epidemics*, a book which has a better claim to authorship by the Physician of Cos than does the Oath [3]. The text of the *Epidemics* reads, literally, 'to practice about diseases two: to help or not to harm,' or, as the Standard English Translation by W. H. S. Jones puts it, 'As to diseases make a habit of two things – to help, or at least, to do no harm.' There is, however, a similar, somewhat longer statement in the Oath: 'I will use treatment to help the sick according to my ability and judgement, but I will never use it to injure or wrong them' ([14], p. 165).

The maxim is quoted in different ways. The Greek text supports the stark 'help or do no harm.' However, one frequently sees the 'at least, do no harm' of the Jones translation, which is also found in the classic French text of E. Littre, 'Avoir, dans les maladies, deux choses en vue: etre utile ou du moins ne pas nuire' ([19], pp. 635–637). Also, the maxim is stated in the form, '*primum non nocere*': 'Above all or first of all, do no harm.' I have tried to trace the origin of this wording without success. Its very ancient ancestry may be a sentence in which Galen rephrases the Hippocratic maxim. However, he adds 'above all' not to the harm phrase, but to the helping phrase: it is necessary that the physician particularly aims at helping the sick; if he cannot, he should not do them harm.[1]

The maxim is found in an unlikely context. The *Epidemics* are a collection of brief case histories recorded by physicians during their 'epidemia' or visits abroad to various Greek islands and cities. Jones says that they are a series of

S. F. Spicker and H. T. Engelhardt. Jr. (eds.), Philosophical Medical Ethics: Its Nature and Significance, 27–41. All Rights Reserved. Copyright © 1977 by D. Reidel Publishing Company, Dordrecht-Holland.

notes jotted down in an order which happened to suggest itself, and never edited. Nevertheless, he calls them 'the most remarkable product of Greek science' ([14], pp. 141–142).

The entire collection consists of clinical descriptions. Chapter XI of Book 1 discusses the clinical sign of coctions of the evacuations. At the end of the chapter a few sentences appear which seem to be unconnected moralisms of copybook quality: 'Declare the past, diagnose the present, foretell the future . . . help or do not harm . . . The art has three factors, the disease, the patient, and the physician. The physician is the servant of the art. The patient must cooperate with the physician in battling the disease.' Having satisfied his conscience, the physician author returns to a discussion of fever.

A rash and untutored exegesis of the text might make a case that these are more than a haphazard batch of moral platitudes dropped into a serious scientific text. They might be quite relevant generalizations about clinical judgement, the 'art' of the text. Clinical judgement, or the art, consists of history, diagnosis, and prognosis. The physician is servant of the art — that is, he must follow or, as the Greek literally says, 'pull his oar along with.' the evidence and logic of clinical judgement. The literal text then says, 'the patient must be with the physician in fighting the disease' — that is, the signs and symptoms of the illness in the patient and the evident effects of interventions provide the matter for clinical judgement. In this context, our maxim is more a scientific statement than a moral platitude: to be of benefit, and not to harm, according to the medical theory of this treatise, would be to do those things and only those which redress the disordered balance of the humors. Each medical intervention, such as bleeding or purging, was designed to do this. To harm would be to fail to intervene when evidence called for intervention or to do so too vigorously or in the wrong way, thus either disturbing the natural movement back to humoral harmony or not encouraging it. To benefit is to balance; to harm is to unbalance or to fail to balance. This is the essence of clinical judgement, which matches the physician's estimate of past, present, and future to events in the patient and determines the manner and timing of his intervention. This is simply good clinical judgement; it is superfluous to think of the maxim as a casual moral admonition interjected into a serious scientific treatise.

This essay, however, will be neither history nor textual exegesis, though both might shed light on the maxim. Originally, I intended to sound the ethical depths of the maxim, but this turned out either too banal or too complex. I have settled for a much less ambitious project: the construction of four ideal types of usage to which the maxim might be put. By 'construction' I mean picking up, out of occasional allusions to and invocations of the maxim, certain hints of an argument which might be put together in order to make some moral point about the practice of medicine. Out of these hints, I shall delineate, very roughly, ideal types of use for the maxim, were such arguments worked out. They are 'ideal' types only in the sense that they are very schematic and bare of the distracting complexity of actual moral discourse.

This is a somewhat haphazard methodology for analysis of moral discourse. It is dictated by the fact that I have no actual examples of extended argument, either by physicians or by philosophers, which I can subject to analysis. I do not know whether the hints of argument would turn deontological or teleological, were they actually worked out. Thus, I construct my ideal out of hints, fragments, and announcements of argument.

I identify my four ideal types of usage as (1) medicine as moral enterprise, (2) due care, (3) risk—benefit ratio, (4) benefit—detriment equation. Each of these uses seems to me to reflect a different purpose and to involve different forms of ethical argument. I will state the purpose which the use seems to serve, briefly suggest the form of ethical argument suited to that purpose, and, without making any critical analysis of the argument, indicate some paths for further exploration. I will then propose an actual but still immature argument, put forth by several authors, in which the maxim makes an important, though somewhat paradoxical appearance. Finally, I will venture two generalizations which may be of some practical value.

I. THE FIRST USE: MEDICINE AS A MORAL ENTERPRISE

Medical skills are designed to effect a change in a physical state or process that distresses, debilitates, or may destroy the life of a person. These skills can, however, be used for other purposes: they can create such states in a healthy person for purposes of venality, revenge, or torture. They can be directed to benefit, but out of motives of personal profit or aggrandisement rather than the good of the patient. When it is said that the first duty of the physician is to do no harm, it may be intended to assert that medicine is a moral enterprise.

Medicine as a moral enterprise might mean that medical skills are, somehow, intrinsically and of themselves, meant to be used for human benefit. 'Do no harm' is a warning against their abuse. Although it would be

difficult to demonstrate the intrinsically beneficial nature of the medical
enterprise, there is at least a hint of this idea throughout Eastern and Western
medicine in the continued insistence that a physician must never refuse to
treat a person in need. The inscription on the Asklepieon at the Acropolis
reads, '(The physician) should be like a god; savior equally of slaves, of
paupers, of rich men, of princes, to all a brother, because we are all brothers.'
The Hindu Oath states, 'You shall assist brahmins, venerable persons, poor
people, women, widows and orphans and anyone you meet on your rounds,
as if they were your relatives.' The Chinese code of Sun Ssu-mais (7th
century, A.D.) affirms, 'Aristocrat or commoner, poor or rich, aged or young,
beautiful or ugly, friend or enemy, native or foreigner, educated or uneducated, all are to be treated equally.'

Indeed, the art is considered in some way as sacred, for it comes from the
hand of God and is intended to heal the creatures of God. The prayer of
Maimonides ends: 'Almighty God, thou has chosen me in thy mercy to
watch over the life and death of thy creatures. I now apply myself to my
profession. Support me in this great task so that it may benefit mankind.' A
long tradition, then, supports the view that the physicians are not morally
free to dispose of their skills entirely as they see fit, but are bound by the
origin, nature, and purpose of their art to use them only for human benefit
([6], pp. 21, 30).

Medicine as a moral enterprise may also mean that, even if the skills are
indifferent in themselves, they so affect areas of unmistakable human good
and evil, such as pain, disability, and death, that their use should be guided by
those needs of others. The physician should be so strongly motivated by the
good of his or her patient that other motives will be banished or
subordinated. Do no harm, then, is an injunction to have certain motives.[2]

Whether one attends to the nature of the enterprise or to the motives of its
practitioners, one cannot fail to notice the importance of 'caring.' To
possess medical skills is to be able to care for the sick. Caring, regardless of
motives or affectivity associated with it, may be defined as the act of picking
up (we say 'assume care') another so that the other's well-being depends, in
some significant respect, upon the decision of the one who cares. To care is to
'appropriate' another, to make the other one's own. As the origin of the
English word 'care' reveals, it is to be troubled by another's trouble. The
agreement to care, even in a most formal sense, is a moral act, for it is the
initiation of that person's manifest need. Here, as in innumerable other
human interactions of the same sort, the possibility of responsible or
irresponsible acts, of praiseworthy or reprehensible behavior, of selfless or

selfish motives, in short, of moral action, arises. It is here that 'do no harm' in its meaning, 'do no mischief,' applies most fittingly. To assume some power over another so that the other will benefit is to assume care [22].

In this first usage, then, 'do no harm' is an injunction which warns practitioners that they enter a moral enterprise and exhorts them to motivations which will focus their skills on the well-being of their patients. The ethical roots of this use are about as deep as those roots go. The maxim here is indeed the first principle or axiom of all morality. In Aquinas' terms, 'This is the first precept of the natural law, good is to be done and promoted and evil is to be avoided.' In John Locke's terms: 'All being equal and independent, no one ought to harm another in his life, health, liberty or possessions' ([1], p. 773; [20], p. 311). In this use, then, the maxim is a self-evident first principle of moral discourse. It serves to affirm the moral nature of medical practice and to enjoin motives agreeable to that nature.

It is stated at a level of such generality that it provides little concrete direction. It would seem only to exclude malicious uses of medical skills. But these are reprehensible on common moral grounds. A physician who excises a kidney not because it is diseased, but because it is the kidney of his enemy, is an evil person who only coincidentally has surgical skills. Similarly, a physician who tortures is a moral reprobate who only *per accidens* has a license to practice medicine.

Any further analysis of this use would take the route of examining the nature of morality itself, the ground of moral principle and the relevance of motive, intentions, and consequences in evaluating the morality of practices.

II. THE SECOND USE: DUE CARE

The second principle of the Principles of Medical Ethics of the AMA requires physicians 'to strive continuously to improve their medical knowledge and skill . . . ' Medicine is based on a fusion of several sciences, joined to clinical experience. Use of the science and the experience in clinical judgement requires accurate information, clear reasoning, sensitive observation, and occasionally, manual dexterity. Each of these is attained and improved through exercise and through critical reappraisal by oneself and others. They are reappraised in view of certain standards. Attending to these standards and applying them to particular patients is 'due care.' Benefit means applying due care; harming means failing to do so, with the result that the patient is not cured or is caused new detriment. The maxim here refers both to medical practices in general, calling for their continued improvement by research, and to the skills of particular practitioners, demanding continued study and upgrading.

Due care follows reasonably from the maxim in its first use. If medicine is a moral enterprise, under the imperative of benefiting the patient, the specific acts of medicine, diagnosis and therapy, should meet the standards, general and personal, which will assure, with some certainty, the beneficial outcome. Just as the maxim in its first use stated the ethical tone implied in assuming care, so in this use, it urges the one who has assumed care to take care. It enjoins careful assessment, careful procedures, careful evaluation, careful follow-up. For example, it is an act of carelessness, unfortunately not uncommon, for a physician to fail to perform a thorough rectal examination on a patient suffering from rectal bleeding. A casual diagnosis of hemorrhoids masks the presence of rectal cancer. It is a careless act to treat a bothersome, but hardly lethal, bronchitis with the antibiotic chloramphenicol which, while very effective, can have fatal complications and is properly indicated only in serious infections, such as typhoid fever. It is careless to ignore, as happened in a leading malpractice case, persistent foul odor from a leg cast which, to the careful practitioner, would suggest the inception of gangrene.

This second use is where questions of morality become issues of legality, for claims of malpractice frequently assert failure to take due care in accord with accepted standards of practice. Several questions arise: has a physician been negligent? What are accepted standards? What is the boundary between negligence and the fallibility intrinsic to medical knowledge and reasoning [12]? However, there are more objective questions about the very nature of medical knowledge. Contemporary biomedical science permits elaborate description of diseases, but may inhibit recognition of illness in a particular patient; contemporary therapies can have significant theoretical and practical effects in general, but may be very difficult to assess in particular patients. The concept of due care, then, not only enjoins carefulness in the practitioner, but also reexamination of biomedical epistemology [5].

The moral roots of this use lie close to the maxims of prudence, which Kant described. The former use has a deontological tone: it constitutes the morality of the practice and permits no exceptions. This use admits of degrees of carefulness, from the long process of diagnosis and treatment of neoplasms to the quick, harried repair of serious trauma. It is hypothetical, in that it enjoins care in view of effecting certain outcomes. Further analysis of this second use would take the route of examining the role of the procedurally correct in moral behavior, of the nature of prudential decisions, of the categorical or hypothetical nature of rules, and of the ascription of responsibility.

III. THE THIRD USE: RISK–BENEFIT RATIO

The assessment of medical procedures which is carried out to create standards of due care reveals that most procedures are uncertain in their outcome. Some procedures promise an almost certain benefit, which may not eventuate in a particular application. Other procedures which will benefit entail certain or probable harm. It has become possible, because of epidemiological and statistical methods, to determine in quantitative terms some of these possibilities. Thus, the experience of open heart surgery for replacement of multiple valves shows mortality risk of 5% to 20%; use of the anaesthetic halothane carries a risk of causing hepatic dysfunction estimated to be in the range of 1 in 10,000 cases. Clinical trials are constantly being designed and carried out to determine efficacy and safety of operations and drugs.

Due care requires that these statistics be developed. The careful practitioner will be aware of them as he attempts to match therapy to disease, although one's own experience, one's clinical intuitions, and one's understanding of the nature of statistics should breed caution in their use. 'Medical statistics,' writes Pappworth, 'are like bikinis, concealing what is vital while revealing much that is interesting' ([25], p. 41). Still, the practitioner can use them to steer clear of dangerous or inefficacious treatment. However, any particular patient is a statistic of one. Each patient will respond uniquely; there will be allergic or idiosyncratic reactions. Here, the practitioner approaching the individual patient must base a risk–benefit assessment, not so much on statistics, as on a focused, full knowledge of the person and the illness. That knowledge will never comprehend the uniqueness of the person, but can, by refined experience and sophisticated clinical methodology, draw closer and closer to that uniqueness [9].

However, this statistical and clinical risk–benefit equation is not only an element in the diagnostic and therapeutic judgements of the practitioner. It is also an element in the decision of the patient to accept treatment. Physicians may know, statistically and experientially, how much risk of failure or of harm a procedure entails. But patients alone can know how much risk they wish to run and how much they desire the possible benefits. Each person has a 'risk budget,' as Charles Fried has described it. They calculate in rough

ways, out of experiences, emotions, and energy, the extent of security and
danger they will accept in their lives [11].

The Oxford English Dictionary defines risk as 'exposure to mischance or
peril'. Although the risk is an actuality, as a set of circumstances constituting
the exposure, the harm is a possibility. Decisions taken about risks are
decisions to place oneself in an exposed position, to dispense with certain
securities and protections. When persons do so, they are more uncertain
about the consequent situation than they would otherwise be, but only in
relation to a certain plan of life, for there is, of course, a radical uncertainty
about every next situation, gives the contingency of existence. But the risks
taken within life plans have to do with voluntary steps into more exposed,
less protected states of affairs.

In this usage, 'do no harm' refers, on the one hand, to the physician's
educated assessment of risks. It commands that those procedures be selected
which carry the best chance for success with the lowest risk of harm. It is in
this sense that one may hear physicians occasionally rephrase the maxim as
'do as little harm as possible.' On the other hand, it refers to the patient's
own assessment of how those risks and chances fit a lifestyle, with certain
goals and certain strengths and weaknesses. Here the maxim fits into a
utilitarian form of ethical discourse. The objective statement of the equation
is translated into a personal felicific calculus and choices are made in terms of
how a calculation would appear to maximize the goods and minimize the evils
of a person's experienced life in its present and future.

In this usage, it becomes necessary to begin to specify 'harm' more fully
than in the previous usages. It is usual in the medical context to think of
harm primarily in terms of physical detriments. However, if the equation
which includes the physical detriments is incorporated into a personal felicific
calculus, the scope of harm is expanded.

The wider meaning is common in the law. Joel Feinberg nicely summarizes
the legal use of 'harm':

It has become common, especially in legal writing, to take the object of harm always to
be an *interest* . . . a humanly inflicted harm is concerned as the violation of one of a
person's interests, an injury to something in which he has a genuine stake. In the lawyer's
usage, an interest is something a person always possesses in some condition, something
that can grow and flourish or diminish and decay, but which can rarely be totally lost.
Other persons can be said to promote or hinder an individual's interest in bodily health,
or in the avoidance of damaging or offensive physical contacts, or in the safety and
security of his person, his family, his friends and his property ([8], p. 26).

Let us begin more empirically by defining 'harm' as intrusion by physical
means upon the physical integrity of oneself or another, leaving an effect of

some duration. The intrusion may come from a voluntary or involuntary agent or from an inanimate object or power. I can be harmed by man or beast, by lead weight or lightning. The intrusion comes about because no effort is made or no effort succeeds in warding it off. Its effect is more than transient, as a hurt can be, but remains debilitating for a time or permanently. It reduces one's ability to defend oneself, leaving a wounded integrity.

We can, without distortion, expand this primitive notion from the physical to the psychological realm, although psychological integrity is more vague. But perhaps it can be defined as the ability to respond appropriately and effectively to intellectual and emotional challenges, such as loss or danger. Here the agents of harm remain the same, but the means move beyond the physical to the psychological — threats, lies, ridicule.

Finally, physical and psychological integrity imply social integrity, being able to maintain oneself as an integer by initiating action and responding to others in an ongoing weave of relationships. This integrity can be harmed by cutting off contacts, by distorting communication, by rendering efforts of self-preservation ineffectual.

The notion of personal integrity in physical and psychological and social being is not equivalent to splendid isolation. Intrinsic to the notion of integrity is that one person may, must, and often does allow others to enter the spaces of his or her integrity. Thus, it has been said, *'volenti non fit injuria.'* Injury is not done to one who is willing. Further, one may sometimes enter another's integrity, showing clearly by the manner of entry the intention of supporting or strengthening another's wounded integrity.

I suspect that at the heart of harming and being harmed is the notion of the ability to respond to challenge. A harmful act is one which cannot be warded off, and its harmful effect is decreased ability to defend oneself physically, psychologically, or socially. Response, measured and timely, is the sign of integrity.

I propose, then, to define 'to harm' as any action or event which results in prolonged diminished ability to respond to physical, psychological, or social challenge. In this usage, then, the risk to physical integrity is assumed into the wider scope of risks to the personal integrity of patients. Patients alone are capable of assessing this personal integrity, because it is coterminous with their selfhood. However, it is not uncommon that the patient is incapable of making or expressing his or her assessment. When this happens, someone must make a surrogate assessment. In such cases, the surrogate, who may or may not be the physician, must attempt to be 'in the place of the other.' We will not discuss the complexities of this question here. We only

note that if the surrogate is a physician, his duty to do no harm may extend
not only to controlling the risk of physical harm, but to adopting the felicific
calculus of the other, incorporating in schematic form the entire range of
possible effects on personal integrity.

IV. THE FOURTH USE: THE BENEFIT–DETRIMENT EQUATION

Many medical procedures not only carry risk of harm, but do, necessarily,
cause a detriment at the same time as they effect a benefit. Any amputation
will, in one and the same act, remove a diseased part in order to save life and
always leave the patient with a physical and, sometimes, a psychological
deficit. Administration of powerful alkylating agents, such as nitrogen
mustards, for treatment of lymphomas, produces almost invariably
unpleasant and sometimes serious side effects. Drawing blood for careful
monitoring of a tiny premature baby's blood gases significantly reduces the
baby's blood volume. Some of these necessarily associated detriments can be
remedied; some must be borne.

In situations such as these, the maxim might be rephrased as, 'Do no harm
unless that harm is necessarily associated with a compensating benefit.' A
certain benefit must be balanced against a certain detriment. Here again, as in
the previous risk–benefit usage, a felicific calculus can be employed. How
does one sum the benefits and the detriments in terms of a desired life plan?
Here also the physician knows the ratio, uses it to eliminate disproportionate
approaches, and informs the patient about the effects of the therapeutic plan
which seems most reasonable. Here again, the patient alone is in a position to
make the calculation. One chooses to live even as a quadriplegic; another
prefers the limited life on dialysis to the risks of transplantation.

There are, however, certain problems of benefit–detriment which do not
fit easily into the felicific calculus. These are problems in which the benefit
accrues to one party and the detriments to another. Three current problems
in bioethics are of this type: abortion, allocation of scarce biomedical
resources, and non-therapeutic experimentation on subjects incapable of
consent. A fourth problem is on the horizon: sterilization of carriers of
deleterious genes. In such cases, certain non-moral evils are visited upon some
in order that others might benefit. Classical utilitarian reasoning, although
vaunting its solution to such problems, has generally been considered at its
weakest in coming to grips with the distribution of benefits and burdens to
different parties.

Another manner of moral reasoning, traditionally called the Principle of Double Effect, was designed to deal with problems of this sort. Although much criticized in recent years, from within and without the camp of Roman Catholic moral theologians, who were its creators, it seems at least to ask the right question: under what circumstances can one be said to act morally when one of the manifold effects of that action is a non-moral evil? The death of a fetus, the danger to a non-consenting subject, refusal of dialysis, the imposed sterility of a dysgenic male are all non-moral evils. Is their occurrence or permission justified by some good, presumably 'greater,' for some other or others?

The Double Effect approach to this question is distinctly more deonto-logical than the felicific calculus. In its most traditional form, it depends on the distinction between directly intended and indirectly intended or merely permitted effects. The object of the direct intention must be a good in itself or, at least, be morally indifferent. In the ethical theory which engendered the double effect, statement about intention and object, although they appear teleological, are in fact considerations about the character of the act itself. Thus, an act good in itself could cause a foreseen, but unintended evil result, but no good result, no matter how great, could justify an act vitiated with bad intent or by an intrinsically evil object. Recent attempts by Catholic theologians to untangle this ethical intricacy have turned on the notion that 'proportionate reason' is not merely a 'serious reason' but rather an explanation of how the evil effect is an inextricable by-product of a good which one is obliged to perform. Outside the theologians' camp, Phillipa Foote argues that it is the concept of positive and negative duties, rather than the intended and the foreseen, that determines the justifiability of an evil effect ([7], [17], [23], [10]).

We will not enter the debate about the strengths and weaknesses of double effect reasoning. We simply note that, in arguments about the morality of multiple effects, participants often believe that some of these are undesirable and, perhaps, immoral. They also believe that something other than 'greater good of another or of the greater number' must be proposed to justify the commission or permission of an evil effect. They seek for 'serious' or 'overriding' reasons which are at least implicitly deontological. The abortion debate, in some of its forms, is the classic example. Abortion is a medical act which has several consequences: the mother's well-being and the death of the fetus. Many make an ethical case for abortion by admitting the undesirable, evil (non-moral), and perhaps immoral result of fetal death, but cite one or several reasons which they consider 'to override' or 'to justify' that effect.

Freedom to one's own body is taken as such a reason, a principle which is clearly deontological.

In this use, then, 'do no harm' is an imperative introducing double effect reasoning. It calls for the proposal of serious or proportionate reasons for allowing a detriment which is necessarily concomitant with a benefit. Further analysis of this use may follow the path of deontological questions about duties, about intrinsic evil, or into the theories about 'good reasons' as determinants of morality.

V. A PARADOXICAL USE

Recently, several authors have invoked the principle 'do no harm' to justify involuntary euthanasia. Engelhardt writes:

In the field of medicine, the need is to recognize an ethical category, a concept of wrongful continuance of existence, . . . (which) presupposes that life can be of a negative value such that the medical maxim *primum non nocere* would not require sustaining life. ([4], p. 187; [15]).

The proposal is, at first sight, paradoxical. Does not one harm another by allowing him/her to die? Can sustaining life be properly called harming?

A review of the use of the maxim may put the proposal in perspective. If 'do no harm' means having always the motive to care for the other, termination of painful or seriously debilitated existence might be considered a 'caring act.' However, this appears to beg the question: can deprivation of life, of any quality, be a good for the one deprived? The second usage, due care, at first sight, seems irrelevant, for it is primarily procedural. However, it may be highly relevant. Due care consists of assessing medical actions in relation to certain goals. It might be argued that sustaining life of low quality is not a goal of medical actions since medicine is concerned only with restoration of health in some functional sense. Thus, medical actions which cannot achieve this are improper and may be ethically discontinued. The physician judges this action to be beyond his or her responsibility. The third usage, risk—benefit equation, bears only on the question, often moot, about whether continued care might possibly bring about restoration. The fourth use, benefit—detriment equation, is most often invoked. If used as felicific calculus it is flawed by being always a surrogate judgement and also by the logical peculiarities inherent in the suggestion that some one would be 'better off dead.' It seems that both benefit and detriment must be experienced in order to be weighed.

Finally, if the fourth use is seen as a good reasons argument, the good reasons must be scrutinized in terms of some broader ethical theory which gives the criteria whereby a reason is measured as good. Richard McCormick, for example, proposes a theological ethical theory:

In all of these instances – instances where the life could be saved – the discussion is couched in terms of the means necessary to preserve life. But often enough it is the kind of the quality of life thus saved (painful, poverty-stricken and deprived, away from home and friends, oppressive) that establishes the means as extraordinary. *That* type of life would be an excessive hardship for the individual. It would distort and jeopardize his grasp on the overall meaning of life. Why? Because, it can be argued, human relationships – which are the very possibility of growth in love of God and neighbor – would be so threatened, strained, or submerged that they would no longer function as the heart and meaning of the individual's life as they should. Something other than the 'higher, more important good' would occupy first place. Life, the condition of other values and achievements, would usurp the place of these and become itself the ultimate value. When that happens, the value of human life has been distorted out of context [24].

At this early stage of this difficult discussion, I would suggest that it is legitimate to invoke the 'do no harm' maxim as a justification for termination of life. The logic of this justification, however, must move through usages two and four, 'due care' and 'good reasons.' The substance of the argument is difficult to make because standards of due care for the dying and the irretrievably comatose are very insufficiently developed by physicians, and because theories of good reason for action are very skimpily designed by philosophers. Physicians who do not understand the 'end of medicine' and philosophers who do not appreciate the 'end of man' are unlikely to succeed in providing the substance of that argument ([16], [13]).

VI. CONCLUSION

In conclusion, I wish to draw several generalizations about the 'do no harm' argument. First, arguments rather than argument seem more appropriate. The maxim serves in a variety of ways, each of which represents a somewhat different mode of ethical discourse. We have noted several: a deontological principle, a counsel of prudence, a calculation of acceptability, a rule of double effect. When the maxim appears, its role as one or another of these should be recognized and the argument analyzed accordingly. Secondly, the maxim as deontological principle and counsel of prudence is directed at the physician as moral agent, urging that he or she have certain motives, intentions, and ways of judging. As felicific calculus and as rule of double effect, it is directed primarily at the patient and only indirectly at the physician, for it is the recipient of care who must accept risks and find reasons proportionate. Only occasionally will the physician have to exercise surrogate judgement about these. The 'do no harm' maxim, in these uses affirms that physician ethics must be centered on respect for persons and their autonomy. The benefit to others commanded by the deontological principle which initiates the moral enterprise of medicine is seen more clearly to be the benefit of fostering the independence of patients. Harming touches not only the body, but the person in his or her personality and community.

In conclusion, it may appear that dwelling on the negative apodosis, 'do no harm,' rather than upon the positive protasis, 'be of benefit,' creates the impression of a minimalist morality. This may be. But if we recall the version of the maxim, 'at least do no harm,' we may see it, not so much as a morality of lower limits, but as an admonition to humility. When good persons possess great powers and wield them on behalf of others, they sometimes fail to recognize the harm done as they ply their beneficent tools. The medical profession has such power and has, most often, the intention of using it well. They must become sensitive to its shadow side. A character in a recent novel states the case for humility well:

I was less morally ambitious than you . . . I didn't aspire to do good; that seemed too difficult. I only wanted not to do harm ([21], p. 271).

Only wanting not to do harm, we may conclude, is difficult enough!

University of California Health Policy Program,
San Francisco, California

NOTES

[1] Professor O. Temkin writes, 'I do not know the origin of *primum non nocere* though I feel certain that it has its own roots in the Hippocratic passage. But as with other old medical dicta, it is very difficult, if not impossible, to trace the exact origin' (personal communication to author). The Latin version of Galen contains the elements of both 'primum' and 'at least,' reading, 'oportet enim medicum imprimis aegrorum auxilio animum intendere sin minus ipsos tamen non laedere.' Galen's own comment on the text is interesting: 'Those studying medicine, I am aware, believe, as I once did, that it was unworthy of the Great Hippocrates to lay down the precept, "help and do no harm." But the truth of this statement is manifest to those who have attained some experience . . . for one sees many famous physicians guilty of inopportune use of too strong remedies.' (*Galeni in Hippocratis Epid* I, ii, [53], 148–9.)

[2] Both these thoughts are combined in a curious passage by Thomas Percival: To a young physician it is of great importance to have clear and definite ideas of the end of his profession; of the means for their attainment, and of the comparative value and

dignity of each. Wealth, rank and independence, with all the benefits resulting from them, are the primary ends which he holds in view and they are interesting, wise and laudable. But knowledge, benevolence and active virtue, the means to be adopted in their acquisition are of still higher estimation. He has the privilege and felicity of practicing an art, even more intrinsically excellent in its mediate than in its ultimate objects. The former, therefore, have a claim to uniform preeminence. (Leake, C. (ed.): 1975, *Percival's Medical Ethics*, Krieger, Huntington, New York, p. 100.)

BIBLIOGRAPHY

1. Aquinas: 1945, *Basic Writings of Saint Thomas Aquinas*, A. C. Pegis (ed.), Random House, New York, II, 773 (I–II [94], [2]).
2. Beecher, H.: 1970, *Research and the Individual*, Little–Brown, Boston.
3. Edelstein, L.: 1967, 'The Genuine Works of Hippocrates', *Ancient Medicine*, The Johns Hopkins Press, Baltimore.
4. Engelhardt, H. T.: 1975, 'Aiding the Death of Young Children', in M. Kohl (ed.), *Beneficent Euthanasia*, Prometheus Books, Buffalo.
5. Engelhardt, H. T. and Spicker, S.: 1975, *Evaluation and Explanation in the Biochemical Sciences*, Reidel, Dordrecht-Boston.
6. Etziony, M. B.: 1973, *The Physicians Creed*, Charles C. Thomas, Springfield.
7. Fagothy, A.: 1963, *Right and Reason*, C. V. Mosby, St. Louis.
8. Feinberg, J.: 1973, *Social Philosophy*, Prentice-Hall, Englewood Cliffs.
9. Feinstein, A.: 1967, *Clinical Judgement*, Krieger, Huntington, New York.
10. Foote, P.: 1967, 'The Problem of Abortion and The Doctrine of Double Effect', *Oxford Review* No. 5, 5–15.
11. Fried, C.: 1971, *Anatomy of Values*, Harvard University Press, Cambridge.
12. Gorovitz, S. and MacIntyre, A.: 1975, 'Toward A Theory of Medical Fallibility', *Hastings Center Report* 5, 13–23.
13. Gustafson, J. M.: 1975, *The Contributions of Theology to Medical Ethics*, Marquette University, Milwaukee.
14. Jones, W. H. S.: 1923, *Hippocrates I*, Harvard University Press, Cambridge.
15. Jonsen, A. R. *et al.*: 1975, 'Ethical Issues in Neonatal Intensive Care', *Pediatrics* 55, 756–768.
16. Kass, L.: 1970, 'Regarding the End of Medicine and the Pursuit of Health', *The Public Interest* 40, 11–42.
17. Knauer, P.: 1967, 'The Hermeneutic Principle of Double Effect', *Natural Law Forum* 12, 132–162.
18. Kramer, C.: 1968, *The Negligent Doctor*, Crown, New York.
19. Littre, E.: 1840, *Oeuvres Completes d'Hippocrate*, Paris, 1839–1861, II, pp. 635–7.
20. Locke, J.: 1965, *Second Treatise*, 6, P. Lasletti (ed.), Mentor Books, New York.
21. Lurie, A.: 1975, *The War Between the Taits*, Random House, New York.
22. Mayerhoff, M.: 1971, *On Caring*, Harper and Row, New York.
23. McCormick, R.: 1973, *Ambiguity in Moral Choice*, Marquette University, Milwaukee.
24. McCormick, R.: 1974, 'To Live or Let Die', *Journal of the American Medical Association* 229, 173–175.
25. Pappworth, M. H.: 1971, *Primer of Medicine*, Appleton-Century-Crofts, New York.

LOUIS LASAGNA

DISCUSSION OF 'DO NO HARM'

In discussions of medical ethics, there is an ever-present danger — of confusing clichés with profundity and eternal verities. It is my unshakable belief that *primum non nocere* has become just such a cliché. Used by people who know neither its origin nor the time-bound quality of its original advice, the phrase has become a refuge for everyone from malpractice lawyers to therapeutic nihilists. Yet an examination of the concept can be useful in arriving at a moralistic *modus vivendi* for today's world.

Let me not mince words. I see no validity to the notion that 'above all' [or even first of all] do no harm is either 'the prime principle of medical ethics' or 'the answer to the malpractice crisis.'

Much more attractive (to me at least) is the Jones translation of what is available to us as part of the Hippocratic corpus of medical works: 'to help or at least to do no harm.' Patients want to be helped, first and foremost. To be kept from harm is not irrelevant, but it is in a sense a *negative* goal. In ancient times, when the therapeutic cupboard was relatively bare of excellent remedies but brimming with measures of questionable merit but indubitable capacity for harm, it certainly behooved the physician, if incapable of providing succor, at least not to add iatrogenic woe to nature's ills.

But in 1975 surely all that has changed. Not that physicians are incapable of inflicting harm — far from it! Our potent chemicals, our complicated machines, our daring surgical maneuvers, our 'spare parts' capability provide us with infinitely more power for harm than our ancestors possessed. But we also possess infinitely more power for good than did our forebears. Furthermore, every diagnostic, therapeutic, or prophylactic weapon has two edges, and there is no 'safe' drug, vaccine, anesthetic, or surgical procedure.

The proper medical and moral stance for today's physician, therefore, is not to avoid harm at all costs, but to optimize treatment. In what ways are these positions different? In some respects, not at all. As in times of yore, a therapeutic maneuver that is not necessary and carries even the slightest risk poses a cost—benefit situation that is unacceptable (although one might not rule out use of a placebo in such a case).

On the other hand, one should not hesitate to use penicillin to treat

S. F. Spicker and H. T. Engelhardt, Jr. (eds.), Philosophical Medical Ethics: Its Nature and Significance, 43—46. *All Rights Reserved. Copyright* © 1977 *by D. Reidel Publishing Company, Dordrecht-Holland.*

pneumococcal pneumonia or chloramphenicol to treat typhoid fever, despite the ability of each of these antibiotics (rarely) to kill, because the untreated diseases are even more deadly. Two years ago an article appeared entitled 'Amphotericin Pharmacophobia' which showed the dangerous extremes to which a misguided adherence to *Primum non nocere* can lead. The article documented the deaths of five patients whose serious (and ultimately fatal) fungal infections were untreated for fear of toxicity from the antibiotic that offered them at least a chance for survival!

The explosion in our knowledge presents the conscientious physician with ever-increasing problems. He must now not only take a history to ferret out the possibility of penicillin allergy, but may have to test some patients with penicillin antigens before deciding to use this antibiotic. Knowing that tetracyclines can stain the teeth of children, he must avoid these antibiotics in the young whenever possible. Since antibiotics are usually eliminated to a large extent by the kidneys, the doctor must adjust the dosage and dosage interval of antibiotics in patients whose renal function is compromised. The doctor must eschew the simultaneous use of drugs which, given together, can cause serious toxicity or nullify each other's therapeutic benefits.

There are other, more positive aspects to optimizing therapy. Venereal disease or hypertension undiagnosed and untreated is serious indeed, so the physician's responsibility in minimizing the harm from these diseases requires him to acquire the characteristics of a detective, a diplomat, a salesman, a psychiatrist, a minister, and a pharmacologist. For minor illnesses, on the other hand, the physician's role may be to encourage self-diagnosis and even self-treatment, to spare the patient and the doctor the greater time, expense, and hazard of professional diagnostic and therapeutic adventures.

I referred earlier to the time-bound quality of our therapeutic risk—benefit ratios. At one time bleeding, puking and purging were orthodox therapy. Today they are denigrated, although periodic bleeding is still a method of choice for the hemic plethora that characterizes a disease known as polycythemia vera. The implantation of valves in the heart and great vessels, the use of coronary by-pass surgery, the availability of chronic renal dialysis, our power to transplant kidneys, hearts, and livers and to breathe for people whose own respiratory centers have failed have all contributed new factors to the cost-benefit equation and cause us constantly to reevaluate the calculus of our optimal therapy approach.

Is medicine primarily a 'moral enterprise'? I doubt it, any more than plumbing or auto repair is. Physicians rarely cure or save lives, and spend most of their time trying to provide some comfort, relieve symptoms, and perhaps prolong life. The moral issues come up in situations that constitute only a small fraction of the physician's practice. The dramatic life-and-death issues (euthanasia, abortion, etc.) are difficult (and also time-bound, incidentally) but relatively uncommon occurrences for the typical physician.

There are, however, opportunities for the physician to manifest behavior that is at best unprofessional and at worst immoral. A physician's personal hang-ups about dying patients, or smelly ones, or noisy, lying drunks, his fears about financial ruin from malpractice suits, his desire to get to the golf course rather than stop at the scene of an auto accident to tender help, his preference for a 9 to 5 work schedule rather than one that makes his time not his own but his patients', a willingness to strike for higher wages – these are factors that at least alter the traditional view that physicians often have about themselves or that attracts them into medicine in the first place.

The physician's attempt to function morally and ethically is increasingly hampered by contrary advice from laws or regulations. The Helsinki Declaration says that 'the doctor must be free to use a new therapeutic measure if in his judgement it offers hope of saving life, re-establishing health, or alleviating suffering,' but FDA tells him that his personal judgement is not trustworthy and that if he prescribes a drug for an indication that is not recognized as legitimate by our regulators, he is legally liable if damage ensues, no matter how many other countries have approved the drug for that purpose.

No drug is likely to be approved for marketing in the U.S. that has not successfully undergone controlled trials in this country, even if impeccable foreign trials have already been performed. How can one reconcile one's professional responsibility to his patient and perform such a trial, comparing the new drug with either an old drug or a placebo already shown by competent scientists to be inferior to the new treatment?

What is the right thing for the doctor to do – in an attempt to minimize harm to the patient – if obtaining 'fully informed consent' will frighten the patient out of his wits or make it likely that the patient will make a decision against his own welfare? Is it really enough to say that people ought to be allowed to make the wrong decision if they so desire?

May the patient who wishes a 'surrogate' to make a decision on his behalf choose his own doctor to be that surrogate, or must he choose a 'neutral' ombudsman whom he neither knows nor trusts? If a patient has carefully decided that death is preferable to life (and not simply in a moment of severe depression), can we not agree that in such a case deprivation of life *is* a good? (*I* certainly think so, although I also believe that such instances are rare, and that one must be on guard against the physician who will terminate the patient's life for his [the doctor's] *own* peace of mind, or the family's rather than that of the patient.)

But what *of* the family? Is the individual always sacrosanct? Why is one person's welfare more important than the collective welfare of a group of persons? Military triage or triage during a civil catastrophe is based on the optimization of *collective* care, in the belief that if two surgeons working at capacity can save either ten moderately wounded men or two seriously wounded ones, the ten should take priority over the two. Is this sort of statistical morality invidious? If *not*, then may one not ask whether it is ethical or moral or just to inflict huge hospital bills and economic catastrophe on a family simply to keep 'alive' someone who seems neither sentient nor capable of ever being so again?

Finally, a respectful plea for pluralism and fallibilism — or at least a reminder of their existence. In the practice of medicine, men and women of experience and good will may disagree heartily on the best course of action. Sometimes this is the result of different data bases, a situation which may allow for consensus to be reached by providing new information. But often it is a matter of different judgements based on the same data base. As Edwin Newman has put it in his delightful book *Strictly Speaking*: 'Nine justices of the United States Supreme Court may consult the same laws, check the same precedents, and come out with contradictory conclusions, elegantly expressed.'

Discussions of medical ethics all too often lack this ambience of pluralism and fallibilism. The very words 'right' and 'wrong' trap us by their intransigence. So does the fear of moral anarchy, of helpless drift on a dark and uncertain ethical sea. But to accept the validity of differences — and what is more characteristic of life than variability? — to respect and even to seek differences, may in the long run prove our salvation. Perhaps all I have been saying, rather long-windedly, is that 'primum non nocere' strikes me as just the opposite sort of advice — a stern, inflexible commandment carved in stone, with neither the carving nor the stone being of high quality.

University of Rochester,
School of Medicine and Dentistry,
Rochester, New York.

SECTION II

ETHICS AND MEDICAL ETHICS

R. M. HARE

MEDICAL ETHICS: CAN THE
MORAL PHILOSOPHER HELP?

I should like to say at once that if the moral philosopher *cannot* help with the problems of medical ethics, he ought to shut up shop. The problems of medical ethics are so typical of the moral problems that moral philosophy is supposed to be able to help with, that a failure here really would be a sign either of the uselessness of the discipline or of the incompetence of the particular practitioner. I do not want to overstate this point, however. It could be the case that, so far as practical help goes, philosophy is at the stage now at which, not so long ago, medicine was. It has been said that until fairly recently one was more likely to survive one's illnesses if one kept out of the hands of the doctor than if one allowed oneself to be treated — and this was at any rate true of the wounded on battlefields, because the surgeons' instruments were not sterilized. Yet all the same medicine *has* now progressed to a stage at which it saves lives. The change came when certain *methods* got accepted: I mean, not merely such things as aseptic surgery, but also the application to medicine of the scientific method in general, which meant that firm and reliable procedures were adopted for determining whether a certain treatment worked or not; and also the relation of medicine to fundamental knowledge about physiology and biochemistry, which made possible the invention of new treatments to be tested in this way.

The same could be true of philosophy. There have been great philosophers in the past, just as there were great doctors before the advent of modern medicine; but it is only very recently in the history of philosophy that general standards of rigour in argument have improved to such an extent that there is some hope of our establishing our discipline on a firm basis. By 'standards of rigour', I mean such things as the insistence on knowing, and being able to explain, exactly what you mean when you say something, which involves being able to say what follows logically from it and what does not, what it is logically consistent with, and so on. If this is not insisted on, arguments will get lost in the sands. Even now it is insisted on only in certain parts of the philosophical world; you are very likely to meet philosophers who do not accept this requirement of rigour, and my advice to you is that you should

S. F. Spicker and H. T. Engelhardt, Jr. (eds.), Philosophical Medical Ethics: Its Nature and Significance, 49–61. All Rights Reserved. Copyright © 1977 by R. M. Hare, Corpus Christi College, Oxford, England.

regard them in the same light as you would regard a medical man, whether or not he had the right letters after his name, who claimed to have a wonder drug which would cure the common cold, but was not ready to submit it to controlled tests. It is undoubtedly true that many patients will feel much better when they have taken his drug; but since we simply do not know whether it is the drug that has made them feel better, or his personal charisma, or natural causes, he has not contributed to the advance of medicine.

I do not want to give the impression that nobody insisted on rigour in argument until recently; indeed, it was the insistence on knowing what you meant that really got philosophy started. Socrates, Plato, and Aristotle, as well, probably, as some other great men of their time whose works have not come down to us, knew how philosophy ought to be done and made great progress in it; and there have been other periods in which philosophy in this rigorous sense has flourished; but they have always been succeeded by periods of decline in which a kind of superficial excitement was prized above rigour in argument, and so philosophy got lost. It is very important not to let this happen again. For the true philosopher the most exciting thing in the world — perhaps the only exciting thing — is to become really clear about some important question.

I said at the beginning that if philosophers could not help with the problems of medical ethics they might as well shut up shop. But *how* can they help? Not in some of the ways that many people seem to think. The failure to help in *these* ways is indeed the reason why it is thought that philosophy can never help at all. But we must not look for elixirs.

It is very important, for example, to understand that the relation between a philosopher and somebody who is troubled about a question in medical ethics can never be like that between an old-fashioned general practitioner and his patient. Philosophy is much more like the teaching of remedial exercises. Philosophers cannot give their patients pills which the patients can just swallow. Philosophy itself is the medicine, and it has to be understood, to some degree at any rate, by the patient himself, in a way that medical science does not.

Nor does philosophy try to prove to people that they must think this or that, by deducing conclusions from premises which cannot be denied. Some philosophers have thought that they could do this; some still do. What I am now saying is controversial; but I can only tell you what I think in the present state of the controversy. Claims to prove moral conclusions, starting from premises which we cannot deny, always turn out to fail in one of the following ways: either the premises can, after all, be denied; or the argumentation is simply invalid; or it is expressed in an ambiguous way, so that if you take the words one way, the premises can be denied, but if you take them in a way in which the premises cannot be denied, the conclusion does not follow from them.

I will give you an example connected with the problem about abortion. People sometimes think that they can prove that abortion must be wrong by using the following sort of argument. We know that murder is always wrong; we know that killing (sc. intentionally) another innocent human being is murder; we know that the fetus is a human being, and innocent; so we know that killing it is murder, and therefore wrong. There are at least two points at which this argument can be assailed. The first concerns the word 'murder'; the second, the word 'human'. Another word that could give us trouble is 'innocent', and so could 'intentional'; but I shall not have time to talk about those. Now it is perfectly true that on *one* definition of 'murder' it means something like 'wrongful killing'; and in that sense murder must be wrong. But that is not how the word is being taken in the second premise of the argument, that killing another innocent human being is murder. For this premise is being claimed to be undeniable, and to make it so we should have to *define* 'murder' in such a way that it must be true. Some people have indeed defined 'murder' as 'the intentional killing of another innocent human being', though there are difficulties about this definition. But if we used this definition of 'murder', we should make the argument invalid; for it does not follow logically from the fact that a man has intentionally killed another innocent human being that he has done wrong. So even if we were to accept without question that to kill a fetus is to kill an innocent human being, we cannot prove that it is wrong; it is, certainly, murder in the sense defined, but not in the sense in which murder logically has to be wrong.

More interesting is the expression 'human being'. There is no doubt a sense in which the fetus is already a human being; and there is another sense in which it does not become a human being until it is born. How are we to decide in which of these senses the words 'human being' are being used when murder is defined as 'the intentional killing of another innocent human being'? Is this meant to cover fetuses or not? Well, either it is or it is not. If it is, then it is not so self-evident that the killing of *any* innocent human beings, including fetuses (which is what 'murder' will now mean) is wrong. That, indeed, is what we were trying to decide, and we cannot beg the question by *assuming* that it is wrong. On the other hand, if 'human being' does not cover fetuses, then killing fetuses will not be killing human beings, and so will not be murder, and so will not be wrong just because murder is wrong.

At this point it may be objected that deciding to call the fetus a human being is not just an arbitrary decision. Fetuses, it may be said, are *like* human beings in certain important respects. But the question remains, are these respects sufficient to make us include fetuses under the prohibition of murder? On this question, no light has been shed by these verbal maneuvers. Philosophers spend a lot of time talking about words; but at any rate the good philosophers do this precisely in order to *avoid* being deceived by words into evading the substantial questions. The thing is to get the words straight – to decide what you are going to mean by them – and then get on to the real business.

This brings me to what I think is the main – perhaps the only – contribution of the philosopher to the solution of these problems. He comes in because moral problems, of which problems in medical ethics are an example, cannot be discussed without using many words whose meaning and logical properties are not at all clear. These included, in particular, the moral words such as 'wrong'. Philosophy is a training in the study of such tricky words and their logical properties, in order to establish canons of valid argument or reasoning, and so enable people who have mastered it to avoid errors in reasoning (confusions or fallacies), and so answer their moral questions with their eyes open. It is my belief that, once the issues are thoroughly clarified in this way, the problems will not seem so perplexing as they did at first and, the philosophical difficulties having been removed, we can get on with discussing the practical difficulties, which are likely to remain serious.

So much then for the place of philosophy in this business, as I see it. I want now to expound two rival philosophical approaches to problems of medical ethics (both of them consistent with the view about the role of philosophy that I have just been advocating). I am going to call these two approaches the 'absolutist' approach and the 'utilitarian' approach. These names are not particularly helpful ones, and can be misleading; but they are current in philosophical discussions and so I do not want to introduce new names. It is necessary, however, to warn you that 'absolutist' is not here being used in the sense in which it is the opposite of 'relativist' (that is a quite different controversy which need not concern us); and that there are a great many different versions of utilitarianism, some of which are very easily demolished, but others of which are at least extremely plausible. After I have set out these two rival approaches, I shall suggest a way of looking at the matter which combines the virtues and avoids the faults of both of them.

Either of these approaches could be represented as in line with common sense and our ordinary opinions, although if we look closely at the approaches themselves they look inconsistent with each other. This is a sign that common sense and our ordinary opinions may not be entirely self-consistent. I shall be trying to show that, when the issue is fully clarified, we can still go on holding the important parts of our common-sense views, and that this will not land us in inconsistency. But before we can understand this, we shall have to do some fairly difficult philosophy.

Absolutists will often say something like this: there are certain kinds of actions (for example, killing innocent people) which are wrong, and nothing can make them right. The kinds of action in question are specified in fairly simple, general terms, and this, as we shall see, is the most characteristic feature of this approach. Utilitarians, on the other hand, are likely to say that one has to do the best one can in a given situation — to act for the best. It is easy to see how the two approaches can conflict in unusual or difficult cases. For example, absolutists will say that because killing innocent people is always wrong, if you are in a situation in which if you do not kill one innocent person twenty other innocent people will die (though not by your hand), then you ought to be prepared to let the twenty die rather than become guilty of the death of the one. But utilitarians will say that you have to act for the best in the circumstances, and save the twenty at the expense of the one. There is a particularly clear example which is commonly used in philosophical discussions of this subject: twenty-one potholers are coming out of the cave that they are exploring when the front one, who is fatter than the rest, gets stuck in a narrow place; there has been sudden heavy rain and the water is rising in the cave behind them, so that they can only survive if they use such force (e.g., explosives) to remove him as will in fact kill him. I have used this example because it is a particularly clear one; the literature about abortion and other questions in medical ethics is of course full of similar examples.

Let us first look at some of the arguments that are used on both sides of this kind of controversy. Some of these arguments are theoretical and some practical. On the whole it is the theoretical arguments of the utilitarians which are convincing, and the practical arguments of the absolutists. This, as we shall see, points the way to a resolution of the conflict, because a more sophisticated utilitarian theory can absorb enough of the absolutist approach to retain its practical merits.

As an example of a practical argument which is used by absolutists, consider the following. Let us call it the 'slippery slope' argument (another name might be the 'thin end of the wedge' argument). If you once allow abortion in some admittedly very difficult cases, then you have breached irrevocably the principle that it is wrong to kill innocent human beings. You will then find yourself unable to condemn abortion in any cases, or infanticide, or even the plain murder of adults when it seems to you to be 'for the best'. Or, to take another example: if you are prepared to allow the bystanders to kill the driver trapped under the blazing gas tanker to save him from roasting to death, how can you say it is wrong to kill *anybody* who seems to have a greater likelihood of unhappiness in life than of happiness (which perhaps includes a great many of us). And if we can kill somebody when it is for *his* greater good, ought we not in fairness to kill him when it is for the greater good of all, considering their interests impartially? My sister is a doctor, and a colleague once said to her, 'If euthanasia is legalized, we shall start by killing people to put them out of extreme agony, and end up killing them because we want to get away for the weekend.'

What the absolutist is here appealing to is the sanctity of a very simple and general (and, most people will think, a very important) moral principle. We feel that if we once loosen our hold on this principle, anything goes. The utilitarian may reply by saying that life is not so simple as that. In the general run of cases this simple principle that it is wrong to kill innocent people is the one to follow; its general abandonment would have disastrous consequences for people's well-being; we should go perpetually in fear of our lives. So we should very seldom indeed be acting for the best if we did anything to weaken the hold of this principle upon our society or upon ourselves. It is extremely easy to persuade oneself that in one's own particular case it would be for the best to breach the principle; but, just because it is easy to persuade oneself of this, we ought to be on our guard against doing so when, perhaps, an impartial spectator, who knew the facts and the future better than we do, would warn us that we were deceiving ourselves. And that is why most of us think, when we are considering the moral education of our children or the formation of our own characters and of the generally accepted *mores* of society, that it is very important to establish a secure place for these good general principles — principles like the one about killing, or the principle that it is wrong to tell lies or break promises. And we think, most of us, that if it would take a very great deal to make a man break one of these principles, he is a better man than somebody who will break them without a qualm if he can convince himself that it is the best thing to do in the circumstances.

If all this is so, then there are sound *utilitarian* reasons for doing all we can to preserve the good principles by which the absolutist sets store. I want to illustrate this by considering a move which is extremely common in arguments about euthanasia. Medical people often say, 'Our whole training and our attitudes are directed towards the saving of life; how can you ask us to kill people?' Here, you see, it is a question of the attitudes that we think doctors ought to have in general; it is certainly true that unless, in general, a doctor is devoted to the saving of life, he is likely to be a bad doctor. So if a doctor is asked to end a patient's life, or even (though this is not euthanasia strictly speaking) to refrain from saving the life of a patient whom it is far better to let die, he will, if he is a good doctor, feel the greatest reluctance; to do either of these things goes against the grain — the 'grain' being his training as a doctor in the saving of life. Of course, if the advocates of euthanasia or of letting people die in certain cases are right, the doctor ought to overcome this reluctance, provided that he is *certain* that this is a case in which the patient will be better off dead. But there is a practical danger that, if it is overcome in these particular cases, this will lead to a *general* change of attitude on the part of doctors and perhaps also of patients; doctors will stop being thought of, and will stop thinking of themselves, as devoted to the saving of life, and will come instead to be thought of as devoted to doing what *they* think is best for the patient or even for people in general, even if it involves killing him; and this development might not be, taken all in all, for the best.

So here again we might have a *utilitarian* argument for preserving the absolutist principle. I say that we *might* have such an argument. It might, on the other side, be said that the new state of affairs that I envisaged would be better than the old. That would be a matter for investigation. But I have done enough, perhaps, to illustrate the general point that, if we allow the absolutists the practical importance of their good general principles, we can do something to reconcile their position with that of the utilitarians; for we can say that it might be better, even from a utilitarian point of view, in our medical training and in our legislation to seek to preserve the general respect of doctors for the lives of their patients, than to endanger this respect in order to do the best thing (apart from considerations about endangering respect for life) in some relatively rare particular cases.

It will of course be disputed whether this is true: it will be argued on one side that the cases calling for euthanasia or letting die are very numerous and that therefore it would be better to *change* our attitudes; and on the other side that these cases are relatively few, and that they can be looked after in other ways, and that therefore the present attitude is the best one. Or there may be a half-way position (one which is now extremely popular, but which I do not myself find altogether logical) which says that the best attitude to adopt is that killing is absolutely ruled out but it may be all right to let patients die in certain cases. The difficulty here is with the extremely tenuous distinction between killing and letting die — a philosophical problem with which I shall not have time to deal. But at any rate we seem to have reached a point in the argument at which we can investigate, with some hope of discovering the answer, what *is* the best attitude for doctors to adopt to this kind of question. For we can ask, what it would be like if they did adopt one attitude or the other — what it would be like in hospitals and in the homes of dying patients if one attitude or the other were adopted, and which would be the better state of affairs. So the philosophical exercise would have resulted, as all good philosophy should, in returning the problem to the non-philosopher for further investigation, but in a form in which it is better understood, clearer, and therefore easier of solution.

However, I did not really go deep enough into the philosophical aspects of the question. For I left unexamined the problem of how we would decide which state of affairs was 'for the best'. In the short time that remains I want to say a little about this question. In order to be clear about it, I shall have to assume for the sake of argument the truth of a theory about moral reasoning which I hold and have argued for in other places, and apply it to the present problem; I shall not have time now to defend it. But my position is not quite so weak as might appear from what I have just said. For in fact it can be shown that for the purposes of this practical argument my theoretical position has the same effect as a great many of the most well-supported views on how we should argue about moral questions.

Before I put the matter in my own way, I will just give you a list of these views which I say lead to the same results as my own. There is first of all the Christian view that we should do to others as we wish should be done to us (and this means, done to us if we were in precisely the position of the person we are dealing with, including having his desires and interests). Then, secondly, there is the Kantian view that we should act in such a way that we can will the maxim of our action to be a universal law (which entails that it is a law to be applied also if we ourselves were in the position of our patient or victim). Thirdly, there is the so-called 'ideal observer' theory, according to which we should do what would be recommended by an impartial spectator who knew all the facts and had the interests of all the parties equally at heart. And fourthly there is the so-called 'rational contractor' view (recently put forward in a very unclear way by Professor John Rawls and a good deal more clearly by his disciple Professor David Richards); this holds that we should do what is required by the principles which a set of people would accept for the future conduct of the society in which they were going to live, if they did not know what particular role in that society each individual one of them was going to fill. Though Rawls and Richards do not think that this view yields the same practical results as the others, I have tried to show elsewhere that it does.

What is common to all these positions (the logical bones of all of them, we might say) is that they require us to adopt certain *universal* principles or prescriptions, to be applied impartially to whoever is affected by them — ourselves or other people. This logical kernel of all these positions is what is stated in its simplest and most economical form by my own theory, which says that in making a moral judgment what we are doing is prescribing universally for all cases of a given precisely specified kind. If we realize that this is what we are doing, and that therefore our prescriptions would have to be followed also in cases in which we were at the receiving end of the actions which we are considering, we shall be led to give equal weight to the equal interests of all the parties in the situation (because in other precisely similar cases *we* would occupy the roles now occupied by the other parties). And this, in turn, will lead us to a form of utilitarianism (though Rawls does not realize that his own theory has this consequence); for the essence of utilitarianism is that we should do the best we can to serve the interests of all the parties affected by our actions, treating the equal interests of each of them as of equal weight. That is what 'acting for the best', as I have been using that expression, really means.

Now there are a great many different varieties of utilitarianism, as I said; and I should certainly confuse you if I tried to tell you what they all are. The variety which I think is generated by a careful application of the theories I have just been listing is one which, fortunately, enables us, in the way I have indicated, to incorporate the important practical insights of the absolutist. Let me try to tell you as clearly as I can how this comes about.

Suppose that we are wondering what universal principles to adopt for the conduct of ourselves and others, and that we are therefore, as I have said, led to seek to do the best we can for the interests of all the parties considered impartially. This at first sight looks as if it will lead to arguments which many doctors will find repugnant. Imagine a doctor who is told that if he gives a patient of his a bottle to kill his wife with, the patient will give him a very large sum of money; the wife is going to have a pretty miserable time if she lives anyway; the husband will benefit enormously if he is rid of her; the doctor himself will spend the money on buying a yacht and thus get a lot of healthy enjoyment; and if he puts in the death certificate that she died of heart failure, nobody will know there was any foul play. So, it might be argued, the doctor has very good utilitarian reasons for supplying the poison. This sort of example can be used to create the impression that utilitarianism is a thoroughly disreputable creed.

But the utilitarian can justly reply that the argument has been altogether too superficial. We have to ask, not only what is for the best on this particular occasion for the parties affected, but what is for the best for society as a whole. All the members of society are likely to be gravely harmed if doctors are brought up with such attitudes that they can even contemplate such an act. The interests of all are therefore best served if doctors simply put such thoughts out of their mind. This sounds like an absolutist sort of thing to say; but there are good utilitarian reasons for saying it. The doctor who would even think of such a thing is a bad doctor and a bad man, and he or anybody else who had a hand in his upbringing was doing something enormously harmful when he allowed such ideas to be entertained. The good doctor, on the other hand, will put such thoughts out of his mind altogether; and it is in the interests of all of us that our doctors should in this respect be good ones.

The point I am trying to make is that, even on the utilitarian view, there are certain principles which we ought all to try to preserve, and that anything which damages the general acceptance of them is always harmful; and that even though in some rare particular cases it might be more in the interests of the parties, taken as a whole, to break these principles, the good doctor and the good man simply will not consider doing it. If he were going to consider it, he would have to be a worse doctor and a worse man, and to have such doctors is worse for society in general than to have the sort that, on the whole, we do have.

However, all this does not answer for us the question, *What are* the good general principles whose general acceptance by doctors would be for the best? How are we to tell what these principles ought to say about killing? Ought they to ban all killing of patients, for example, or ought they to permit euthanasia? And if so, precisely under what conditions ought they to permit it? To deal with these questions clearly, we have to distinguish between two kinds of moral thinking — two levels or two occasions of moral thought; and correspondingly between two sorts or two uses of moral principles.

There is first of all the kind of thinking that we ought to do when we are considering a particular case before us with all its difficulties and temptations and uncertainties — a patient, say, has just collapsed and we are wondering whether we ought to try to revive him. And secondly there is the kind of thinking that we ought to do when we are not faced immediately with a particular problem, but are trying to decide what principles or attitudes doctors ought to have, what guidelines the disciplinary bodies of the medical profession should follow, or what laws the legislature should enact. This is the sort of thinking that we were doing (not terribly well I am afraid) in the Church of England's Working Party on Euthanasia which reported recently. In this second sort of thinking, too, we are allowed to think about particular cases, but in a rather different way. We are not confined to actual cases before us, but can consider hypothetical, even fantastic, cases, like the one about the potholers that I mentioned earlier. And, since we do not have actually to act in the cases which we consider, we can take them at our leisure, find out all about them including what happened *after* the crucial decision was made; or, if we can't find out, *invent* particular details to illustrate particular points. And about each of these cases, when we have been into it in detail, we can decide what ought to be done, or to have been done, in these precise circumstances. So we shall end up with a lot of very *specific* principles (though still universal ones) which say that in all circumstances *just like this*, one ought to do *just that*.

But this ought not to be the end of this kind of thinking; for, you remember, the purpose of it is to give some sort of general guidance about the attitudes of doctors and others, who are *not* going to be able to give the cases in which they find themselves involved nearly so much thought, because they will not have the time or the information. The principles the doctors will need are not highly specific ones, but, rather, general ones which give the best guidance in the ordinary run of cases, and which, therefore, are the best principles for doctors to adopt almost as second nature — though of course in *very* peculiar cases they may find themselves constrained to depart from them. So now we come to the question which I said I had not dealt with — the question of how to select those good general principles which absolutists rightly say we should follow (though they say next to nothing about how the principles are to be *selected* or the selection *justified*). What I have to say about this will make it doubly clear that there is a place for such principles in a utilitarian system and that the reasoning which leads to their selection is in fact utilitarian.

First of all, when we are doing the selection, we ought not to pay too much attention to particular cases, actual or hypothetical, which are not at all usual or which are unlikely to recur. For we are selecting our principles as practical guides in the world as it actually is, and not as it would be if it were composed of incidents out of short stories, or out of philosophical examples. So it makes a difference if, for example, the number of people who die in agony of terminal cancer either is very small, or would be very small if proper care were taken of them. This is the point of the maxim that hard cases make bad law. If we give weight to the cases in proportion to the probability of occurrence of cases of precisely that type, we shall be more likely to adopt principles whose general adoption and preservation will lead to the best results, on the whole, for those who are affected by them.

And we should not be put off if somebody comes along and tells us about some highly peculiar case and says, 'In this case, in which it would obviously be for the best to depart from these principles, either you must agree that we ought to depart from them or you are not really a utilitarian' (of course it does not matter very much what we *call* ourselves). What we should say to him is, 'All right, then, if the case really is so very peculiar and really occurs, we ought to depart from the principle. But since it is so easy to deceive oneself, and since in actual cases we never know enough and never have enough time to think about it, it is very hard to be sure that this *is* a case in which we ought to depart from the principle. Maybe it is; but maybe, on the other hand, the case actually before us, which we have to deal with here and now, is not really so peculiar after all; we are only trying to persuade ourselves that it is peculiar because we want to get away for the week-end. But even if it is peculiar — even if in *this* case we ought to break the good general principle — we shall do so with the greatest misgiving, because it goes against our whole upbringing as doctors; and the occurrence of this case does not in the least mean that the good general principles are no good. They still ought to be our main standby as doctors, and we ought not to do anything to weaken them.' This, I think, would be a sound attitude, and fundamentally a utilitarian attitude, for doctors to preserve, because it is for the best that doctors should preserve it.

Corpus Christi College,
Oxford, England

BIBLIOGRAPHICAL NOTE

I have avoided inserting references into the actual paper, and do not believe in endnotes; but since my treatment of many questions has had to be very superficial, I append some references to places where I have dealt with them in greater depth. Abortion and euthanasia are discussed in my papers in *Philosophy and Public Affairs* 4 (Spring 1975) and *Philosophic Exchange* 2 (Summer 1975). (The Church of England's Working Party Report on Euthanasia was published by the Church Information Office, London, in 1974, and entitled *On Dying Well*.) The formal similarity between the views I listed on p. 12 is explained in my paper 'Rules of War' in *Philosophy and Public Affairs* 1 (Winter 1972) and my review of Rawls' *A Theory of Justice* in *Philosophical Quarterly* 23

(1973). The distinction between the two levels of moral thinking and the relation between my views about the meanings of the moral words and utilitarianism are dealt with in my papers, 'Principles' in *Proceedings of the Aristotelian Society* 72 (1972/3), and 'Ethical Theory and Utilitarianism' in *Contemporary British Philosophy* 4, H. D. Lewis (ed.) (London, 1976). The theoretical basis of all my remarks is to be found in my two books, *The Language of Morals* (Oxford, 1952) and *Freedom and Reason* (Oxford, 1963).

JAMES RACHELS

MEDICAL ETHICS AND THE RULE AGAINST KILLING: COMMENTS ON PROFESSOR HARE'S PAPER

I shall make three brief comments on issues raised by Professor Hare's paper. The first has to do with utilitarianism; the second, with the slippery slope argument; and the third, with the moral rule against killing.

I

Professor Hare thinks that utilitarianism is an acceptable moral theory; in fact, he thinks that it is entailed by his own universal prescriptivism. His reconciliation of utilitarianism and absolutism consists in showing — or at least, suggesting that it might be shown — that there are good *utilitarian* reasons for accepting some absolutist rules. So the 'compromise' between the two approaches is in one sense no compromise at all: the ultimate ethical justifications all turn out to be utilitarian.

But there is a passage in his paper which illustrates very nicely what other philosophers, including myself, find objectionable about utilitarianism. Professor Hare describes a case in which a doctor is offered a large sum of money to supply poison to a man who wants to kill his wife. The wife 'is going to have a pretty miserable time if she lives anyway,' the husband would be happy to be rid of of her, and the doctor would use the money to buy a yacht, which would make him happy. 'So,' Hare continues, 'it might be argued, the doctor has very good utilitarian reasons for supplying the poison. This sort of example can be used to create the impression that utilitarianism is a thoroughly disreputable creed.' And so it can.

What does Hare say about this case? First, he admits that if we only ask what is best *on this particular occasion,* for the parties affected, we must conclude that the doctor ought to supply the poison. However, he says that if we stop here, the argument is 'too superficial,' for we must also ask what is best *for the society as a whole;* and what is best for the society as a whole is for doctors — and others — to be brought up with such attitudes that they cannot even contemplate such an act. So it appears that, by this maneuver,

S.F. Spicker and H.T. Engelhardt, Jr. (eds.), Philosophical Medical Ethics: Its Nature and Significance, 63–69. All Rights Reserved. Copyright © 1977 by D. Reidel Publishing Company, Dordrecht-Holland.

the utilitarian can avoid the embarrassing conclusion that the doctor ought to supply the poison.

Now what is objectionable is the *original* conclusion that in this particular case — forgetting for the moment about society as a whole — the best thing for the doctor to do is to supply the poison. It is not right to kill someone who doesn't want to die, or to provide the wherewithal to a killer, just to get a new yacht or to make the killer happy, and we don't need to bring into account 'the society as a whole' to see this. Even if we limit ourselves to consideration of only the facts of the particular case, it is still wrong. The fact that utilitarianism says otherwise makes it a disreputable creed, even if there are further maneuvers the utilitarian might employ to reverse the original decision. Moreover, notice that even if doctors are brought up to have attitudes that bar them from contemplating this act, the effect of this will be that on some occasions (including this one) they will not contemplate doing *the right thing*. For Professor Hare's proposal is *not* that they shouldn't contemplate supplying the poison because doing so would be wrong. They should be trained not to consider such actions because *other*, similar actions would be wrong, and on the whole it is best just to exclude all of them from consideration rather than to trust people to make individual judgements in each case.

One way to bring out the wrongness of killing the wife in Hare's example is to ask yourself what judgement you would make if *you* were the intended victim. How would the doctor, or the woman's husband, feel about being killed in such circumstances for such reasons? Professor Hare has argued, in many articles and books, that an action cannot be right if it fails to pass this sort of test of universalizability. (They are cited in the *Bibliographical Note* at the end of his paper.) This type of argument gives the conclusion immediately, without bringing in 'the society as a whole,' that supplying the poison would be wrong. If so, then the connection between Professor Hare's universal prescriptivism and utilitarianism is problematic.

II

Professor Hare suggests that the familiar 'slippery slope' argument might be used to show that, on utilitarian grounds, we ought to accept a fairly strict prohibition on euthanasia. 'If euthanasia is legalized, we shall start by killing people to put them out of extreme agony, and end up killing them because we want to get away for the weekend.'

This argument can be taken in two ways. First, it may be taken to mean that, once a certain practice is accepted, from a logical point of view we are committed to accepting certain other practices as well, since there are no good reasons for not going on to accept the additional practices once we have taken the all-important first step. But, the argument continues, the additional practices are plainly unacceptable, therefore the first step had better not be taken. For example, it may be argued plausibly that once we allow abortion in the early stages of pregnancy, there is no reason not to allow abortion a little later on; and then, there will be no good reason not to allow abortion still later, until finally we are allowing abortion at any time during pregnancy. But if third-trimester abortions are permitted, there is no good reason not to permit infanticide as well, since any good reason that can be given for objecting to infanticide can also be given for objecting to third-trimester abortions. And so, it may be concluded, if we do not want to be committed to approving of infanticide, we had better not approve of abortion even in the early stages of pregnancy.

Taken in this way, the slippery slope argument makes a point about *what you are committed to* once certain practices are accepted. It seems clear, though, that if the argument is taken in this way it will not be a sound argument when applied in the case of euthanasia. For there obviously are good reasons for objecting to killing patients in order to get away for the weekend — or for even more respectable purposes, such as securing organs for transplantation — which do not apply to killing in order to put the patient out of extreme agony. Accepting the one does not deprive us of grounds for rejecting the other.

The second way of interpreting the argument is very different. The argument may be taken as claiming that, once certain practices are accepted, *people shall in fact* go on to accept other practices as well. This is simply a claim about what people will do, and not a claim about what they are logically committed to. If we start off by killing people to put them out of extreme agony, *we shall in fact* end up killing them for trivial reasons, regardless of logic and nice distinctions. Therefore, if we want to avoid the latter, we had better avoid the former. This, I take it, is the force of the absolutist argument with which Professor Hare is concerned.

Now I think it is important to be clear about these two very different forms of the slippery slope argument. Not noticing the difference between them can lead to arguing at cross purposes. Thus, someone may argue that euthanasia should not be permitted because if it is then we will *in fact* end up doing terrible things; and someone else may reply, missing the point entirely but not realizing it, that accepting euthanasia in a few special types of cases does not *logically commit* us to the terrible practices which of course we would all abhor. This reply makes a valid point against the first form of the argument, but it leaves the second form untouched.

Whether or not acceptance of euthanasia in a few special types of cases would lead to the moral horror which Professor Hare's sister's colleague suggests is an empirical question and not a philosophical one. Professor Hare has taught us philosophers not to pretend to any special expertise in such empirical matters, and I don't. However, I would like to offer a couple of common-sense reasons for doubting that such horrors would ensue. I should quickly say that I don't think the problem is whether *doctors* in particular would be corrupted. The question concerns people in general: Would a change in people's attitude toward euthanasia lead to a more *general* change in their attitude toward killing? Would the breach of the moral rule against killing in these special circumstances lead to a general decline in our respect for human life? Historical and anthropological evidence suggests that it would not. It is easy to find examples of societies in which the acceptance of killing, in special circumstances, has not had any apparent effects on people's attitude toward killing in general. In Eskimo societies the killing of infants, and feeble old people, was widely accepted as a measure to avoid starvation; but this did not lead to a more general breakdown of respect for life. We can also note that in our own society killing has been, and still is, accepted in many circumstances. Although I am myself opposed to capital punishment, I would think it a feeble argument against the death penalty to say that, if we start off by executing criminals, we will end up executing non-criminals. So far as one can tell, the evidence points the other way: People are able to compartmentalize different types of cases, and keep them separated, fairly well. Therefore, if we carefully define the types of cases in which we think euthanasia is justified, and also set out strict procedures for making the decision to kill in individual cases, I see no reason to think that such a practice would lead people in general to cease valuing human life, or to doctors treating their other patients murderously.

III

Professor Hare emphasizes the question of what rules we ought to follow, and says that we should select rules 'whose general adoption and preservation will lead to the best results' considering the kinds of situations we most commonly find ourselves in. We ought not, he says, worry too much about 'highly peculiar' cases that don't come along very often. So, if we are wondering whether to accept a rule against killing that would rule out euthanasia, 'it makes a difference if the number of people who die in agony of terminal cancer either is very small, or would be very small if proper care were taken of them.' If the number is small enough, then we can safely ignore this sort of case when formulating our principles.

How, then, are we to justify making occasional *exceptions* to the rules, in the 'highly peculiar' cases? Professor Hare says we are to justify it on utilitarian grounds, but with 'the greatest misgiving.' I think that if we approach the matter in this way we shall miss one of the most important aspects of the moral rule against killing. I want now to suggest a way of understanding the point of this rule that may help us to see, in a systematic way, why certain exceptions should or should not be made.

If we take the rule simply to prohibit *killing*, we quickly run into difficulties. Taken in this simple way, the rule would prohibit killing bugs — killing a bug is, after all, no less a case of killing than killing a human. But of course when we object to killing, *this* isn't what we have in mind at all. So we need to specify the rule more closely. At this point someone is sure to suggest that the rule against killing is only a rule against killing *humans* — but this only invites the further question, what is it about humans that makes killing one of them a morally serious matter, while killing a bug is not?

Of course in some societies the doctrine of 'the sanctity of life' is taken as covering *all* life, non-human as well as human. The Jains, for example, are not only vegetarians for this reason, they watch where they step so as to avoid crushing bugs beneath their feet. On the surface, at least, they appear to be more consistent, for if *life* is sacred, why *isn't* the life of a bug sacred? The bug is a living thing just as surely as we are living things.

But our talk of 'life' is crucially ambiguous. We use this word in two very different ways. On the one hand, when we speak of 'life,' we may be referring to *living things*, i.e., to things that are *alive*. Here the contrast is with things that are dead, or with things that are neither alive nor dead, such as rocks. Not only people, but chimpanzees and bugs, and even trees and bushes are living things. On the other hand, when we speak of 'life' we may have in mind a very different sort of concept, that of *having* a life. This is a notion of biography rather than biology. Human beings are not only alive, they *have lives* as well, whereas other sorts of living things, including trees and bushes and bugs, do not have lives. When Drs. Duff and Campbell reported that they allowed 43 infants to die after concluding that in each case 'prognosis for meaningful life was extremely poor or hopeless,' ([1], p. 890) they were using the concept of life in the second sense, in the sense in which one does or does not *have* a life. Only in this sense does it make sense to talk of a meaningful life or a happy life or a good life.

If the concept of life is ambiguous in this way, then so is the concept of the sanctity of life. The doctrine of the sanctity of life could be taken as placing value on things that are alive. If so, then it is as much an offense to the sanctity of life to kill a bug as it is to kill a man. On the other hand, the doctrine may be taken as placing value on *lives* and on the interests that some creatures, including ourselves, have in virtue of the fact that they are the subjects of lives.

So the point of the rule against killing, on the view I am proposing, is not so much the preservation of things that are alive as the protection of lives and the interests of the subjects of lives. There are a number of implications for medical ethics, having to do with how we understand exceptions to the rule. First, if a patient is in an irreversible coma, his *life* has already ended, even though he is still alive. (The temporal boundaries of one's life need not be the same as the temporal boundaries of one's being alive.) That is why no interest of his will be violated by 'pulling the plug.' If we take the point of the rule against killing to be the preservation of living things, then of course killing such a person is a serious violation of the rule; after all, when such a person dies, something that was alive ceases to be alive. But if we take the point of the rule to be the protection of lives, we get a very different result. For no life is destroyed when the plug is pulled on a patient in irreversible coma.

Second, there are implications for the problem of defective newborns. Here we need of course to distinguish the cases according to how bad the defect is. A Tay—Sachs infant is not the subject of a life and never will be, and that is why keeping it alive seems so peculiarly pointless. A Down's infant, on the other hand, will have a life, although a comparatively simple one, and that is why allowing *it* to die is a more serious matter.

Finally, to take the more complicated case of euthanasia for the terminal patient in extreme agony. This case is more complicated because, unlike the person in irreversible coma or the Tay—Sachs infant, this patient does have a life in progress. However, the only effect which killing him, or allowing him to die, would have on his life would be to subtract a terrible part from it. And if the patient himself judges that this would be a benefit and not a harm to him, that judgement is surely a reasonable one. On this, Professor Hare and I agree.

So, returning to Professor Hare's question: What *rule* with respect to killing would it be good for doctors to accept? I don't think it is desirable for us to cling to a strict rule against killing if we understand the point of that rule to be the preservation of living things, simply for the sake of preserving living things. It is desirable, however, that we cling to a rule protecting *lives*. In sketching the implications of such a rule, I think I have only been drawing out the implications of the rule we already have, but which we often misunderstand.

University of Miami,
Coral Gables, Florida

BIBLIOGRAPHY

1. Duff, R. S., and Campbell, A. G. M.: 1973, 'Moral and Ethical Dilemmas in the Special-Care Nursery', *The New England Journal of Medicine* 289, 890–894.

SECTION III

SPECIAL RIGHTS AND DUTIES:
FROM EUTHANASIA TO EXPERIMENTATION

MARVIN KOHL

EUTHANASIA AND THE
RIGHT TO LIFE

I

Despite the frequent assertion that ours is one of the most benevolent of all free societies, we are currently witnessing a remarkably declining interest in helping others, especially in helping the more unfortunate. There are several reasons for this. Sober experience has taught us that we have been careless, that more often than we care to admit, our spending of great sums of public money has not significantly helped the needy, but has enriched the greedy. Part of the disillusionment is the result of our growing awareness of the problem of future shock. Our increasing belief, nay fear, is that we may be changing our society too fast and in a direction few of us wish to go. But probably the most pressing reason is the economic—ethical one. Most of us are willing to help others, when this does not require too great a sacrifice. But sobering economic experience has taught us, not only that the costs of welfare-like programs are high, but that their fiscal appetites are insatiable. Economists warn us of the dangers. Professed philosophers — the high priests of the good life — concur by telling us that morality can neither command that we help others nor require acts of great or unreasonable sacrifice.

Is it too far-fetched to correlate the decline of an avowed faith in a benevolent society (and the consequent revival of all sorts of appeals to fear) with the growing bigotry, intolerance, and remarkable insensitivity to the possibility of euthanasia[1] being morally justified under certain circumstances?

Euthanasia is certainly no new phenomenon in human affairs. But the opposition to it has seldom before raised its head so high among the masses, or led them to organize movements like that of The Right to Life, and to such readiness to reject out-of-hand the limited practice of voluntary beneficent euthanasia. Much of this attitude is due, of course, to the anti-benevolent, anti-welfare state backlash which I just spoke of. Some of it may be the result of what is going on in the abortion movement. Here it is sufficient to note that the unwarranted claim made by many pro-abortionists

S. F. Spicker and H. T. Engelhardt, Jr. (eds.), Philosophical Medical Ethics: Its Nature and Significance, 73–84. All Rights Reserved. Copyright © 1977 by D. Reidel Publishing Company, Dordrecht-Holland.

that the killing of *any* unwanted fetus is kindly killing, or the use of abortion as a birth control method, can only open the doors to an indiscriminate rejection of the more benevolent forms of abortion and euthanasia.

In thus calling attention to the connection between the anti-benevolent sentiment which seems to be growing in certain segments of our society, I would not want to suggest that this accounts for all the opposition to the practice of voluntary beneficent euthanasia. Nor do I think that all the worries about euthanasia can be justly dismissed even if its rejection is a decision in which the lower passions ultimately rule over both reason and sympathy. I wish merely to call attention to the fact that the issues of euthanasia arise out of a variety of fundamental premises, probably the most important being the extent of our commitment to having a benevolent and rational society.

Let us, however, pass from speculation about the causes of opposition and consider a major worry about the practice of voluntary beneficent euthanasia. Notice that the concern here is with *voluntary beneficent euthanasia* and not with worries about or arguments against *involuntary* or the *non-beneficent* varieties. One cannot emphasize this distinction too strongly, for there are powerful and morally sound arguments against the general practice of the latter. Most of these arguments, however, are inapplicable (or ineffective) against voluntary beneficent euthanasia, especially when one further limits this class to terminally ill patients and also offers the option of an assisted suicide. Indeed, it is the failure to make this distinction adequately that gives the arguments of more dogmatic opponents of euthanasia an air of plausibility they would otherwise not have.

This brings us to the question of what acts of voluntary beneficent euthanasia ought to be made legal. Suffice it here to say that I see no compelling reason to oppose the scheme summarily laid out below.[2] In other words, given conceptual and procedural safeguards (the establishment of which cannot be ruled out *a priori* without moral obliquity), there is no telling reason why a kindly and rational person should object to the following policy concerning those afflicted with an incurable disease (or injury) in its terminal state.

1. Within the limits established by the similar rights of others, there must be relief of pain, relief of suffering, respect for the patient's right to refuse treatment, and provision of adequate health care.

2. When a terminally ill or injured individual has signed a 'living will' or expressed, as a result of reflective judgment, the wish to die, he (or she) has the moral right — and ought to have the legal right — to refuse or discontinue medical treatment, especially the use of extraordinary means of life support.

3. When such an afflicted individual is in a state of acute or chronic irreversible coma or is an infant. consent may be obtained indirectly from an authorized representative acting in the patient's behalf, provided that that consent is not contrary to the known preferences of the individual.

4. When such an individual requests and gives free and fully informed consent that his life be terminated, a physician ought to be legally permitted to place at the patient's disposal medication which would end life swiftly and painlessly; and where the patient is not physically able to administer to these needs, a physician should be allowed to induce death, or permit it to occur.

There is a popular tendency nowadays for those who find this proposal offensive to point out that, since the notions of a voluntary request, a kindly act, being terminally ill, and even the term 'euthanasia' itself are in some situations highly problematic, one can never be certain when all these conditions hold and should therefore always refrain from the practice of euthanasia. Few would be more sympathetic than I to such charges when they are properly made. But unless we are to fly in the face of all human experience we must admit that while there are twilight zones, some acts are clearly kind and freely consented to, and some people are clearly terminally ill. In fact, it seems an unpardonable oversight, an extreme form of epistemological skepticism, or a want of intelligence to deny this. For this is like denying that there is a genuine difference between day and night simply because there is no sharp line, but rather a twilight zone, between them.

One other word of caution. Those of us who advocate the legalization of voluntary euthanasia for the terminally ill on the grounds of kindness and rationality are not doing so because we abhor the dying or because we merely wish to empty hospital beds and thereby save money. Nor are we advocating legalization because we favor agism[3] or some clandestine form of population control. *Euthanasia is recommended only as a last resort.* It is not the only kindness that can be shown; but to someone in dire need, it often is the greatest kindness.

My principal purpose in this paper, to which I now turn, is to begin an explication of the notion of rights, in particular the notion of the right to life, in order to see if we can more clearly determine whether or not this right is violated by the limited form of euthanasia here being advocated.

II

The philosophy of rights is certainly one of the most perplexing provinces of moral philosophy. Advocates, especially natural rights theorists, often maintain that men have knowledge of the existence or nature of rights in a way not drastically different from the way we know all sorts of common things, and they generally hold that rights (or something essentially similar) are necessary in order to protect the moral autonomy of the individual against the tyranny of society. On the other hand, bolder opponents argue that there are no such things as rights anterior to the establishment of government or law, that rights-talk is a perpetual vein of nonsense, and that this manner of approaching moral problems is at best not very helpful. In short, we are told that the firmly held American belief in the rights to life, liberty, and the pursuit of happiness is so insecure — both at its foundation and in terms of utility — that cultivated people must hold their breath in their neighborhood for fear of blowing it away.

It is easy enough to show that there is some truth on both sides. Rights, especially when conceived of solely as natural entitlement, are phantomlike. Yet these same 'phantoms,' at least since the eighteenth century, have been bulwarks against government tyranny and continue to play an important role in the ideology of political and legal reform. That they function in this capacity is not surprising when we consider that rights often are viewed, not as ideals, but as moral thresholds which when violated, demand restitution or remedy — sometimes radical or revolutionary change.

Of course, critics would probably be quick to remind us that the utility of rights would not need to be asserted until arguments for their truth had been seriously, if not irreparably, flawed. But this charge, though generally cogent, appears to me to press one part of the argument too hard. For it seems to assume that 'positive' truth (in the sense of correspondence to the facts) and utility are possible in all areas of human inquiry. However, the former is a dubious assumption — clearly so in the area of ethics. If, aside from desiderata such as clarity, definiteness, consistency and scope, only preferability vindications[4] be warranted (as the best of evidence seems to indicate), then the so-called 'paucity of truth vs. utility' argument is less convincing than it initially appears.[5]

In the long list of charges that have been leveled against the utility of rights talk, one of the most convincing is the charge made by R. M. Hare [3]. Because discussions of rights by and large lack clarity and definiteness, because the discussions seem to be incapable of resolving the conflict between competing claims, and because they gain in relative clarity and effectiveness only when they are translated into more basic moral principles, Hare concludes that at the present time such discussions are not very helpful. The charge, taken in this general way, has substance, and I do not wish to quarrel with it.

But when this has been said, we still need to guard against hasty inferences. It is true that rights talk is not very helpful in understanding and resolving conflict at the present time. But it does not follow that this approach has little utility in effecting social or political change. This is shown by the political history of England, France, and the United States at different times. Moreover, at least in this country, there is evidence that one of the dominant reforming ideological currents of our time is essentially grounded in rights-talk. To the extent that this is true, it becomes important for the philosopher interested in the viability or effectiveness of his theory to give careful and critical treatment to the notion of rights. Philosophers who are passing over the subject of rights may also be missing a unique opportunity to improve the human situation. Of course, this is a limited point. For we can draw more than one true picture of the moral world, provided we do not claim that our picture is the only true one. But if championing human rights proves to be the major, or only viable, way of effecting social or political change, then a theory of rights takes on increased significance to the extent that one purports to be doing normative ethics and is interested in improving the human situation.

III

The phrase 'the right to life' continues to be used to cover an almost endless list of desiderata, ranging from having respect for all living creatures to having whatever one needs to live minimally well. Because of this ambiguity, as well as the difficulties alluded to earlier, critical judgment is needed as a corrective. We do not, I suggest, need to specify the precise content underlying all claims to the right to life. That is a seemingly impossible task or one likely to result in the (hardly illuminating) conclusion that a right is some form of entitlement. We need to know, within the context of a given theory or argument, what more precisely is the content of the right to life and on what evidence its disputed claims are based.

Militating against this approach is a tenacious belief that the right to life is a natural right so self-evident in the light of natural reason that its content cannot be satisfactorily explicated. It is hardly possible to find a view in greater accord with this belief than those who claim that rights are simply natural entitlements and who are content to add that the right to life means that each person ought to be entitled to live without others' intervention or that each ought to be left free to live his life. Admittedly, this is a definition of sorts. Speakers of the language, as well as rights theorists, often characterize a right as being 'something to which a human is naturally entitled,' or more narrowly as 'an entitlement to do, have, enjoy or have done.' Moreover, such rough definitions have the advantage of avoiding the brunt of criticism directed against the characterization of rights in terms of claims or powers.

There is nothing strange in entertaining this formulation; it is held by perhaps a majority of natural rights theorists and many intuitivists. But two things *are* surprising: first, that advocates of this doctrine do not see that the purported right to life has, in effect, become synonymous with the right to liberty and therefore that the great trinity has, so to speak, lost its Father; second, it is one thing to say that rights are known by the light of natural reason and another that they are knowable in a way not drastically different from the way we know all sorts of other things. One is tempted to ask, if rights are so knowable then what, even in theory, would not be knowable? But I shall forego this temptation and be content to raise the more modest question, namely, if rights are to be understood merely as natural entitlements, then *what* do we know when we know that a given species possesses them?

Unless I have overlooked an important part of the doctrine, what we purportedly know is this: If there are human rights, then (a) they are possessed by human beings, and (b) it is because of this fact alone [presumably the truth of (a)] that every human being has certain moral entitlements. Is it necessary to add that (a) is true but trivial and that (b) is something of an enigma? For how does it follow that if human rights are the rights of humans we therefore actually have or possess them? I hope it is not too brash to conclude therefore that, aside from the dubious logic, if rights are of this limited nature, then what we know is that we indeed know very little about them, or vastly less than what is being claimed.

It may generally be observed that there are ways out of this charge. Obscurantism or proximate vacuity may be avoided by enriching the notion of a right, or by letting a specific right, such as that of life, liberty, or happiness, carry the great part of the semantic burden, or (and this does not exhaust all possibilities) by doing a little of both. But to define a human right as a human entitlement and then be content only to say that the right to life means that each ought to be entitled to live without other's intervention (or the like) is not the maneuver that allows escape from this charge.

The second of the three approaches I here wish to consider is the claim that the right to life is somehow synonymous with the principle that one ought never to kill an innocent human being. This, when properly examined, is another way of saying that the right to life is inalienable. Since I have treated this question in some depth elsewhere [5], I shall be content to touch only upon some of the more important matters and then add a consideration that heretofore may have been overlooked. I shall not discuss this matter further, since I want to consider other ways of dealing with the right to life.

To say that one ought never kill an innocent human being is, in part, to say that such killings are always morally wrong. Unless we are to regress to 'light of natural reason' talk or ascribe a supernatural origin to the claim (thereby consecrating and perhaps placing it beyond discussion or criticism), I take this to mean that wrongful killing is an unjustifiable intrinsic or extrinsic injury. Now if the latter be the sole ground, it is difficult to understand how the prohibition could be arrived at without considering probable consequences, and even more difficult to understand why, given conceptual and procedural safeguards, a limited practice of euthanasia should be ruled out *a priori*. On the other hand, if it is a combination of both modes, or if the prohibition rests solely upon the notion of an unjustifiable intrinsic injury, then the question is whether such injury necessarily will, or is reasonably likely, to occur given the provisos outlined earlier. If not, then why the prohibition?

I use the phrase 'reasonably likely,' because it should be recognized that, even with the establishment of the most careful safeguards, there is some possibility, however remote, of accident, negligence, or intentional malevolence. There is simply no way to eliminate these factors completely. Of course, advocates of euthanasia can say that, since this is true of every social policy, it is therefore not telling against any particular program. But since this is a question of helping to terminate the lives of fellow human beings, we should, I believe, be extremely cautious. There is perhaps no easy answer. Yet for those who consider this 'remote risk objection' telling, I should like to ask: Under what circumstances would the practice or legalization of voluntary euthanasia be morally conceivable? What are the consequences of a public policy that denies, because of remote consequences, help to those generally in dire need? And is it not better that men and women, being fully informed, should be free to decide whether or not they wish to run that risk?

Before leaving this line of thought, I should like to bring the issue into sharper focus by moving from the level of theory to a concrete example.

Few cases have received more publicity and stirred the interest of the general public more then that of Karen Ann Quinlan. The case is unusually complex. Yet several things seem clear: first, Joseph Quinlan asked that the respirator be removed and that his daughter be allowed to die; second, Karen was quoted as saying, on three different occasions, that she never wanted to be kept alive by extraordinary means (so that there has been no evidence that the removal of Karen from the machine would be contrary to her known preferences); third, none of her doctors claimed that Karen was in any technical sense dead; fourth, because there has been evidence that she is comatose with irreversible damage to at least one part of her brain, there has been neither any immediacy in terms of relieving pain nor a way of having her directly express her own preferences; and, finally, Judge Muir denied the plaintiff's request, indicating that 'such an authorization would be homicide,' and that it would be a violation of the right to life, presumably Karen's constitutional right [7].

The question of a constitutional right to life is even more problematical than the one we have raised, and it is best, I think, to leave it aside. But the question of why the removal of Karen Quinlan from the life-support machine should be viewed as an act of murder may profitably be raised from the present moral perspective.

With regard to this question, I would say that if it is reasonable to regard wrongful killing as an unjustifiable intrinsic or extrinsic injury and if the removal of Karen Quinlan from the machine is not, in the strict sense of the term, an injury to anyone, then it is reasonable to conclude that it is not an act of wrongful killing. Admittedly, to harm others is to violate their interests. So, even if there is the interest in being alive only if one's life could be radically different, some harm has been done. But to say this is to admit neither that the act in question is predominantly harmful nor that it is an injury.

We injure a man when we deny or deprive him of some important or vital need he rationally prefers to have. In this sense, a man who removes a minor part of a toenail without permission, while someone is asleep, may or may not be harming him, but it is difficult to see how this could constitute injury. On the other hand, to remove the entire limb would normally constitute an injury unless, of course, it was gangrenous. Similarly, killing a man is generally considered an injury, because it generally violates the conditions mentioned. But to say that it must always be an injury is to assume that life is always preferable to death, which begs the question.

In saying this, I am not suggesting|that this notion of injury is unproblematic, which indeed it is not. I am only urging that given the circumstances of the Quinlan case, the removal of Karen from the machine is not an injury, and to that extent is not an act of wrongful killing.

IV

A more helpful discussion of the question of what a holder of the right to life is entitled to is presented by Judith Jarvis Thomson in her now almost classic paper on abortion [8]. Thomson explains briefly why there is so much trouble concerning this right[6] and then characterizes three possible positions. The right of life according to this analysis

(a)   includes having a right to be given at least the bare minimum one needs for continued life;

(b)   does not include the right to be given anything, but amounts to and only to, the right not to be killed by anybody;

(c)   consists not in the right not to be killed, but rather in the right not to be killed unjustly.

Thomson then contends that views (a) and (b) are implausible by advancing some ingenious counter-examples.

It is obvious from what has been said that I share Professor Thomson's views concerning (b). But I do not find her rejection of (a) entirely convincing, although it does raise important questions.

Consider, for instance, her claim that the right to life cannot include the entitlement that one be given at least the bare minimum one needs for continued life. She writes:

... Suppose that what in fact *is* the bare minimum a man needs for continued life is something he has no right at all to be given? If I am sick unto death, and the only thing that will save my life is the touch of Henry Fonda's cool hand on my fevered brow, then all the same, I have no right to be given the touch of Henry Fonda's cool hand on my fevered brow ([9], p. 55).

Thomson correctly reminds us that all general rights have their just limits. So the right to do X, where X is a general entitlement, is never the right to do or obtain whatever is required to do X. To be more specific, if someone argues that having a right to life includes having a right to be given at least the bare minimum one needs for continued life *whatever* that might require, then they are mistaken.

Weighty as Thomson's arguments are, they carry little or no weight against those who agree with the principle that all rights have their just limits but also maintain that the right to life seems to require that, in the distribution of goods, some regard for necessities of life on the part of all citizens should be attended to. Without adequate provision for physical sustenance and basic health care, the right to life seems at best to be incomplete and, at worse, a sorrowful misdescription.

For example, suppose that what, in fact, is the bare minimum a man needs for continuing life is not the touch of Henry Fonda's cool hand, but some food. Is not the holder of the right to life, subject to provisos I will shortly describe, entitled to that food? And suppose a man needs a blood transfusion, is he not similarly entitled?

Now there are some formidable problems. But, quite apart from the familiar difficulties of how we would deal with enemies or persons who, although capable, refused or knowingly neglected to contribute their fair share, we would, I think, want to say that a man is entitled to that food or blood provided this does not deprive another of an essentially similar right. That is to say, the right to life provides some positive entitlements and, although it may override other rights or claims, when sensibly interpreted cannot be understood to override another person's right to life.

It must be admitted, by way of conclusion, that the business of mapping out the proper domain to be covered by the term 'right to life' is largely an unfinished activity. But I do think it fruitful to start by holding that a moral right is in itself a moral principle, and/or an entitlement called for by moral principles (or their like); it is permissible for its possessor; it entails *prima facie* obligations on the part of society, or at least a *prima facie* obligation on the part of another individual; and it is a moral threshold such that when it is seriously violated, remedy or restitution is required. A right, in this sense, is a double entitlement: The holder is entitled to some type of treatment or opportunity and also entitled to redress if that is not provided. So, to the extent neither is justly accorded, civil disobedience or a more extreme method of redress is warranted.

On this view, when a society capable of providing minimal subsistence and health care does not do so because of essentially ideological or purported moral reasons, it violates the rights of its members so affected. This is based − but not solely − upon the general recognition that knowingly to allow people to suffer or die from lack of proper diet, basic and vital health treatment, or their like, when this could have been reasonably avoided (and to say that this is fully consistent with even the *prima facie* right to life), is to make a hollow mockery of that right.

In short, the right to life is imperfectly but perhaps best conceived of as the right (1) to have the bare minimum one needs for continued life whatever that may require, provided this does not violate anyone else's similar right, that available resources do not make this an impossible task, and that reasonable provision is made for the indolent, misanthropic, or enemies; (2) to have protection against unjust assault or interference with these vital interests; and, (3) subject to the proviso that no more force be used than the occasion necessitates, to seek redress if that prove necessary.

If we assume that the right to life can be so defined, then I see no likely conflict between it and the practice of voluntary beneficent euthanasia. This limited form of euthanasia has its share of difficulties. But these difficulties arise because we do not know how to attain that without also having something which we do not want, and not because we have violated a basic human right.

State University of New York,
College at Fredonia,
Fredonia, New York

NOTES

[1] In this paper I shall use the term 'euthanasia' only to refer to active euthanasia, that is, the deliberate inducement of a relatively painless quick death. By 'beneficent euthanasia' is in part meant 'the inducement of a relatively painless quick death, the intention and actual consequences of which are the kindest possible treatment of an unfortunate individual.'
[2] For a full discussion of my treatment of this question, see Kohl ([5], part 3; 6).
[3] 'Agism' is 'the discrimination against people on the basis of their chronological age.'
[4] '... by a preferability vindication we understand an argument which establishes the justificandum as the preferable means for achieving the end.' Katz [4]. Cf. Feigl [1,2].
[5] It would also be foolishness to contend that even with a more adequate conception of a right, the problem of existence becomes significantly less intractable. But what I fail to see is, why, if there is a chasm between the *ought* and the *is*, the gulf is any greater concerning rights than with other kinds of moral principles.
[6] A source of much of the trouble, she tells us, is that the right to life is treated as if it were unproblematic, which it is not ([8], p. 55). In a more recent paper she adds that this characteristic is true of all rights and 'that all rights are problematic presumably in that we cannot say (without much difficulty) what the bearer of that right is minimally positively entitled to.' [9]

BIBLIOGRAPHY

1. Feigl, H.: 1950, 'De Principiis non est disputendum ...?', in M. Clack (ed.), *Philosophical Analysis*, Cornell University Press, Ithaca, New York, pp. 119–156.
2. Feigl, H.: 1952, 'Validation and Vindication: An Analysis of the Nature and Limits of Ethical Arguments', in W. Sellars and J. Hospers (eds.), *Readings in Ethical Theory*, Appleton-Century Crofts, New York, pp. 667–680.
3. Hare, R. M.: 1975, 'Abortion and the Golden Rule', *Philosophy and Public Affairs* (4), 202–204.

4. Katz, J. J.: 1962, *The Problem of Induction and Its Solution,* University of Chicago Press, Chicago, pp. 27–28.
5. Kohl, M.: 1974, *The Morality of Killing*, Humanities Press, New York.
6. Kohl, M. (ed.): 1975, *Beneficent Euthanasia*, Prometheus Books, Buffalo, New York, pp. ix–xix, 130–141.
7. Muir, Robert, Jr.: 1975, Opinion, In the Matter of Karen Quinlan: An Alleged Incompetent. Superior Court of New Jersey, Chancery Division, Morris County, No. C-201-75, Nov. 10, 1975, pp. 33, 41.
8. Thomson, J. J.: 1971, 'A Defense of Abortion', *Philosophy and Public Affairs* 1, 50–59.
9. Thomson, J. J.: 1973, 'Rights and Deaths', *Philosophy and Public Affairs* 2, 148.

JOHN TROYER

EUTHANASIA, THE RIGHT TO LIFE, AND MORAL STRUCTURES: A REPLY TO PROFESSOR KOHL

I. INTRODUCTION

If I understand him correctly, Professor Kohl has two goals which he hopes to achieve in his paper:

1.   He wants to set out, with a precision sufficient to allow translation into statute law, a set of conditions under which euthanasia is morally permissible.

2.   He wants to defend these conditions against the charge that acts meeting them are morally impermissible because they violate the killed person's right to life.

In attempting to accomplish his second goal, Professor Kohl exhibits a good deal of (understandable) perplexity about rights in general and the right to life in particular. Unfortunately I sometimes find it hard to discern Professor Kohl's exact views on these difficult topics. Nor am I at all certain of the truth in these matters. Still, where he leads I must follow (albeit with considerable trepidation), and I begin my commentary with two sections on rights. I conclude with a section on euthanasia and legislation.

II. THE RIGHT TO LIFE

Professor Kohl finds at least the appearance of conflict between his claim that every person has a right to life. The main goal of his paper, as I understand it, is to show that no act of euthanasia meeting his conditions violates the killed person's right to life. In this section I will argue for the following three theses:

1.   Under the most natural reading of 'Jones has a right to life', there is no reason to suppose that Jones's right to life is violated by any act of euthanasia to which he consents.

S.F. Spicker and H. T. Engelhardt, Jr. (eds.), Philosophical Medical Ethics: Its Nature and Significance, 85–95. *All Rights Reserved. Copyright* © 1977 *by D. Reidel Publishing Company, Dordrecht-Holland.*

2.   The only plausible reading of 'Jones has a right to life' which entails that all acts of euthanasia are morally impermissible also entails that Jones's suicide is morally impermissible.

3.   None of Professor Kohl's arguments shows that suicide is morally permissible.

As far as I can see, this means that Professor Kohl's central arguments, while interesting and important, do nothing to establish his main claim.

To see that the right to life, given its most natural reading, is compatible with at least some acts of euthanasia we have only to note that the right to do x is in general compatible with the right not to do x. Thus the right to life is at least *prima facie* compatible with the right to death. Of course there may be cases in which the right to do x entails the duty to do x, but I can't offhand think of any; nor can I think of any reason to believe that the right to life would be among them, were there any. So in the absence of good arguments to the contrary, we seem justified in assuming that Jones's right to live is compatible with his right to die.

Are there any good arguments to the contrary? I see only bad ones. One such is suggested by Professor Kohl's remark that the 'unalienability' of the right to life is significant. Perhaps it is, but not in any obvious way. Surely the fact that Jones's right to do x is unalienable does not entail that Jones has a duty to do x. At most it means that no matter what he or others do, Jones will retain the right to do x. Consider the following scenario, set in Arthurian Britain:

Arthur, having spied on Gueniver for months (while allegedly searching for the grail), notices that her exuberant exercise of her right to travel makes it exceedingly difficult to find her. He therefore approaches her and offers to do her laundry, if only she'll restrict her roaming. She agrees and they strike a bargain. Later Sir Lancelot happens by, is struck by Gueniver's beauty, and asks to let him show her Cornwall. 'Alas,' she says, 'I'd love to go, but I've bartered away my right to travel.' 'Never fear,' Lancelot replies, 'your right to travel is *unalienable.*'

And off Gwen goes. Or perhaps she doesn't. The moral of the story is that she needn't. The fact that the right to travel is unalienable is perfectly compatible with the fact that anyone possessing it also possesses the unalienable right to refrain from travel.

Of course Professor Kohl does not mean to suggest that the unalienability argument, as I have interpreted it, merits serious consideration. Instead he interprets it as the claim that to say Jones's right to life is unalienable is just 'another way of saying' that one ought never to kill the innocent. It seems to me a very odd other way of saying this, but suppose we take 'Jones has an unalienable right to life' to mean 'If Jones is innocent, then no one has a right to kill him': does this interpretation of the right to life render it incompatible with euthanasia? Well, 'Yes and No'. It depends on how we read 'If Jones is innocent, then no one has a right to kill him'. If we read it strongly, taking 'no one' to mean 'no one at all', then it entails that no one has a right to commit suicide. I assume that if this is so, then no one has a right to commit euthanasia. On the other hand, a 'weak' reading is more plausible and less conclusive. A weak reading is just one which interprets 'no one' as 'no one but Jones' (or, weaker still, as 'no one who lacks Jones's permission'). Thus when I say 'No one has a right to stick his thumb in my ear', a strong reading would entail that I don't myself have a right to stick my thumb in my ear, a weak reading would entail only that no one else has a right to stick his thumb in my ear (or, weaker still, that no one lacking my permission has a right to stick his thumb in my ear). Since in these contexts we often use 'no one' to mean 'no one but me', or the like, I think it would be unreasonable to interpret the right to life, construed as the right not to be killed if innocent, as a prohibition against suicide.

I don't, incidentally, mean to imply that the right to commit suicide entails, by itself, the right to commit euthanasia. At best it provides some basis for some arguments the conclusion to which is the right to commit some acts of euthanasia. One (inadequate) argument would proceed as follows: If Jones has a right to do x, and if Jones asks Smith to help him to do x (or to do x for him), then Smith has a right to help Jones to do x (or to do x for Jones).[1]

Up to this point I have argued that the right to life, given any natural reading of 'the right to life', is at least *prima facie* compatible with the moral permissibility of certain acts of euthanasia. Yet Professor Kohl is certainly correct in thinking that many who oppose euthanasia do so because it violates what they choose to call 'the right to life' — mistakenly, since what they intend to refer to is the duty to refrain from killing the innocent, *no matter what*, and even if the innocent in question is oneself.[2] Unfortunately Kohl says nothing which can be construed as an argument against such proponents of 'the right to life'. If they are his intended opponents (and if not, who is?), Professor Kohl needs to show (at least) that suicide is sometimes morally permissible. This he does not do. At one point he claims that killing is wrong only if it does someone an 'injury', but I doubt that a person who thought that suicide is always immoral would accept this premise. John Finnis, for example, writes:

> Considered as a fully deliberate choice (which it doubtless only rather rarely is), suicide is a paradigm case of an action that is always wrong because it cannot but be characterized as a choice directly against a fundamental value, life ([1], p. 129).

I think Mr. Finnis is wrong, but I doubt that I could convince him of this and I doubt that he would be more moved by what Professor Kohl says about the right to life. I am not myself convinced by Professor Kohl's claim that killing is wrong only if it causes the killed person some injury, for Professor Kohl defines an injury as a denial or deprivation of an important need which the possessor would rationally prefer to have. But surely it is wrong to kill Jones, if Jones wants to live, even if Jones's desire to live is irrational. Or so it seems to me. It is certainly not *generally* true that it is morally permissible to do to Jones anything that fails to cause him injury, and I see no reason to suspect that killing Jones would be one of the special cases.

III. RIGHTS AND MORAL STRUCTURES

Professor Kohl is suspicious of talk of rights in general. In fact he seems to hold that such talk should be prohibited as unacceptably fuzzy and unhelpful, were it not useful in promoting social and political advances. Such a position may seem dubious — at least it seems so to me — but it is in line with Professor Kohl's general belief that ethical judgements should be evaluated not by 'positive' truth, but by various pragmatic considerations.

I couldn't disagree more, but this is scarcely the place to debate such basic issues. Rather, I will attempt to say a bit about rights in general and why I think they must be taken seriously, even if this provides no immediate benefits or resolutions to ethical problems.

Rights have traditionally, at least in one tradition, been taken to come in two forms, natural and 'social'. Natural rights are those a person possesses no matter what social relations obtain, social rights are those which depend on particular social arrangements. Of course rights may be both natural and social, e.g., the right to travel. Perhaps it will help to clarify this, and some of the difficulties in talk about rights, if we set out two hopelessly crude formulations of the right to travel, parsed first as a natural right, then as a social one:

TN   In a state of nature, each person has a right to go where he wants, so long as he does not infringe on anyone else's right to do the same.

TS   In the contemporary U.S.A., each citizen has a right to travel on the public ways, so long as his doing so does not infringe on anyone else's right to do the same.

Why do I say that these formulations of the right to travel are hopelessly crude? Chiefly because I believe people have both a natural and a social right to travel, though they have nothing like the rights embodied in *TN* and *TS*. Suppose, for example, that you are sunbathing in a state of nature (i.e., *au naturel*); I do not have a right to travel across your toes, much less your midriff. And surely I have no right to travel up and down your spine — except, of course, in special circumstances, as when I am a chiropractor and you have paid me to do so. These restrictions on my right to travel are scarcely captured by the clause disallowing infringements on anyone else's right to do the same. Nor is it at all clear how we should rephrase *TN* so that it says what we want it to say. In fact attempts at reformulation lead fairly quickly to the hypothesis that 'anyone else's right to do the same' should be replaced with something like 'anyone else's rights', and such a reformulation looks suspiciously as if it will render talk about rights incredibly complex or completely vacuous.[3]

It is, of course, this tendency of rights to 'bump into one another', and the attendant difficulty of formulating rules for determining right of way, that account for much of the skepticism concerning talk about rights. Still, I think such skepticism is misplaced; it is surely better to take the difficulty as a sign of where the work lies than as an excuse to give up talk about rights.

Why? Well, the notion of a right seems to capture an important aspect of the structure of most people's moral beliefs. To borrow some terminology from Robert Nozick, most people's moral beliefs constitute neither a 'maximixing' nor a 'deductive' structure; they come closer to constituting a maximizing structure with 'side-constraints', where a side-constraint is essentially a marker for a right ([2], pp. 2–7; [3], pp. 28–35). Rights, so construed, are neither absolute nor reducible. Let me explain these claims in order. To say that rights are not absolute is to say that every right is such that it may be overridden. All rights, as far as I can see, are what W.D. Ross called *prima facie* ([5], pp. 18–36). This makes things extremely messy, as the balancing of *prima facie* rights is a problem without any known algorithm, but it seems to be the way things are. We might try to save some small and circumscribed set of rights as absolute, but I see little hope for even limited success along these lines. The Catholic Church's best efforts led first to the obscurity of the doctrine of double effect and then to the repugnant (to me) conclusion that it is morally preferable to let a mother and baby die than to save one by killing the other.[4] I seriously doubt that anyone can do better than this, and even if someone could there would remain a great many rights which, while clearly not absolute, still merit recognition. The claim that rights are irreducible means simply that we do not *now* have any means of replacing talk about rights with talk about what is right (or wrong), what we ought (or ought not) to do, etc.

Thus rights are here to stay, barring the heroic measure of discarding the basic structure of most people's moral beliefs. There may be reasons sufficient to justify such a drastic procedure, but the difficulty of balancing rights is scarcely one such, especially as any immediate and wholesale jettison of people's considered moral beliefs would leave ethical theory as a study without a subject matter.

What we need, then, is some method of determining what rights people have, together with some procedure for weighing these, both one against the other and each against the promotion of the common good. It is often claimed that the major problem in ethical theory lies in reducing talk about what ought to be done to talk about what is; it seems to me that there is a problem just as difficult, and perhaps more crucial, in reducing talk about rights to talk about what ought to be done, The only significant steps toward a resolution of this latter problem of which I am aware occur in the works of W. D. Ross, John Rawls, and Robert Nozick ([3; 4; 5]). And until such a resolution is accomplished, we can say only that:

1.   Understanding talk about rights is crucial, if we are correctly to determine what we ought to do.

2.   To say that Jones has a right to do *x* is never to say more than that Jones has a *prima facie* right to do *x*.

3.   There is (at present) no way, in general, to proceed from premises about rights to conclusions about what one ought to do. (E.g., in some cases we ought to violate someone's rights, though in others we ought not to do someting *just because* it violates someone's rights.)

These conclusions, while skeptical, scarcely seem damning. They are jointly compatible with the claim that eventually ethical theory will make complete sense of talk about rights, i.e., explain what rights people have and why, provide a method for resolving conflicts among rights and between rights and the common good, etc. After all, ethics is a young science with an incredibly complex subject matter, and there is little reason to suppose that it would have, at this point, even the right concepts for formulating principles adequate to its purposes. Of course it is logically possible that ethics is less like medicine in the 17th century than witch-theory in the 18th, but I see no reason to believe this and considerable reason to doubt it. So I doubt it.

IV. EUTHANASIA AND LEGISLATION

If what I have contended above is correct, the case for the moral permissibility of euthanasia is not established by Professor Kohl's arguments. Nor is it clear how it might be established conclusively. As I noted, my own inclination would be to begin by arguing for the right to commit suicide (in at least some cases), and to proceed to argue for a (limited) right to euthanasia as an 'extension' of this right. But the latter argument might be extremely difficult to formulate. I noted earlier that it does not in general follow, from the fact that Jones has a right to to do x, that Smith has a right to help Jones to do x, even if Jones asks for Smith's help. And of course there is a further step to the conclusion that Smith has a right to do x for Jones, even if Jones asks him to. Nor will it help to suppose that Jones can transfer his right to commit suicide, supposing that he has such, to Smith. For the right to commit suicide is, by its very nature, non-transferable. Smith can help Jones kill himself, but there is no way for Smith to commit Jones's suicide.

Perhaps there are other and better ways to establish the right to commit euthanasia, but I see none. Professor Kohl, in his book on the morality of killing, attempts to show that in some cases euthanasia is the kind and beneficent thing to do. He is quite convincing on this; unfortunately his argument will not show that euthanasia is morally permissible in such cases unless he can show that kind and beneficent actions are always morally permissible. Perhaps they are, but neither Professor Kohl nor I believe that they are.

Nonetheless it may be possible to make a good case for *legalizing* certain acts of euthanasia even in the absence of a demonstration that such acts are morally permissible. After all, we do not generally demand that all acts which are not demonstrably morally permissible be made illegal. Thank God. Thus many states have rescinded their laws against suicide (curious enough laws to begin with) in deference to a respect for the value of 'self-determination', And if it could be shown that the only arguments against the moral permissibility of suicide rested on theological premises of a controversial nature, this would surely be *some* reason for making suicide legal.[5]

Suppose, then, that we treat Professor Kohl's criteria for permissible euthanasia as proposals not about what can be shown to be morally permissible, but about what should be made legal. Will they stand up, taken in this light? Well, to begin with, they cover a wide range of quite different cases. As I understand him, Professor Kohl would lump the following cases (and many others) together:

1. Cases where a competent adult decides to refuse medical treatment necessary for his continued existence. (For example, a leukemia victim who refuses remission therapy.)

2. Cases in which a patient in coma, suffering from a terminal illness or injury, has signed a 'living will' stating that in such circumstances he wants life-support systems (or the like) to be withdrawn.

3. Cases in which a similarly afflicted patient has an 'authorized representative' who states that the withdrawal of life support systems is not 'contrary to the known preferences of the individual'.

4. Cases in which a competent and informed terminally ill patient asks for the means to commit suicide.

5. Cases in which a competent and informed terminally ill patient, unable to commit suicide, asks that a doctor kill him.

6. Cases in which an infant with a terminal illness or injury has an 'authorized representative' who consents to its killing.

7. More or less anomalous cases, like that of Karen Quinlan.

In all these cases, Professor Kohl argues that 'euthanasia' should be legal.

Perhaps he is right in this, but there are some problems. Before stating some of these, it is perhaps worth noting that many of the cases which Professor Kohl describes could be handled without making euthanasia legal. For example if suicide, and the right to assist a suicide, were legal, cases of sorts 1 and 4 would be handled. (I assume here that if suicide should be legal, there should also be a legal right to refuse any medical treatment, even if such treatment is necessary to prolong one's life.) And if a reasonable definition of 'brain death' were adopted, various cases of sorts 2, 3, and 7 could be treated as Professor Kohl wishes. Finally, recognition of 'living wills' would handle the remaining cases of sort 2.[6] What sort of problem cases would remain? As far as I can see, the following:

1'.   Cases in which a terminally ill patient who wishes to commit suicide is unable to do so.

2'.   Cases in which we cannot ascertain a terminally ill patient's wishes. These will include patients who are comatose and those who are otherwise unable to communicate their desires (e.g., infants).

3'.   The remaining anomalous cases, like that of Karen Quinlan.

Suppose we consider these in order. The first class of cases could be handled by making it legal to kill a person (in certain circumstances) if he wishes to commit suicide but is unable to do so. Of course such cases raise many difficulties. Why is he unable to do so? Is he physically unable, or psychologically so, or what? The cases in which he is physically incapable of committing suicide, and cannot accomplish his ends by refusing further treatment, seem to me likely to be few and far between. But this is no reason for failing to provide for them, if we can do so reasonably. However, the difficulties of doing so are significant. How, for example, are we to tell if the person is competent to make a decision? Perhaps a law could be drafted which (more or less) guaranteed that any decision which satisfied its provisions would be competent, but I do not myself see how to draft such a law. Nor do I think it would be right to draft a law which made it *mandatory* for a doctor to kill a patient who expresses a wish to kill himself but is unable to do so.

But whatever the difficulties of cases of class 1', they are the easiest of the lot. With cases of sort 2' we begin to ask for the legal permission to kill people, admittedly only terminally ill people, who may wish to live. Granted some 'authorized representative' of the patient must consent, but on what basis would that consent be granted? Not, presumably, on the basis of any knowledge of the patient's wishes. Now perhaps I am simply in error, but it seems to me wrong to make it legal for someone else to decide that I, when terminally ill and unable to communicate my desires, ought to be killed. What if my incommunicable desire is that I be kept alive as long as possible? Of course it might be objected that if I fear this I ought not to authorize any representative to make such decisions. But from Professor Kohl's inclusion of infants, I infer that Jones's authorized representative need not be authorized by Jones. In any event, there is considerable doubt in my mind as to whether people ought to be able to authorize someone to say whether or not they should be killed.

Cases like that of Karen Quinlan raise still more problems. For here we have people who are not dead, and who are not even terminally ill. That is, there is no illness or injury which they have which will inevitably kill them. If some authorized representative, not necessarily authorized by them, is to be able to decide whether they should be killed, some strong argument to justify this seems to me necessary. I cannot find this argument in Prof. Kohl's paper.

Of course there may be strong arguments for the moral permissibility of killing people like Karen Quinlan, and equally strong or stronger arguments for making it legal to kill them. But I doubt that such arguments can be made on the grounds that such killings are kind or merciful. After all, there is no reason to believe that Ms. Quinlan is in pain, or otherwise in need of whatever relief death brings. And if a patient is in fact in pain or discomfort there are almost always means of alleviating this short of killing him. (Since all I know of Ms. Quinlan's case is what I read in the papers, and since those who read other papers understand the case differently, I would not wish to tie the point of this paragraph to the accuracy of my account of Ms. Quinlan's condition; my point would stand —or fall — even if there were no cases like the one I describe here.)

In any event, if Jones is comatose but might recover (i.e., has some probability greater than zero of recovering) consciousness, it is surely more charitable to preserve his possibility of recovery than to annul it. Suppose that Jones were the only person you loved, or — which may or may not amount to the same thing — who loved you; surely from Jones's point of view even a one in a million chance of recovery is preferable to no chance at all. Of course it may be that the chances of recovery are so slim, and the costs of preserving them so great, that it is unreasonable (or even immoral) to preserve them. (This is perhaps quite likely to be the case if the costs of preserving Jones are such that Smith and Robinson, who would otherwise live, must die.) But then killing Jones, while it may be morally justifiable, is not justifiable on the grounds that it is kind to Jones to kill him.

I hate to end on a note which suggests that I unthinkingly endorse the 'primitive' morality of common sense and common maxims — though considering the favored alternatives this might not be so bad — but I do believe that in many cases there is a great deal to be said for the principle that one should live and let live.

University of Connecticut, Storrs, Connecticut

NOTES

[1] This argument is inadequate because some instances of it have true premises and false conclusions. Thus Jones may have a right to have sexual relations with Mrs. Jones, though Smith lacks such a right, even though Jones has asked Smith to carry out Jones's legitimate rights. Perhaps this difficulty, and others, could be met by adding a clause demanding that Smith's proxy activity not violate the rights of any others; and perhaps not.

[2] Of course not all opponents of suicide and the like misuse the phrase 'the right to life.' John Finnis, for example, is quite clear on this point:

> In other words, rights (such as 'the right to life') are not the fundamental rationale for the judgment that the killing of other (innocent) persons is impermissible. What is impermissible is an intention set against the value of human life ... no one speaks of his 'right to life' as against himself, as something that would explain why *his* act of self-killing would be wrongful ([1], p. 130).

[3] The problems with *TS* are even more obvious. I have a right to travel on the Mass. Pike, but not if I'm riding my tricycle or my Saint Bernard. Nor does an inmate of a state prison have a right to wander the lanes of Farmington. And on and on.

[4] Note that if all rights and duties are *prima facie,* then even establishing that there is a duty not to kill the innocent will not show that we ought never to kill the innocent.

[5] I happen to believe that the only strong arguments for the moral impermissibility of suicide (i.e., all suicide) rest on demonstrably false theological premises, but I cannot establish this here. And I may not be able to establish it at all.

[6] I do not mean to imply, of course, that the legalization of living wills is unproblematic. It raises, among other issues, that of 'informed consent,' and few more difficult issues, from a practical point of view, could be broached. Consider, for example, the question of whether a person who believes (falsely) in his eternal heavenly existence following earthly death can give his 'informed' consent in a living will.

BIBLIOGRAPHY

1. Finnis, J.: 1973, 'The Rights and Wrongs of Abortion', *Philosophy and Public Affairs* 2, 117, 145.
2. Nozick, R.: 1968, 'Moral Complications and Moral Structures', *Natural Law Forum* 13, 1–50.
3. Nozick, R.: 1974, *Anarchy, State and Utopia,* Basic Books, New York.
4. Ross, W. D.: 1930, *The Right and the Good*, Oxford University Press, London.
5. Rawls, J.: 1971, *A Theory of Justice*, Harvard University Press, Cambridge.

SIDNEY MORGENBESSER

EXPERIMENTATION AND CONSENT: A NOTE

It is becoming the received view that governmental control or supervision of medical experiments and actions undertaken in light of their results is necessary not only to minimize the chances of the occurrences of such medical tragedies as the thalidomide one ([40; 38], Chap. 1; [34]) but also of such medical scandals as the Tuskegee syphilis study.[1] This view about the role and function of governmental agencies is not without its problems, some of which I shall consider below; but I shall begin by accepting it as reasonable [7, 3, 13, 30]. Similarly for its sister thesis that governmental supervision does not or ought not merely forbid or merely aim to avoid harm, but also to allow if not to facilitate and encourage reasonable medical experiments — where a medical experiment is reasonable if (as a first approximation), the expected positive benefits from the experiments outweigh the expected hazards and relevant rights are respected. Nothing special here about 'reasonable'; the thesis about reasonable experiments can be viewed as an instance as it were of the principle — if such an august baptism is in place — that actions are, if not justified, then at least reasonable and not merely permissible if their promised good outweighs their threatened bad and relevant rights are not crushed in their execution. Needless to say, the principle, though not empty, since it seems to rule out certain forms of utilitarianism, is weak; at best, it stipulates a sufficient or perhaps a conditional necessary condition for reasonableness. Still there may be a point of introducing it here in order to indicate that there need not be any special moral principle to guide medical practice action and moral medical reasoning.[2] Medical ethics begins when relevant rights and their relative stringencies are specified and relevant utilities ranked; moral medical perplexity frequently arises when new areas of medical experimentation (e.g., gene transplants, fetal research) are first glimpsed and then partially conquered. New areas are dramatic ones and receive much heralded attention, but old ones have their problems too — often equal if not more socially pressing ones — as some fugitive observations about the familiar and old areas of drug research to which I have already alluded may indicate.

Recently the FDA has been criticized for being too stringent, for blocking

S. F. Spicker and H. T. Engelhardt, Jr. (eds.), Philosophical Medical Ethics: Its Nature and Significance, 97–110. All Rights Reserved. Copyright © 1977 by D. Reidel Publishing Company, Dordrecht-Holland.

the marketing and general availability of new and potentially useful drugs. The justice of this criticism is debatable, but not the implied criterion for FDA or federal guidance, provided that 'new' is short for such longer expressions as 'functionally new, and not at best merely structurally new but medically a substitute for an already available drug' [17, 31, 37]. Research directed towards the discovery and marketing of a new form of a sugar-coated aspirin for children may be deemed reasonable on the grounds previously suggested; those who take the new aspirin may very well positively benefit. Still, it might be more reasonable to direct social resources and the time and energy of doctors and chemists away from the discovery of substitutes for Bayer, St. Joseph's, and other such. To be sure there might be social benefits (e.g., lower prices) if such substitutes for available aspirin are found, although that is debatable; still greater social benefits might accrue if research were directed elsewhere. To deal with this issue we might suggest that the FDA or some other federal agency suggest some federal policy on this matter — either to tax redundant research or to offer proper incentives. But why wait for Federal action or why be dependent upon it? Perhaps there are other ways to deal with the problem. One such way is to appeal to the various ethics committees which we will discuss below and insist that they judge not merely whether a proposed experiment is reasonable, but more reasonable than others, or even rule that a doctor S is justified in performing experiment T only if of all experiments available to S it is the one with highest expected utility, assuming relevant rights are respected. But ethics committees have no rights to deal with these matters; by law they must be concerned with the relative benefits and risks expected from the specific drug being tested; opportunity costs cannot be considered. Moreover, I doubt whether such committees would want to deal with these issues; they respect the rights of scientists to test the hypotheses that interest them. Furthermore, it seems otiose to have committees discuss alternatives available to scientists without considering the role of drug-companies; frequently alternatives available to individual scientists and doctors are available only because drug companies believe them to be potentially profitable. And unless we believe that there is a pre-established harmony between high probability and high social welfare, our problem remains — even if we call upon scientists to put pressure upon drug companies. Of course there is another way out. We could take the recent rhetoric of the corporations about their social responsibilities seriously and argue that the drug companies have relevant obligations [1]. But I do not put much stock in this move, not only because I am suspicious of the rhetoric. In light of generally accepted beliefs about the rights of private enterprises, I do not see how we could establish the claim that drug corporations are specially obligated in the manner in question; we do not put similar demands upon all private enterprises. At best, we can, I think, argue that the Federal government has a *prima facie* obligation to invest in areas of research which are either neglected or cannot be adequately financed by private enterprise. Needless to say, these beliefs about private enterprise are not sacrosanct; they can and ought to be challenged [24]. But I hope I will be forgiven if I drop my own challenge and be allowed one or two meta-observations about recent discussions of medical ethics.

It seems to me that much of the latter has concentrated on what may be called the micro- and has neglected the macro- aspects of medical experimentation; has focused, often quite movingly, on the rights of participants in medical experiments; and has bypassed consideration of the various institutional arrangements which, as it were, generate and sustain these experiments. Radical critics, with whom I am much in sympathy, have on the other hand emphasized the macro-aspects, have neglected the micro-, and have occasionally forgotten that some micro-problems are invariant ones and must be dealt with no matter what the social arrangements be. I shall attempt to deal with some of the latter issues in what follows.

Participants in medical experiments have a right of informed consent; doctors and others responsible for medical experiments have an obligation to inform the participants and obtain their informed consent. Though the thesis is reasonable and reasonably clear, there are some problems with the term 'experiment'; that term and its kin have been used in a number of ways in discussion about medical ethics, at least three of which deserve or require attention.[3]

Some doctors claim that there need not be any special laws or directives about special areas of medical experimentation; as they put it, all medical procedures are experimental. It seems that here a procedure is called experimental if there are risks and uncertainties accompanying its employment; in this sense perhaps all medical procedures may be called experimental. A dentist X-raying a patient, a doctor prescribing an old and oft-used drug may be engaged in or prescribing experimental procedures. We could appeal to our principle and say that the dentist X-raying the patient must obtain the informed consent of the patient; or alternatively that the doctor has no right to order the patient but only to advise him. But there really is no need to appeal to our principle; a doctor has no right to order a patient to do T even if there were no risks and uncertainties surrounding T. One could argue that when there are no risks and uncertainties, the doctor may be somewhat more pre-emptory with his advice. But if, as frequently claimed, all medical practice is experimental, there is no need to debate this point ([32], pp. 127–130).

On any account, in arguing for informed consent in what may be called standard cases of medical therapy and care, we are, I think, arguing for a relatively weak form of informed consent.[4] We want the doctors to reason with the patient − as a friend, as Plato put it; we are not demanding that the doctors provide the patient with a signed-by-the-doctor-document describing the relevant risks and uncertainties with the procedure which the patient then either decides to follow or neglects. Neither are we necessarily arguing that the patient not adopt the option of waiving his right and − out of trust, say − tell the doctor to go ahead, propose a treatment and not bother to inform him of relevant risks and benefits, or of alternative treatment. Neither need we demand that the doctor obtain the consent of an ethics committee before he advises his patient, and that it become law that such committees be constituted. In standard medical cases informed consent of a relatively weak kind is perhaps the only relevant kind.

Our attitude changes − understandably so when the procedure is experimental in a second sense, namely, when it is new − e.g., a new form of surgery. Here we might or should demand that more stringent requirements about informed consent be met, if only because there is little direct evidence for the assigning of probabilities. But (as far as I know) there is no legal or universally accepted requirement for a stronger form of informed consent in experimental situations of the second type. To be sure, when a surgeon does undertake to perform a new type of operation, he must obtain the written consent of the patient, but that is only because he must obtain the written consent in all cases of surgery and frequently obtains it only to protect himself. The whole area of consent in surgery, and especially consent in new types of cases, needs rethinking. I would suggest that no new type of surgery be allowed to proceed unless it has been approved of by a relevant ethics committee ([14]; [26], pp. 15–18, 73–81, 90; [38], pp. 27–36; [35; 28]).

Such committees play a role, and an important one, when medical experimentation in still a third sense is undertaken. Roughly speaking, an undertaking is called a biomedical experiment in this sense if it is instituted to gather data in a statistically significant way which may be used to test a medical hypothesis, or, more generally, to test a medically related hypothesis. (I shall say that a hypothesis is a medical hypothesis if it is of the form 'If S . . . then . . .'

where '*S*' stands in place of an action which doctors can be expected to be able to undertake and execute; the hypothesis that heart disease may be due to cultural stress will not in this context be considered a medical, but a medically related one. Often experiments in hospitals consist of the collection of questionnaire-data gathered to test hypotheses about the social or psychological causes of disease or ill health and are only medically related hypotheses.)

There are different types of experiments which call for different types of participation and which involve different types of rights. In the immediate sequel paralleling the opening section, I shall restrict myself to some aspects of drug experimentation and their stages. Drug experimentation frequently goes through (1) stage A, experimentation on animals; (2) stage B, experimentation on human 'volunteers' to test for toxicity; (3) stage C, experimentation upon patients who are ill and may be helped by the new drug. There are relevant FDA rulings which allow for the transition between stages, and ethics committees play a role in stages B and C. If the C-stage experimentation is successful, drugs are released for general use and they become experimental in the first sense of the term; problems about drugs and informed consent do not, as already indicated, disappear.

In experiments of the third type we frequently have informed consent of a strong type; the doctor must obtain the signed consent of those participating, he must inform the patient and participant of relevant risks and benefits and of alternative treatments, and he must obtain the consent of the relevant ethics committees who try to assure that participation in the experiments is voluntary, that relevant information is transmitted, and that participants can make rational decisions. Each of these terms, 'rational', 'voluntary', 'informed', 'consent', is a difficult one and may conceptually involve each other; much discussion has occurred about them both singly and collectively. But there is a preliminary question. Why have these committees in the first place? I am not sure of the proper answer; obviously there may be many.

Two reasons which are frequently given for these committees do not seem to me to be decisive ones. It is occasionally claimed that these committees are needed in order to solve complicated moral problems which arise in medical experimentation and which cannot or should not be solved by the individual doctor or scientist in charge of the experiment ([11; 2], pp. 29–57). But this answer falsely assumes that these committees solve moral issues in the relevant respect, that they can or do stipulate relevant moral criteria to be employed as guidelines for permissible research. But they do not. The guidelines, the criteria, are given to the committees either by a state legislature or the N.I.H.; the committees interpret them; the committees are committees of casuistry. It is also on occasion claimed that these committees are needed in order to have public control over the medical profession, that these committees are there in order to have a public say over medical investigation. But this latter argument falsely assumes that these committees are largely composed of lay people. They are not; in hospitals one or two non-medical outsiders are members of such committees; they are a distinct minority. On these committees the medical profession almost polices itself. And as far as hospitals at least are concerned I think it is fitting that this be the case. The medical staff should take primary responsibility for the care of the patients and for offering and discussing alternatives with them.

Notice, in passing, that I am only discussing the ethics committees in hospitals. I do think that there should be more public participation by members of the community in the decisions about the overall running of the hospital and about the role of the hospital in its communities [9]. I also think (for a variety of reasons which I cannot review here) that ethics committees in prisons should (if research there continues) be composed of at least an equal number of doctors and non-doctors, with a large representation of persons who know about and have been concerned with the rights of prisoners. The history of research in prisons is abominable; the rights of prisoners who participate in medical experimentation need special attention and protection.[5]

I return to our topic and suggest that ethics committees play modest but important roles, serving as sources of knowledge for doctors who frequently find it difficult to know how to construct a proper and informative consent form and overestimate such difficulties. In addition, the committees frequently defend patients in wards whose rights are not as well protected as those of private patients; they cause doctors to be clear about risks and remind them of the rights of patients. There is finally an important and methodological point. Often there is no way of knowing whether the information given to participants in a new experiment is reasonable except by comparing the experiment with previous ones and with the information given them; committees are agents for such comparisons. Committees are therefore useful sources of information and serve as a sort of collective memory for the hospital. There are of course problems. Committees can become lax and overlenient and too reasonable about the interpretation of risks and benefits. I do not know how they are reviewed; they ought to be, at least on occasion. Committees could in principle assume too much power and veto projects which fully informed patients and others might assent to. But this danger is not I think a pressing one. There is pressure on the committee from the general medical staff not to block experiments.

Notice that the presence of these committees weakens one defense that is often offered for the practice of informed consent. Those participating in experiments may be presumed to be concerned with their interests. Properly informed, they would not consent to experiments that run the risk of unduly injuring them; doctors would be blocked from undertaking risky experiments. Hence the prudential justification of the practice of informed consent. But this answer — this argument from prudence — is not that compelling; the committees could be expected to block risky and unwise experiments. Note further that these committees are expected to encourage those who participate in experiments to give their *informed* consent and not to waive their rights. Of course there is no way a committee can assure that a patient who participates in an experiment considers the options or requests further detailed information. Ultimately it is up to the doctors in charge of the experiment and their associates to encourage deliberation and discussion. But the principle is clear; the patient is to be encouraged. Why? I presume that part of the answer is obvious. We prize autonomy and think it desirable that people be encouraged to take responsibility and are given the relevant information that enables them to make responsible decisions.[6] It may of course be true that autonomy is rationally desirable, that no agent can rationally desire not to make up his mind on the basis of evidence, and that no agent can rationally desire that someone else have the moral authority to dictate to him what to do here, that no agent can rationally desire that the doctor have the authority to order him. Perhaps; but the emphasis upon autonomy neglects one essential feature about informed consent. If I deliberate whether to go to a ball game and finally decide to go, I do not consent to go; a mother after deliberating might consent to have her child go to a game with the other children in the class. If I consent, I have a special role to play, I have a special authority. A patient who consents does so because he has a special authority; alternatively, the doctor has no right to risk bodily injury to the patient without the latter's consent. Given the patient's rights in the matter, we find it desirable that he exercise them in an autonomous manner. At least, to a first approximation, this is how the matter appears to me, qualifications below.

Perhaps all this is overelaborate and all that is required here is to appeal, as some have, to the principle of respect for persons and to argue that the doctors show their respect for the patient and for those who participate in experiments by discussing the experiment with them and by trying to elicit their consent ([5], pp. 107–140). But I doubt that the principle carries the relevant weight. If the principle of respect for persons entails that no one who participates in an experiment is ever rightfully misled, then I think the principle debatable. Consider the oft-discussed experiments in which people are approached and asked whether they would be willing to sign a document which is a copy of the Bill of Rights but which they are misled to believe is a copy of a proposed bit of novel legislation. I do not think that these types of experiments are obviously reprehensible [39].

It is worth noting in concluding this section that, according to many, the emphasis upon rights of patients and duties of doctors is misplaced. They argue that we should discuss the situation not in terms of rights and obligations which are fitting in a court of law, but in terms of concern and care. Notice, however, that the community indicates what it cares about by stipulating relevant rights and duties; there need not be any conflict between the ethics of care and the ethics of right. Decent ethics committees may when they care go beyond the call of duty, but if they do not heed the patient's rights, they do not care.

The difficulties with the principle of informed consent that I have considered and that arise in the interpretation and justification are, I think, manageable ones. But other problems remain about whose solution I am not at all clear. Three such problems which are frequently raised by doctors are: (1) that the obligation upon the doctor to get informed consent may lead to conflict with other obligations: the principle of informed consent cannot be considered to be, as many seem to claim, a sovereign principle [21; 19]; (2) that demands of experimental design, especially when randomness in assignment is introduced, preclude complete honesty by doctors: the principle of informed consent clashes with the demands of experimental design, or so it is claimed; (3) that the obligation to cure may lead to conflict with the obligation to withhold treatment until the experiment is completed.

Doctors who treat patients [in the experimental situation of the first type introduced at the beginning of the paper] have another obligation, namely, the obligation to cure or try to cure the patient. I agree that these obligations may on occasion conflict and that the obligation to cure is more stringent. The doctor need not lie to the patient; he may not be obligated to be completely candid about the treatment. But no such conflict in obligation arises in stage B of experimental situations of the third kind. Is there another kind?

Scientists often inform us that they have the obligation to increase knowledge and that such obligations may take precedence over the obligation to inform participants in experiments. But I see no such obligation on the part of the scientist, although it may be socially desirable that the scientist feel obligated to try to increase knowledge. Moreover, even if we assume that there is such an obligation, I do not see how we can show that it is more stringent than the one to inform those involved in experiments. Perhaps the scientists mean to inform us that the potential value of the knowledge we may gain from medical experiments is so great that we may think it reasonable to neglect the disutilities that arise when participants and patients are for some reason not informed. But I do not think this answer is morally acceptable. It is not simply a question of weighing utilities; we ought not use people or trample on their rights just for the sake of public good ([2], chaps. 3–4; [33]).

A slightly different problem arises when we consider some of the issues generated by recent gene-transplant experiments. Here it is not the right of patients that is involved; nor is it a matter of considering the expected medical benefits that matter. Traditionally we have assigned – quite properly in my opinion –– high utility to the freedom of scientific research and we have not – once again quite properly in my opinion – insisted that a scientist may engage in a scientific research project only if the research promises much in the way of non-epistemic social benefits. But we have done so, I think, because we have not believed that such research is directly harmful, although we have often worried that knowledge gained may be misused later. We or others may put elementary mechanics to bad use and we do not blame the scientist; we would blame Galileo had he dropped his opponents from the Tower of Pisa in order to test his hypothesis. Galileo couldn't have appealed to the principle of freedom of inquiry; neither do I think should scientists who are involved in research on gene-transplants, if as is claimed, such research may be harmful. There is a complication. The potential harm is not restricted to those directly involved; the population as a whole may be affected by the escaping bacteria. The consent of the population at large cannot be directly obtained; a group that speaks in the name of the community is required, but only if there is danger of direct harm as a result of the experiment.

Conflicts of obligation may arise in stage C experiments; here the doctor is both obligated to try to cure his patient and obligated to experiment or to heed the results of the experiment before he uses a new drug in therapy. May not a doctor who is trying to cure his patient mislead his patient about the experimental set-up and do so on the belief that (1) participation in the experiment may be potentially helpful to the patient, (2) the patient may not voluntarily agree to participate, or (3) would not agree if the details of the experiment were clearly articulated to the patient, if for example the patient were informed that he would be assigned at random either to group A receiving an old drug or group B — the new one.[7]

Doctors apparently often reason in some such manner and think themselves justified in slightly misleading participants in experiments. There are many consent forms which do not describe the nature of the experimental design and which read that the participants will be treated in a scientifically approved manner. I cannot speak with any assurance on this issue, but I believe that the consent forms just described are not acceptable and that more candor is required. I add that there are reports about patients being informed about 'random' assignments and not being disturbed by the information.

Notice further that since assignments are at random the doctor cannot argue that it would definitely be beneficial to a patient to participate in an experiment: the patient might receive the old drug. At best the doctor could argue that it might be beneficial to the patient in the long run that an experiment be conducted. I cannot see how a doctor can argue that his obligation to cure the patient may justify him in not informing the patient about the experimental design; he could at best argue that his obligation to cure the patient may require him to perform an experiment and then have more available knowledge which he might use to cure the patient — but only if he is in the position to perform an experiment which is morally admissible.

But we are not done. What if the doctor honestly believes and with some justification that a new drug is better, why should he in light of his obligation to cure his patient withhold treatment till the experiment is completed? Why should patient A be assigned at random — or otherwise to a group that will receive the old drug, if the doctor believes the new drug to be better? Does not the obligation to cure override the obligation to be guided by the results of experiments?

Once again I have no definite answer, and can only offer the outline of one. Since we are at a comparatively early stage of familiarity with the drug, we do not believe that the doctor in question has a right to be that convinced, or be that assured. We use two types of inductive knowledge, knowledge about the drug in question and higher-order inductive knowledge that drugs that often seem to be promising turn out to be hazardous. In light of this higher-order knowledge we do not think that the doctor can act immediately upon his beliefs and just go ahead and use the new drug as a standard form of therapy. Of course, the situation is different if the old drugs have not been helping the patient at all and the patient is seriously ill.

Incidentally, why should a patient agree to participate in an experiment? If the patient assigns high utility to participating either because he is altruistic or wants to be involved in a project which aims to increase knowledge, then our question admits of a relatively easy answer. Our question remains as a relevant one, however, about others who are — and quite understandably — solely concerned with their health and recovery.

A possible answer for some types of cases suggests itself. Assume patient A is told about new drug B_1 which may be better than drug B_2 which he has been receiving, and assume that he uses the higher-order inductive knowledge that drug B_1 may turn out to be worse, then I think he should want an experiment to be performed. Now if A is optimistic, he may want to take drug B_1, and he should ask that those who are participating in the experiment be allowed to choose which drug they take. A's request would not be unreasonable, perhaps, if there is no known causal connection between being optimistic or pessimistic and being cured by either drug, and some of the problems about openness about randomness might be avoidable. But I readily admit that this is only a possible answer with obvious pitfalls about statistical design and is an answer for only certain types of cases. Is it rational to agree to take a placebo? I raise this question only to remind the reader of many issues I have not considered. These untouched issues include some of the following:

1. Many recent books and articles have argued, often convincingly, that experimenters are frequently callous about the suffering they cause animals in experiments; many restrictions are obviously needed. But I know of no convincing argument that proves that animals can never be used for experimental purposes . Even critics of our current practices seem to agree that the suffering (if any) of animals in experiments may be justified if the results of the experiments can be used to treat diseases that afflict humans or even other animals.

Often the view is expressed that animal sacrifice may be justified because animals lead a lower type of life than do humans. Needless to say, this view opens up a Pandora's box of questions and difficulties. Can we 'sacrifice' a demented person for the sake of a sane one? Do all animals lead a lower type of life than all humans? I presume that proper answers must consider (a) the pain inflicted, (b) the level of life of those used in experiments, and (c) the moral relationship between those experimented upon and those approving the experimental practices [29; 4] .

2. My co-contributor to this symposium, Dr. Natalie Abrams, has dealt with many of the problems that must be considered before we conclude that prisoner participation in stage B experimentation is justified. I add two minor observations.

(a) If we all volunteered, either out of altruism or obligation, our problem could disappear; no need then to use prisoners, etc. The data amassed by Titmuss suggests that altruistic volunteering may be forthcoming; the benefits we all derive from the results of experiments suggest that we are all obligated to 'volunteer'. Not so, as long as the profits go to the drug companies. Under current conditions, stock holders in drug companies should perhaps be obligated to volunteer.

(b) The proposed benefit—risk ratio applicable in stage C is not applicable here; the person in stage B does not stand to gain medically from the experiment. I know of no good discussion of the relevant benefits or just compensation to be given to those who participate in stage B experiments. I do not think that we could justify an experiment solely on the grounds that the utility from knowledge gained is great and compensates for the disutility of the suffering or inconvenience caused to the participants. The law is frequently evasive on this point, I think.

There is a strong case to be made out for the thesis that those who participate in medical experiments should be insured (by the N.I.H., drug companies, etc.) against risks. But even if there is proper insurance, I do not think that an ethics committee could agree to an experiment in which there is a serious probability (let us say 0.03 and above) that a patient may lose his life even if the participant knows of the risks and agrees. I am primarily considering cases where those who participate do so in hope of financial gain; society must have other ways of fulfilling its obligation to the poor. I do not think that ethics committees should play a role when a doctor experiments upon himself.

Columbia University,
New York City, New York

NOTES

[1] The literature on violation of rights in medical experimentation is immense. The most important volume is Katz [16]. Also relevant: Pappworth [23], Curran [8]. For the Tuskegee study see Restak [27].
[2] See Nozick [22]. Proposed actions that violate moral rights can be viewed as prima

facie morally inaccessible; among the morally accessible, some are reasonable; a proposed action that is at least as reasonable as any alternative one is the rational one to do. For a few words about 'accessible' actions see my fleeting remarks in Held [15].

[3] Charles Fried's important monograph [12] is relevant for most of the issues I am considering. See also Vischer [36].

[4] There is interesting material on standard cases of therapy. See the interesting historical study by Entralgo [10].

[5] The story is an ancient one; see Siegler and Osmund ([32], p. 124). For discussion of recent research see Mitford [20].

[6] See the discussion of autonomy in Landerson [18]; references listed there are plentiful.

[7] In my view, to use a therapy widely without its having been subjected to a clinical trial is amoral and anti-social. See G. Pickering's discussion ([26], p. 49), and Lord Platt's discussion in Cohen ([6], pp. 76−77).

BIBLIOGRAPHY

1. Arrow, K.: 1972, 'Uncertainty and the Welfare Economics of Medical Care', *American Economic Review* 53 (5), 941−973.
2. Barber, B. *et al.* (eds.): 1972, *Research on Human Subjects*, Russell Sage Foundation, New York.
3. Beecher, H.K.: 1966, 'Ethics and Clinical Research', *New England Journal of Medicine* 274, 1254−60.
4. Brophy, B.: 1975, 'The Silent Victims', *New Statesman and Nation* 89, 278−279.
5. Campbell, A. V.: 1972, *Moral Dilemmas in Medicine*. Longmans, New York.
6. Cohen, H. C.: 1971, *Morals and Medicine*, Oxford Univ. Press, Oxford.
7. Coleman, L.: 1974, 'Terrified Consent', *Physician's World*, May 1974, p.1.
8. Curran, W.: 1970, 'Governmental Regulation of the Use of Human Subjects in Medical Research', in P. A. Freund (ed.), *Experimentation with Human Subjects*, George Braziller, New York.
9. Dellums, R. V.: 1974, Discussion, *Congressional Record*, March 19, 121, & 1287.
10. Entralgo, P. L.: 1969, *Doctor and Patient*, McGraw-Hill, New York.
11. Etzioni, A.: 1973, *Genetic Fix*, New York.
12. Fried, C.: 1974, *Medical Experimentation*, North Holland/American Elsevier, New York.
13 Fuchs, V.: 1974, *Who Shall Live?* Basic Books, New York, Chap. 5.
14. Guttentag, O. E.: 1968, 'Ethical Problems in Human Experimentation', in E. F. Torrey (ed.), *Ethical Issues in Medicine*, Little, Brown and Co., Boston, pp. 195−226.
15. Held, V. *et al.* (eds.): 1974, *Philosophy, Morality, and International Affairs*, Oxford Univ. Press, Oxford, pp. 221−223.
16. Katz, J.: 1972, *Experimentation with Human Beings*, Russell Sage Foundation, New York.
17. Klass, A.: 1975, *There's Gold in Them Thar Pills*, Penguin Books, Baltimore, pp. 115−128.
18. Landerson, R. R.: 1975, 'Theory of Personal Autonomy', *Ethics* 86 (1): 30−48.
19. Meyer, B. C.: 1968, 'Truth and the Physician', in E. F. Torrey (ed.), *Ethical Issues in Medicine*, Little, Brown and Co., Boston, pp. 159−177.
20. Mitford, J.: 1973, *Kind and Usual Punishment*, Random House, New York, Chap. 9.
21. Myers, M. J.: 1967, 'Informed Consent in Medicine?', *California Law Review* SJ, 1396.

22. Nozick, R.: 1974, *Anarchy, State and Utopia*, Basic Books, New York, pp. 28–35.
23. Pappworth, M. H.: 1968, *Human Guinea Pigs*, Beacon Press, Boston.
24. Powers, C. W. (ed.): 1972, *People-Profits: The Ethics of Investment*, Council on Religion and Economic Affairs, New York.
25. Poynter, N.: 1974, *Medicine and Man*, Penguin Books, Baltimore.
26. Proceedings, Round Table Conference of CIOMS -- WHO – UNESCO, Geneva, Oct. 1969: 1960, *Medical Research – Priorities and Responsibilities*, World Health Organization, Geneva.
27. Restak, R.: 1975, *Premeditated Man*, Viking Press, New York, pp.111–114; 120–121.
28. Robbins, H.: 1974, 'The Statistical Mode of Thought', in J. Neyman (ed.), *The Heritage of Copernicus,* MIT Press, Cambridge, pp. 419–430.
29. Ryder, R.: 1973, 'Experiments on Animals', in S. Godlovitch *et al.* (eds.), *Animals, Men and Morals*, Grove Press, New York.
30. Schwartz, H.: 1975, 'Will Medicine Be Strangled in the Law?' *New York Times*, Feb. 25, p. 35.
31. Schwartzman, D.: 1975, *The Expected Return from Pharmaceutical Research*, American Enterprise Institute for Public Policy Research, Washington, D. C., pp. 49–52.
32. Siegler, M. and Osmund, J.: 1973, *Models of Madness, Models of Medicine,* Macmillan, New York.
33. Sjoberg, G.: 1967, *Ethics, Politics, and Social Research*, Routledge and Kegan Paul, London.
34. Sjostrom, H. and Nilsson, R.: 1973, *Thalidomide and the Power of the Drug Companies*, Basic Books, New York.
35. Sutherland, N. S.: 1975, 'Doctor in the Doghouse', A Review of *Medical Nemesis* by Ivan Illich, *Times Literary Supplement*, Mar. 21, p. 295.
36. Vischer, M. B.: 1975, *Ethical Constraints in Medical Research*, Charles C. Thomas, Springfield, Ill., pp. 12–16, 34–39.
37. Wardell, W.: 1975, 'Development in the Introduction of New Drugs in the United States and Britain, 1971–1974', in R. B. Helms (ed.), *Drug Development and Marketing*, American Enterprise Institute for Public Policy Research, Washington, D. C., pp. 175–182.
38. Wardell, W. and Lasagna, L.: 1975, *Regulation and Drug Development,* American Enterprise Institute for Public Policy Research, Washington, D. C.
39. Warwick, D. P.: 1975, 'Social Scientists Ought to Stop Lying', *Psychology Today* 8, 38–40. 105–106.
40. Young, J. H.: 1967, *Medical Messiahs*, Princeton Univ. Press, Princeton.

NATALIE ABRAMS

MEDICAL EXPERIMENTATION: THE
CONSENT OF PRISONERS AND CHILDREN

The purpose of this paper is to examine some arguments concerning the use of special subjects, i.e., prisoners and children, in human experimentation. It is the difficulty of obtaining informed consent which presents the problem for these categories of subjects. In the case of prisoners, the issue is usually whether or not the prison situation itself and/or any possible threats or rewards could be coercive and thus limit the prisoner's freedom to consent to participation. In the case of children, the difficult issue is usually presented in terms of proxy consent. Since the child himself cannot consent, the question asked is in what situations should proxy consent be permissible.

In the following paper, I will consider a number of different philosophical positions concerning the distinction between offers and threats in order to see what they imply for the prison situation. Although many problems still remain to be solved both in the development of an adequate position concerning threats and offers and in its application to the prisoner situation, I hope my discussion indicates some different possible approaches to the problem which can then be pursued further. I will try to argue for allowing the possibility of experimentation on prisoners. Furthermore, I shall claim that some of our misgivings about the use of prisoner 'volunteers' have less to do with a concern for their autonomy and more to do with our personal conceptions about the purpose of incarceration. The major portion of the paper will concern the prisoner question. Concerning the issue of children, I shall argue that presenting the problem in terms of proxy consent is incorrect and, if applied as such, would have important practical consequences.

By focusing on these particular problems in human experimentation, I do not mean to convey the impression that they are necessarily the most important or pressing issues. I do believe, however, that we are already aware of the general areas in which there are difficulties and that what is now important is to attempt to consider more carefully particular aspects of the problem of experimentation. It is for this reason that I have chosen not to devote this paper to a presentation of the many different ethical problems involved in human experimentation but rather to concentrate on a relatively

S. F. Spicker and H. T. Engelhardt, Jr. (eds.), Philosophical Medical Ethics: Its Nature and Significance, 111–124. All Rights Reserved. Copyright © 1977 by D. Reidel Publishing Company, Dordrecht-Holland.

narrow issue and to try to see the relevance of particular philosophical interpretations.

The requirement of 'informed consent' involves two separate issues. One is that the subject be informed of all relevant information necessary for making his decision. The second part of the requirement is that the decision be 'free' and issue from the person himself. This latter point is the basic idea behind the demand for 'consent,' and it is this second part of the problem with which I will be concerned. There do not seem to be any special difficulties involved in informing a prisoner versus informing any individual of the necessary information.

Crucial to the prison situation is the question of whether or not threats and/or offers are coercive and limit the prisoner's ability to refuse to participate in experiments. The dispute generally revolves around two points: first, whether or not offers are coercive; and, secondly, what are the criteria for the distinction between threats and offers. Even if it were granted that offers were not coercive but threats were, the problem would still remain as to when an individual is confronted with a threat and when he is confronted with an offer.

One possible approach to this question is presented by Virginia Held in her article, 'Coercion and Coercive Offers' [4]. As suggested by this title, Professor Held argues that the relevant distinction to be made is not that between threats and offers but rather between what she calls 'initial' versus 'final' coercion ([4], p. 60). 'Initial' coercion occurs in a situation in which there is at least the possibility of resistance. For example, I can sign a loyalty oath and take a government job or I can refuse the oath and not take the job. Even though the pressure may be great, I can literally refuse the oath. In a situation of 'final' coercion, on the other hand, resistance is not even possible. An example she gives of 'final' coercion is the existence of a high fence preventing entrance to a government building. Here, it would not be possible to overcome the resistance ([4], p. 59).

The degree of coercion involved is, however, different from this distinction between kinds. The degree of coercion is a 'function of the undesirability of the outcome and the probability of its occurring' ([4], p. 59). Held argues that, when the degree of coercion remains constant, 'initial' coercion, in which there is at least the possibility of resistance, is preferable to 'final' coercion. Our ordinary distinction, then, between threats versus offers would simply be a distinction between different degrees of coercion, not different kinds. Some so-called offers and threats we can resist and some we cannot. Therefore, some offers and some threats would fall under what she calls 'initial' coercion, although, as Held admits, it is probably true that most offers present instances of 'initial' coercion, whereas most threats present instances of 'final' coercion.

In the prisoner situation, therefore, in order to determine whether or not the prisoner has been coerced, the important question is not strictly whether the prisoner has been offered a reward or threatened, but rather whether or not he could have resisted (initial versus final coercion) and how undesirable and probable the alternatives were (degree of coercion).

There seems to be a serious difficulty, however, with this interpretation. If 'initial' coercion is defined as that which one literally could resist, or that kind of coercion 'in which the person coerced could in some sense have supplied the deficiency of will' ([4], p. 60) whereas 'final' coercion could not be resisted, one would have to have this information first. That is, one would have to know which alternatives could be resisted before a situation could be properly classified as either one of 'initial' or 'final' coercion. But it is just this information which is missing in most morally troublesome cases of possible coercion. Unless one limits discussion only to cases in which some physical restriction is operative, the problem is always at what point does a threat or an offer actually restrict or limit an individual's freedom, such that he could not choose the other alternative, even though not physically coerced. Unless one begs this question and assumes that all non-physical coercion *could* be resisted simply by supplying the deficiency of will, the important difficulty of determining in which situations people could and could not resist still remains.

The following statement by Held is definitely true: 'There are forms of coercion . . . where the person coerced did what he did against his will, but might himself have supplied the deficiency of will, and there are forms of coercion where the person coerced did what he did against his will, but might in no way himself have summoned the courage to resist' ([4], pp. 58–59). However, the distinction between these two kinds of situations cannot be made simply by appealing to external circumstances, such as 'high fences.' Furthermore, and more importantly, Held considers a situation one of 'initial' coercion even if the only way the person could have resisted is 'if his character had been different' ([4], p. 58). To repeat an argument usually presented in connection with the free-will dispute, the significant question is not whether the person could have chosen differently if he had had a different personality or set of desires, but whether the person, as he was in that same situation, could have chosen otherwise. It is this question which must be answered before a situation can be identified as one of 'initial' or 'final' coercion.

Held's analysis, therefore, does not seem to provide much guidance in the prisoner situation. Assuming no one is arguing for physical coercion as a means of obtaining subjects for experimentation, all likely forms of coercion in the prison situation would fall into the category of 'initial' coercion, the least objectionable variety, and yet, one still cannot know whether or not the alternatives as presented to the prisoners do, in fact, overcome their wills to the extent that they could not supply any deficiency.

Another approach to this problem is given by Gerald Dworkin in his article 'Acting Freely' [1]. Here, Dworkin argues that an individual is acting freely, i.e., is not coerced, if he does not mind doing that action for that reason ([1], p. 377). For example, I am acting freely when I give money to a charity if I do not mind giving away money to help other people, but I am not acting freely if I give money to a kidnapper, provided that I object to giving him money as a means to securing my child's safety. The main objection with which Dworkin has to contend is the claim that all actions could be reinterpreted in such a way that a person always does what he wants to do, or always acts for reasons which he accepts, and is therefore never coerced. This argument states that the most that offers or threats could do would be to change the person's 'wants' or 'desires' by changing the consequences of performing the given alternatives. According to this interpretation, the individual's freedom is in no way restricted. This, of course, should not imply that there is nothing objectionable to such threats and offers. It simply argues that the disturbing feature of these situations is not that an individual's freedom is limited. Hence, when I hand money over to the kidnapper I am still doing what I want to do, i.e., I am saving my child's life. When I give up money to the highwayman, I am also acting for reasons which I accept, i.e., I am saving my own life.

Dworkin opposes this interpretation by rejecting the redescription of the act in question (handing over the money) as 'saving the child' or 'preserving his life' ([1], p. 372). Applying this dispute to the prison situation, the question would then be whether, if a prisoner consents to experimentation for the purpose of receiving additional money or an early parole, he is in fact doing what he wants to do. Can his participation in the experiment be redescribed as contributing to his own support, or aiding his family (either by gaining extra money or early parole), reasons for which he certainly might not mind acting? If it is argued that the redescription is appropriate, then the prisoner's freedom to refuse participation is not restricted by additional rewards or threats, no matter how great. All that is happening is that his desires are altered by the changed consequences.

One could reject this argument in a number of different ways. Dworkin would do so by rejecting the redescription of the acts (i.e., participation would not be the same as helping one's family, etc.). A second way of rejecting the argument is to claim that even if one's freedom is not violated by these threats and offers, they are still objectionable. I discuss this on page 122.

A third possible rejection involves distinguishing between two different kinds of freedom. One conception of freedom is dependent upon one's ability to do what one desires. On this view, a person is free provided that he can do what he wants even if he could not choose otherwise. This kind of freedom exists only in cases in which the individual just happens to want to do what he has to do. Although this view might not capture the usual meaning of the word 'freedom,' there is certainly some sense in which we would want to say of such an individual that he was not coerced. If one accepts this notion of freedom, then the prisoner could still be said to be free when he participates in the experiment, provided that the redescription of his actions is accepted. That is, the prisoner is free in this sense if by participating for money, or other reward, he can be said to be doing what he wants.

While accepting this redescription, however, there is another sense of 'freedom' in which it would have to be said that the prisoner still is not free, even if he is doing what he wants to do. This other kind of freedom is referred to by Joel Feinberg as 'dispositional liberty' ([2], pp. 5–6). According to this view, a person is free only if he can do considerably more than what he wants to do. Maximizing freedom, in this sense, would be maximizing the number of available alternatives 'whatever the effect on the person's state of mind' ([2], p. 6). By adopting the view of dispositional liberty, the prisoner might not be making a free decision about participation, even if by participating he is doing what he wants to do. To be free in the dispositional sense, the prisoner must have been able to have chosen otherwise. One might even go so far as to say that by not providing the option of volunteering for experimentation, the prisoner is being denied his 'dispositional liberty' in this area. The question then would be whether or not this is a legitimate restriction of liberty for prisoners. The choice may actually be whether it is less coercive to affect a person's decision, i.e., limit his freedom, by possibly influencing his desires (through altering consequences) or by restricting or eliminating options. This decision would undoubtedly depend upon other values and would require a separate investigation.

A third approach to the distinction between threats and offers is presented by Robert Nozick in his article 'Coercion' [6]. Nozick argues that whereas threats are coercive, offers normally are not. What remains, therefore, is to stipulate the criteria for distinguishing between when a person is presented with a threat or an offer. Nozick states that 'whether someone makes a threat against Q's doing an action or an offer to Q to do the action depends upon how the consequences he says he will bring about change the consequences of Q's action from what they would have been in the normal or natural or expected course of events. If it makes the consequences of Q's action worse than they would have been in the normal and expected course of events, it is a threat; if it makes the consequences better, it is an offer. The term 'expected' is meant to shift between or straddle the predicted and morally required' ([6], p. 112).

In order to apply this distinction to any particular situation, the first step is to find out what the expected course of events would be. In the prisoner situation, if the prisoner would have obtained parole in one year and by participating in an experiment he either is told or assumes that he will be released earlier, then the prisoner is being presented with an offer and is not coerced. On the other hand, if by refusing to participate his sentence would be lengthened or he would not get out when normally expected, he is being threatened and his freedom restricted. The same argument can be made concerning money, using as a base the amount of money the prisoner would normally receive for his duties.

The above discussion is fairly straightforward and unproblematic. Difficulties arise, however, when one begins to question or doubt the acceptability of using the normal course of events as a basis for judgment. Certain cases make it appear as if the base should be not what would have happened in the normal course of events, but rather what should have occurred. One example which Nozick presents points up this problem quite clearly. Consider the case in which a slave owner usually beats his slave every day but one day states that he will not beat him if the slave performs a certain action for him ([6], pp. 115–116). Is the owner threatening to beat the slave or is he offering not to do so? How this situation is interpreted depends upon what facts one uses as a base. Considered in relation to what usually occurs, the slave is being presented with an offer. Considered in relation to what would be morally expected to occur (i.e., owners should not beat slaves), the slave is being threatened. It is obvious from this, that the kind of situation used as a base is of central importance to the question of whether someone is being presented with a threat or an offer.

The problem which needs to be solved is whether one should use the normal course of events or the morally expected course of events as a base. Nozick suggests that when the 'normal and morally expected course of events diverge, the one of these which is to be used in deciding whether a conditional announcement of an action constitutes a threat or an offer is the course of events that the recipient of the action prefers' ([6], p. 116). Hence, in the slave case, assuming the slave would prefer the morally expected course of events, i.e., not to be beaten, it is this which should be used as the basis for decision. The slave would therefore be threatened by the owner's announcement.

Applying this interpretation to the prisoner situation, the question is then what the morally expected course of events would be and whether the prisoner would prefer the normal or the morally expected course of events. Determination of what the morally expected course of events would be must be considered as part of a general theory of punishment and cannot be discussed here. However, there are definite practical results which would have to be considered while evaluating what situation to use as a base.

The general implication of categorizing something as a threat instead of an offer, with the assumption that threats are coercive, whereas offers are not, is that threats should be avoided as much as possible. If threats are thought to limit freedom, once something is seen as a threat, one should try to eliminate it or prevent it from operating as such. This attitude has consequences for the above interpretation.

On the one hand, the slave obviously prefers the morally expected course of events and if this is used as the base the slave must be seen as threatened. Hence, since threats are coercive, the owner should not be allowed to present his ultimatum, i.e., he should be prevented from saying, 'Do x and you will not be beaten.' On the other hand, if the owner is prevented from making his 'threat' the slave will not have the opportunity to do something which would prevent a beating. Therefore, whereas the slave might prefer that the morally expected course of events were the normal course of events, this by no means implies that the slave would prefer to use the morally expected course of events as a base, for by using it as a base, the owner's ultimatum is viewed as a threat and hence should be prevented. The criterion for choosing between the normally and the morally expected course of events as base should not be simply which set of events the individual would prefer to exist. If the individual's hypothetical preferences are to enter into the decision, it should be whether the person would prefer the ultimatum to be seen as a threat or an offer. On this view, the important decision would have to be whether the individual would want the option to be presented to him. Obviously, if he would desire to be confronted with the ultimatum, then it should be seen as an offer and permitted. If he would not want to be presented with the option, it should be seen as a threat and hence prevented. Here, classifying something as a threat or an offer becomes a derivative matter, dependent upon the individual's hypothetical preferences concerning being presented with the option or the ultimatum.

As previously stated, the above discussion is premised on the assumption that threats are coercive, whereas offers are not. It is only on this assumption that it can be argued that if something is classified as a threat, it should be prevented, whereas if it is an offer, it should be allowed. Nozick argues for his claim that threats are coercive and offers are not by appealing to the decision referred to above, i.e., whether the individual would want (in a hypothetical sense) to be put in the threat or offer situation.

Although the decisions which an individual might make within a threat versus an offer situation cannot be clearly distinguished in terms of whose will is operating, the hypothetical decision about whether or not one would want to enter the threat or offer situation can be distinguished. Nozick claims that it is this latter decision which is more indicative of the existence of free choice. He concludes that the 'rational man' would want to be put in the offer situation but not in the threat situation, and Nozick uses this point to argue for his claim that a person's decision in the offer situation is, therefore, more his own choice, it is more his will which is operative here than in the threat situation ([6], p. 133). My argument is that whether or not one wants to be put in the situation, in addition to being a possible indicator of whose will is operating, is also the preference which should be consulted initially when deciding which situation to use as base.

If one accepts Nozick's claim that threats are coercive whereas offers are not (with the hidden assumption that threats, as instances of coercion, should be prevented whereas offers allowed) one must not use as a base simply the individual's preferences about which situation he would want to exist. Using this simple preference as the deciding factor, conjoined with the above assumptions about threats, can be seen to lead to objectionable conclusions, namely those seen in the slave case.

Now it is necessary to consider the prisoner situation in relation to the above model. Previously the prisoner case was discussed in terms of the normal course of events. Assuming that the morally expected course of events is better from the prisoner's point of view (i.e., he should be receiving more money or he should receive parole earlier), if one accepts Nozick's argument, the morally expected course of events should be used as a base. This would mean that the prisoner would be threatened by an opportunity for early parole or more money in return for participation in an experiment and, hence, the possibility of participating should be eliminated. In practical terms, however, the same objection can be made here as in the slave case. By using the morally expected course of events as the base and classifying the situation as presenting a threat (assuming threats should be prevented), the prisoner would not have the opportunity to gain more money or an early parole (just as the slave would not be able to prevent a beating). Here again, the prisoner might very well prefer using the normal course of events as the base and not preclude the opportunity to receive benefits.

To see more clearly the difference between my argument and Nozick's, consider the following two cases. In the first case, assume that the morally expected course of events and the normal course of events are the same. Presenting the option of shortened sentence or more money would then be making an offer (i.e., offering to raise the prisoner above the morally necessary level) and, as such, should be allowed. The same result would be reached on my interpretation as well, but from a different starting point. The important question here would be whether the prisoner would want the option to participate presented to him, if by participating, he could gain advantages, but by refusing, he would lose none. I am claiming that the choice would be in favor of having the option. In the second case, however, there is a difference between the two interpretations. Assume, here, that the normal course of events is different from the morally expected situation. On Nozick's view, receiving advantages through experimentation would have to be seen as simply bringing the individual closer to the morally desirable level and hence is a threat and should be prevented. On the interpretation I am suggesting, however, this would not follow. Again, the important question is whether the prisoner would want to be presented with the option, i.e., whether, given his present situation, he would want (hypothetically) to be presented with the possibility of gaining advantages by participating, even though he should have those advantages already. My argument is that it is quite possible here that the prisoner would prefer to be presented with the ultimatum. The only way it would be obvious that he would refuse would be if the alternative involved a choice between receiving the benefits by participating or receiving the benefits independent of any action on his part. As noted earlier, however, this is unfortunately not his alternative.

One possible way out of these difficulties of choosing the correct situation as base, at least in the prisoner case, is to argue that experimentation should be permitted if and only if no benefits are in any way dependent upon participation. It is thought that this requirement prevents the necessity of deciding whether the prisoners are being coerced by the benefits. In addition to the practical difficulties involved in this recommendation, i.e., trying to prevent advantages from indirectly accruing to participants, there is the more important difficulty of controlling intangible advantages. Besides money and early parole, another very strong reason for 'volunteering' is the desire to gain self-respect or to feel a sense of pride or self-worth which often comes from believing that one has made a personal sacrifice for other people ([5], p. 452). It is impossible to eliminate this advantage (as it might be possible to eliminate monetary gains) and yet it seems to present even greater problems than external benefits.

One problem is essentially the same as that discussed in relation to the slave situation, except it is even more difficult here to determine what the base situations would be. If one uses the normal course of events as the base, and assumes that the prisoner would have a relatively low level of self-esteem and that allowing him to participate in the experiment would raise this, then the prisoner is being made an offer and should be allowed to participate. If one used the morally expected course of events as the base, the situation is more complicated. Should a prisoner have a feeling of pride and self-esteem at that point in his life (assuming, of course, that he has been properly charged and convicted)? If the answer is affirmative, i.e., everyone has value and perhaps it is his failure to recognize this which prompted the crime in the first place, then the morally expected course of events (what should be the case) is that the prisoner should have a sense of his own worth. Using this as the base, and assuming that the prisoner does not feel about himself as he should feel, participation in experimentation would simply bring him up to the 'moral subsistence level' ([3], p. 36) and must be considered a threat. As such the option to participate should be eliminated, and, as in the slave case, the prisoner would not be allowed the opportunity to gain an advantage. He would not be allowed the opportunity to bring himself up to the level at which it is thought he should be. If the answer to the above question is negative, i.e., the prisoner should not at that point feel great self-esteem (perhaps one should only feel pride at doing good deeds), only then would the opportunity to participate be seen as an offer and permitted. Using the morally expected situation as the base, therefore, creates the following dilemma. If it is assumed that the prisoner should feel what he does not feel, he is thereby prevented from engaging in an activity which would provide him with what he should, but does not have — self-esteem. If it is assumed that the prisoner should not feel particularly different about himself, it is only then that he would be allowed to participate.

It might be argued that the implication of using the morally expected course of events as a base and classifying something as a threat and therefore trying to prevent it, is that the individual should be given the benefit or brought up to the morally desirable level without requiring him to do anything. In other words, calling something a threat, and consequently precluding it, does not mean that the individual would not be given the advantage. Rather, it might be argued, in the ideal case, that the threat should be forbidden and the advantage provided. For example, the prisoner should be given money, parole, medical care, etc., independent of any participation. This certainly would be the desirable approach, i.e., to bring the morally expected state of affairs into existence independent of any action on the individual's part.

Besides the practical difficulties involved in doing this, there is a special difficulty concerning the benefit of self-esteem. It is easy to make sense of giving a person money, medical care, or parole, but how does one 'give' another self-esteem without the necessity of some action on the part of the would-be recipient? How could the morally-expected state of affairs even be brought into existence without the individual doing something? Self-esteem cannot be handed out in the same way that money and medical care can. The choice then seems to be that either the person is allowed to engage in some meaningful activity which would give him the opportunity to gain self-respect, or the morally expected state of affairs cannot be brought into existence at all. There is no reason that the activity must be participation in human experimentation, but whatever the activity is, the same charge could be levied. That is, if the prisoner should feel a certain way and he does not, and if this activity is simply bringing him up to the 'moral subsistence level,' the opportunity to engage in the activity is threatening him and should be forbidden. It is a strange argument which would work to prevent the realization of something which is thought to be morally necessary, a feeling of self-respect.

Thus it would seem, that unless one is going to bring the morally desirable course of events into existence, independent of action on the part of any individual (which, obviously, would be the best alternative), there are situations in which it could be said that prisoners should be given the option to participate in human experimentation, i.e., when they would want the alternative to be presented to them. As Nozick argues, it is this preference which would seem to be the best available guide for determining the extent to which the decision would be their own, and, hence, they could be said to give 'consent.' In addition, allowing participation might be the only way of providing an opportunity to realize the morally desirable state of affairs. Furthermore, we should be equally as concerned about erring in the direction of not recognizing consent when it is freely given as we are about assuming that it is free when it may not be. It is just as much an affront to an individual not to recognize and accept a decision as his own, as it is to assume that the decision is his when it was the result of coercion.

The above discussion is premised on the assumption that if prisoners can give free consent to experimentation, then they should be allowed to participate. I should like to suggest now that the issue of 'free consent' is not the only troublesome problem involved in prisoner participation in human experimentation. In addition, there is also the question of whether prisoners should be allowed to gain benefits by participating, i.e., even if there is no problem concerning consent. This second question regarding benefits is being confused with the first regarding consent whenever the distinction between the following two questions is not made: first, is it justifiable to give additional benefits to those who participate (since there might not have been free consent); and secondly, is it justifiable to give additional benefits to those who participate (because, e.g., prisoners should not have such benefits or participation is not the proper means of obtaining such benefits). It can be seen that these questions address two separate problems.

The answer to the second question is very much dependent on the conception of punishment which is being employed. On the retributive theory, it might be argued that a certain punishment is mandatory because there is some way in which the prisoner deserves the sentence and any alteration in the punishment would be inappropriate. There is also the issue here of whether the punishment is simply the deprivation of liberty or must also involve other deprivations as well, e.g., in terms of money, self-respect, loneliness. Should conditions be made as nice as possible for the prisoner while he is being punished (i.e., not free) or are other indignities also part of his punishment? On the deterrent theory, a criminal is incarcerated in order to prevent him or others from committing the crime in the future. If benefits such as early parole counteract the deterrent effect, they might have to be prevented. On the reformative or rehabilitative theory, a criminal is deprived of his liberty and treated in such a way as to alter his character for the future. It might seem that the opportunity to participate in experiments which would benefit society might possibly be used as one kind of indicator of rehabilitation. Although it is not possible to consider here this second question of the appropriateness of gaining benefits by participation in human experimentation, based on conflicting theories of punishment, I hope it is clear from the above, that this is an entirely separate question from the one involving consent and should be examined separately.

My final point concerns the issue of proxy consent for children. The central question here is usually thought to be in what cases parents or guardians should be allowed to offer consent for those in their care. The assumption is made that since the children cannot consent for themselves the parent or guardian should be asked to consent for them since they would have the children's best interests at heart.

While I do not at all dispute the assumption that in the majority of cases parents or guardians would be most concerned with the best interests of the children, I do object to the use of the phrase 'proxy consent' to refer to consent by parents for children. This is not consent at all. It is the nature of any consent that it must issue from the individual in question and not from a second party for the individual. Thus, when 'proxy consent' is sought, what is really being used as a basis for judgment are standards (whether of care, treatment, or well-being). That is, when a parent is asked to give 'proxy consent' to any kind of intervention, the requirement of consent is actually being by-passed (perhaps because it is not thought possible to obtain) in favor of a decision on the basis of standards of well-being. The parent is being asked to state what procedures he or she thinks is in the best interest of the child. The distinction between a decision based on consent and a decision based on standards of well-being can be seen clearly if one simply recognizes that a decision based on consent must be accepted regardless of whether or not the decision appears to be in the best interest of the person in question.

If the parental decision is really interpreted as 'proxy consent' then, assuming the parents are fully informed and are in a position to make a 'free' choice, the decision of the parents must be respected. A decision based on consent must be accepted simply because of its source. On the other hand, if the parental decision is used as an alternative method to consent, i.e., as a guide in trying to make a decision based on the standard of the child's well-being, the parental decision could be overturned by the court (e.g., by arguing that the standards employed were not those actually in the best interest of the child).

Considering the parental decision as one of 'proxy consent' versus decision on the basis of standards would, therefore, seem to have implications for the authority given to parents or guardians in such situations. In actual fact, standards of well-being are usually employed in deciding on the proper treatment or use of children in medical situations. This should be recognized as such and the idea of proxy consent seen as it really is, i.e., as only a practical method of reaching a decision based on standards by appealing to the judgment of those who are thought to decide on the basis of the child's best interest.

This paper by no means presents a definitive answer to the difficult question of whether or not there are legitimate ethical objections to the use of prisoners in human experimentation. The discussion has been limited in a number of ways. First, I have considered only the question of the possible coercive effects of threats and offers and the ways in which they might preclude free consent. As I hope was made clear, there are other serious questions about the use of prisoners in experimentation (which are not discussed here). These questions must not be confused with the consent issue and are intimately dependent upon the theory of punishment which is being employed. Furthermore, I do not claim to have presented either a full analysis of the distinction between threats and offers or drawn final conclusions about the prisoner situation. What I do hope to have done is to indicate a number of different approaches which might be used in evaluating the prisoner situation, as well as to point out some of the areas in which problems might arise. I also hope that the significance of philosophical analysis for dealing with the ethical problems involved in using prisoners for human experimentation is made clear.

*New York University Medical Center
and Bellevue Hospital,
New York City, New York*

BIBLIOGRAPHY

1. Dworkin, G.: 1970, 'Acting Freely', *Nous* 4, 367–383.
2. Feinberg, J.: 1973, *Social Philosophy*, Prentice-Hall, New Jersey.
3. Freedman, B : 1975, 'A Moral Theory of Informed Consent', *Hastings Center Report* 5 (4), 32–39.
4. Held, V.: 1972, 'Coercion and Coercive Offers', in Pennock and Chapman (eds.), *Coercion*, Aldine-Atherton, New York.
5. Lasagna, L.: 1969, 'Special Subjects in Human Experimentation', *Daedalus* 98 (2), 449–462.
6. Nozick, R.: 1963, 'Coercion', in P. Haslett (ed.), *Philosophy, Politics, and Society*, Fourth Series, Barnes and Noble, New York.

SECTION IV

CHANGING HUMAN NATURE:
MEDICINE IN THE SERVICE OF VIRTUE

JOSEPH OWENS

ARISTOTELIAN ETHICS, MEDICINE, AND THE
CHANGING NATURE OF MAN

I

If we ask how the unrestrained man's ignorance is dissipated and he returns to a state of knowledge, the explanation is the same as in the case of drunkenness and sleep, and is not peculiar to failure of self-restraint. We must go for it to physiology. (Aristotle, *Ethica Nicomachea*, VII 3,1147b6–9; trans. H. Rackham).

For the ultimate means of catalyzing moral ignorance and restoring moral knowledge in a weak-willed man, Aristotle falls back in this passage of the *Nicomachean Ethics* upon the knowledge of a man's physiological condition. The instance he brings forward is that of a person to whom the eating of sweets is not permitted. Overwhelming appetite for them is pushing the man towards eating a delicacy in front of him, while more considered judgment tells him not to. Since the man is weak-willed, his intellectual inclination to follow his better judgment does not prevail against sense impulse. In this particular instance he goes ahead to enjoy the forbidden object.

The passage does not receive too much attention from commentators on the *Ethics*, as it refers to a solution outside their proper field.[1] Yet it has crucial importance for the understanding of Aristotelian ethics in its relation to medicine and the changing nature of man. For Aristotle, strange as it may perhaps appear 'at first sight, the ultimate remedy here is not to be looked for in properly ethical considerations. Rather, it is to be sought in the type of knowledge provided by the physiologists. The eating of the delicacy is regarded by him as taking place in moral *ignorance*. In the Socratic tradition of Greek moral optimism a faulty opinion could not be allowed to prevail over knowledge, man's highest and rightfully dominant possession. No man should knowingly be able to do wrong. The judgment that sweets should not be eaten here and now is undoubtedly present in the weak-willed man's intellect. But it cannot be there as knowledge, against this background. It is present only as a corresponding proposition would be in the mind of a drunkard reeling off verses of elevated poetry, or in an ordinary actor reciting epic lines on the stage. It is not related to the inebriate or the actor as his own, and accordingly is not actual moral knowledge. But the weak-willed man

S. F. Spicker and H. T. Engelhardt, Jr. (eds.), Philosophical Medical Ethics: Its Nature and Significance, 127–142. All Rights Reserved. Copyright © 1977 by D. Reidel Publishing Company, Dordrecht-Holland.

is not totally depraved. He did indeed have the moral knowledge before succumbing to the impulse. He still retains the knowledge, though only in an habitual state. As moral knowledge it is dormant and ineffective. From the viewpoint of actuality there is only moral ignorance.

The latent moral knowledge, however, is definitely referred to by the recital of the words and the concomitant presence of the moral proposition in the weak-willed man's consciousness. How is it to be restored to actuality? How may the moral ignorance in which the man acts be broken through? Surprisingly, Aristotle does not invoke any specifically ethical aids. Without further ado he drops the characteristically moral procedure and states bluntly that the method is to be learned from the physiologists.

This way of dealing with weakness of will may at first strike today's reader as somewhat unusual in the setting of Greek intellectualism. Yet a little reflection will show that the whole passage fits appropriately enough into the general framework of the Aristotelian *Ethics*. The first point to note is that the passage is not asking how ethics can help medicine, but rather how physiology, which is applied by medicine, can help ethics in cases such as the one under discussion. This brings up the general question of how medicine is related to ethics for Aristotle. The bearing of the question is quite significant. Ethics is for him the supreme practical science, the science that governs all the other sciences, arts and crafts, and that directs all human conduct (*Ethica Nicomachea*, I 1–2,1094a1–b11). It has the right to call upon any of them, and explicitly upon the knowledge of human nature (*Ethica Nicomachea*, I 13,1102a18–b28), for whatever help it needs.[2] The reason is that for Aristotle ethics directs man towards the highest goal of his being, his supreme destiny. All other purposes in a man's life are subordinate to that end, and are meant to contribute towards its attainment. This supreme goal consists in the highest kind of intellectual life, namely, the exercise of man's highest faculty, the intellect, upon its highest object. Because of this one common goal, ethics for the community (the *polis*) and ethics for the individual coincide. Their purpose, the highest kind of human intellectual life, is exactly the same (*Ethica Nicomachea*, I 2,1094b6–11). All other types of activity are subordinated to its pursuit. They are meant to help towards it. One requisite, of course, is bodily health, the goal of medical interest (*Ethica Nicomachea*, I 7,1097a15–24). In this way, and in this way only, does Aristotle regard medicine as subordinate to ethics.

Aristotle was the son of a practicing medical man ([9], V.1). In accord with the wording of the Hippocratic oath ([23], I298, line 13), he may be presumed to have received the medical instruction and training customarily given the sons of a medical practitioner. He regularly speaks of medical knowledge with high respect, and makes accurate use of medical illustrations and similes throughout his writings. Yet his own bent was primarily philosophical. His main interest in practical life centered on the supreme destiny of man, towards which bodily health was but a means and a necessary condition. Against that background the question 'Can ethics be of help to medicine?' would have seemed to him wrongly placed. With Plato (*Republic*, III, 389BC) he would most likely agree that ethics could help keep the patient from deceiving the physician about medical symptoms, and could, like rhetoric, (*Gorgias*, 456B) persuade him to submit to the prescribed medical or surgical treatment.[3] But these considerations would be only incidental. Aristotle's overall understanding of the relation between ethics and medicine would place the essential question as 'How can medicine help ethics?' The appeal to physiological knowledge in the case of the weak-willed man would accordingly be but an instance in which the question was found to apply. From this angle the passage quoted at the beginning of the present paper fits neatly enough into the general Aristotelian conception of practical knowledge.

Secondly, the problem here evoked calls for an understanding of Aristotle's notion of practical science itself. For him, the reasoned development of moral knowledge may be called 'practical science' (*Topica*, VI 6,145a15–18) or 'political science' (*Rhetorica*, I 4,1359b10–11; 17–18), and is classed under 'practical' in his divisions of the sciences (*Metaphysica*, E 1.1025b18–1026a23; K 7,1064a10–b4). His basic distinction between the kinds of human knowledge lies between the theoretical on the one hand, and the practical and productive on the other. Theoretical knowledge deals with an object just as it stands, detached in itself, before one's intellectual gaze. The grounds of theoretical knowledge are accordingly located entirely within the object itself. The knowledge does not vary with the personal conditions of the agent at the moment. In Euclidean geometry, for instance, the angles of a triangle are and remain equal to two right angles regardless of the changing dispositions of the knowing agent. Whether the mathematician is good or depraved, strong-willed or weak-willed, sick or well, the geometrical theorem remains unaffected.

Moral knowledge, on the other hand, is worked into and imbedded in the habituation of the agent in a way that allows it to be described as going along with his nature.[4] So constituted, it is obviously changeable with the changing conditions of the man. Culture, habituation, physical and psychic conditions will affect it radically. A German boy brought up from childhood in the Hitler Jugend will tell you that he could see things only from a Nazi viewpoint until the bubble burst in the experience of post-war conditions and the outlook of his earlier years was changed completely. People educated in a strictly Victorian atmosphere will alter their moral judgments drastically with absorption into the spirit of mid-twentieth century permissiveness. Prolonged anger or deep sexual passion will gradually change one's judgment about what one should do. Because changing conditions so profoundly affect moral decisions, they are an essential aspect to be reckoned with in dealing with this type of knowledge. Consequently the physiological dispositions may be expected to play an essential part in the development or the restoration of truly moral cognition. That is just what the Aristotelian passage under consideration presupposes. Again it is found to be quite at home in the broad picture of Aristotle's ethics. To go back to the instances before his own eyes (*Ethica Nicomachea*, I 5,1095b14—1096a7), instead of the modern ones used just now to illustrate his meaning, different types of men do things for the ultimate purposes of pleasure, reputation and public standing, or intellectual activity. They are obviously making their judgments in accord with the type of life they lead. Their personal dispositions determine their differing judgments about what is good for them to do.

The third question that arises from the wording of the Aristotelian passage is what the term 'physiologist' meant exactly at the time. As Aristotle uses the word elsewhere ([5], 835b41—49), and as it was used by others in the epoch, it meant 'one who inquires into natural causes and phenomena' ([25], s.v.). Specifically it referred to the type of investigator who studied nature in the tradition that was followed from Thales onward. The object was to explain natural events in the light of their ultimate causes. For Aristotle, nature in this sense necessarily implied change. For him, change in fact pervaded the sensible world like a sort of life (*Physica*, VIII 1,250b14—15) for the things constituted by nature.

By 'physiologist,' then, Aristotle did not mean specifically a medical practitioner. He had at his disposal, and made regular use of ([5], 338a21—53), the precise Greek terms for medical man and the art of medicine. However, in the *Ethics* (*Ethica Nicomachea*, I 13,1102a21—22) he has in mind 'the more cultured type of medical practitioners,' who have devoted great attention to the knowledge of the body. In the historical setting this could not mean anything else than the study of the human body in the Hippocratic tradition, which was in turn couched in the natural philosophy of the Presocratics.[5] Nature as envisaged by the Presocratics was the ground for medical discourse.[6] Even the objection of the author of *Ancient Medicine*, XX, against what philosophers and physicians have written about nature, does not bear on any separation of medicine from the ancient physiology but rather on the necessity of correct medical knowledge for the understanding of what nature really is.[7]

But what did 'nature' mean for Aristotle himself in this context? He recognizes a number of senses for the term. Its two basic significations in Greek tradition were the stable constitution of a thing and the thing's growth or development.[8] Against this historical background of both change and permanence, Aristotle seems to take the best of both worlds. He finds the basic philosophical meaning of 'nature' to be the *unchangeable* components of *changeable* things. The components are matter, which lacks all determination just of itself, and form, which provides stable determination. Things constituted by these two components exist 'by nature', for instance, animals and their parts, and plants and simple bodies. Since the matter is able to lose one form and acquire another, natural things have to be changeable things.[9] Other meanings of 'nature,' such as the actual process of growth or development, or substances composed of form and matter, or the essential constitution of a thing, will in this context be philosophically consequent upon the basic notions of matter and form.

In man, this will mean for Aristotle that there is a form called the soul, and matter, which of itself has no specific or individual character. The man, the human being, is the composite of the two. The two, as in any living body, form a unit, a single living thing (*De Anima*, II 1,412a3—b8). Consequently there is in a man but the one substantial being, the one agent, the one human nature that is his from birth to death.

II

What, then, is Aristotle's view on the changing nature of man? Certainly in the framework just probed, the formal component of a man, the soul, is essentially unchangeable. It remains the same in the man from embryonic state till death. It makes him and keeps him a human being throughout his entire existence. It likewise makes him and keeps him the same individual throughout his career.[10]

On the other, since motion pervades bodies as a sort of life, there is incessant change in the human composite. A man is changing every moment, waking or sleeping. He is changeable through birth, nutrition, growth, activity and death. Yet from womb to tomb he remains the same substance, the same thing, the same human being. There is no dualism at all here. Body and soul are but the one substance for Aristotle. They are a unit, a single thing, not two existents. The body is not just matter, but the composite of matter and soul. Soul is included in the body as its basic form.[11] To speak of the soul as doing something is but a shorthand way of saying that the man is doing it through his soul or by means of his soul (*De Anima*, I 4,408b11–15). There is but the one agent, the human composite.

Aristotle, it is true, regularly contrasts soul with body in the way of speaking of his time, which is also the way of speaking in our time. Actions or functions that are wholly conditioned by spatial and temporal considerations, which follow upon the composite being, can readily be attributed to the body. Those that transcend the conditions of space and time can be attributed to the soul, for instance, actions that involve universality or free choice.[12] But in either case it is the same agent, the man, who is performing the activity. He remains the same because his soul does not change in substance, no matter how much it develops in its activities and consequent habituation.

The Aristotelian ethics is developed in the framework of these two aspects of the same man, namely, the unchangeable form and the changeable composite body. Because changeable as a composite, a man is educable. He is able to be trained and habituated from his earliest years. According to the way he is trained and educated, he will form his judgments of conduct. If brought up to live only for sense pleasure, his motivation will hardly rise above the bestial level. If trained to live for glory and reputation, he will be conditioned for war and public life. If educated to place intellectual pursuits above all else, he will for Aristotle be given the correct human orientation. Even if he himself does not have too much bent for intellectual interests in his personal life, but is brought up to respect and do what is right (*to kalon*) in the well-ordered community, he will be living a life that is directed towards ensuring the proper overall conditions for intellectual engagement. In this way he will be living, though of course only on a secondary level, for the truly human goal (*Ethica Nicomachea*, I 4–5,1095a14 ff.; X 7–8,1177a12–1178b7).

Proper education, then, is what habituates a man from childhood to pursue the *kalon*, the right thing. The habituation is envisaged as extending throughout the whole gamut of human endeavors in enabling the correct mean to be known and attained in all conduct. It engenders the virtues of wisdom, justice, temperance, and courage, along with their subordinate qualities. It prompts the deliberation necessary to determine the correct mean for human conduct under the incessantly changing circumstances of the ambient and the varying dispositions of the man himself. In view of these ever changing conditions, hard and fast rules cannot hope to be decisive – the decision in every case depends upon the judgment of the correctly habituated man (*Ethica Nicomachea*, II 6,1107a1—2). He alone can determine the correct mean in each new situation, the mean which is the high point of excellence (a6—8). In some cases this high point will always coincide with one of the extremes, for instance, 'adultery, theft, murder' (a11—12). There is no morally right time or right manner or right person with any of these. They are always wrong. The tenet that moral norms are flexible is itself flexible, and flexible enough to allow for norms that hold absolutely (*haplôs* — a17). The tenet itself is changeable according to the situation. Where the components of the situation add up to theft or murder or adultery, the high point of moral excellence is located in the extreme of avoiding them completely. Even in the theoretical order the stand that everything is changeable is untenable in its complete universality, for that would mean that it itself is changeable into its opposite. It thereby, to avoid being self-destructive, allows for something that is unchangeable. Correspondingly the tenet that in the practical order the norms are of their nature flexible has of itself enough flexibility for the admission of absolute norms. Where the morally good and wise man judges that a type of conduct like adultery or murder is always wrong regardless of circumstances, the high point of excellence never varies with the changing ambient. Decidedly Aristotle's views do not come under the notion of the currently popular 'situation ethics.'

From these considerations does not a clear enough picture emerge of the way Aristotle conceives the changing nature of man in relation to ethical knowledge? In its formal element, the soul, man's nature is basically permanent and unchanging. In that regard a man does not make his own nature, and he is unable to change it. He remains always a man, a human being, and always has to be regarded as such. Permanently his nature is intellectual and free, regardless of what may happen to him amid the tragedies of human life. This stands in opposition to much contemporary existentialist writing, in which a man in contrast to something irrational makes his own nature and becomes what he is. But is it not sufficiently obvious that we are free not because we choose to be but because we are so by nature?[13] A man's nature antecedes his choice, and endows him with an aspect of permanence that is not within his power to discard.

Nevertheless, with his nature presupposed, it is man's freedom conditioned by deliberation that sets up the moral order.[14] As an agent a man is a composite of soul and body. By nature this composite is changeable. It can be habituated according to the moral and intellectual virtues. If in current language habit is to be regarded as a second nature, the habituation in which

correct moral knowledge is ingrained from the earliest years of a man's
upbringing may well be termed his changing nature. As the speaking of a
language or the playing of a musical instrument becomes ingrained in a person
through long and careful habituation, and allows him to adapt gracefully his
speech or his performance to the exceedingly intricate themes he may be
required to express, so the morally habituated man is equipped to make the
correct moral judgment in the incessantly changing circumstances of human
life.

But bodily dispositions, both physical and psychic, can change. A man
who had no noticeable urge for alcohol or sedatives may gradually develop
the opposite disposition towards them. A sudden burst of anger, an
overwhelming impulse of greed, a surge of sexual passion, may prompt a man
to act against the judgment made on the basis of his lifelong habituation. The
impulse runs contrary to the moral habituation, and drives the man in an
entirely opposite direction when it comes to predominate. This means that
the habituation is no longer actually functioning, and accordingly that the
moral knowledge embedded in it is not actual. The man is literally in a
condition of moral ignorance. Moral motivation cannot be appealed to. The
physical or psychic disposition of the man has to change before there can be
question of moral guidance. The study of how this change takes place is not
something on the properly moral level. It pertains to the study of the physical
and psychic dispositions of the man. That was the province of the ancient
'physiology.' It is no longer a matter of free choice, the ground of the moral
order.

Consequently Aristotle, for all his emphasis on correct education from
childhood on, could not say with Democritus that 'teaching transforms man,
and in transforming him makes his nature' ([8] , 69B 33). Rather, for Aristotle
the basic nature of a man antecedes his education, and provides the combined
permanence and changeability required for it. Nor could he acquiesce entirely
in the other well-known saying of Democritus: 'Medical science cures diseases
of body, but wisdom rids soul of passions' [7, 24]. For Aristotle the
dichotomy could not be that clear-cut. For him there are situations in which
wisdom is powerless to rid the soul of a passion, and recourse must be had to
the type of knowledge that is applied by medical science.

III

These reflections should allow sufficient understanding of the passage quoted
at the beginning of the discussion. Aristotle's weak-willed man acted through
ignorance, because at the moment of going into action he was oriented in

actuality towards the delectable object alone. His lifelong habituation, in which his moral knowledge was embedded, had been pushed completely out of actuality by the contrary tendency in the sudden impulse of sense appetite. He could not tend in two completely opposite directions at the same time, once one of the tendencies became fully dominant. His will is not strong enough to resist the take-over by the sense impulse. His moral habituation fades out of actuality, and with it his moral knowledge. Actually — and it is the actuality that matters for his conduct — he is in a state of ignorance.

How is this ignorance to be broken through? Certainly not by moral reasoning or persuasion, for it has rendered moral knowledge inoperative. The immediate cause is physical or psychic. The cause of the ignorance is a change that has taken place in the composite, in the body. The study of it pertains accordingly to the physiologist. To him will belong the task of investigating how the physical and psychic conditions of the man keep changing, with the gradual result that the sense appetite is satisfied or lessened or assuaged and the normal equilibrium of the body is restored. The man's moral habituation and the knowledge it concretizes will no longer be impeded from coming into actuality.

That is the general picture. The passage in question does fit neatly enough into the overall conceptions of Aristotle's moral philosophy. In detail, however, the answers to present-day questions are not found ready-made in his own writings. He is indeed explicit in asserting the obvious fact that the passions and emotions cause bodily changes: '... for it is evident that anger, sexual desire, and certain other passions, actually alter the state of the body, and in some cases even cause madness' (*Ethica Nicomachea*, VII 3,1147a15–17; trans. Rackham). But he does not explain in detail how sense impulse prevents moral knowledge from functioning and how the physiologist would account for the subsiding and disappearing of passion. He remains content with a merely factual description of what takes place, and with the assertion that the causal account will be the same as in the cases of sleep and drunkenness.

With regard to sleep we do have a detailed Aristotelian account.[15] Sleep is an affection of the composite of soul and body, in things that are endowed with sense perception (*De Somno et Vigilia*, 1,453b11–454a19). It is 'as it were, a tie, imposed on sense-perception, while its loosening (λύσις) or remission constitutes the being awake' (*De Somno et Vigilia*, 1,454b26–27). So far the parallelism is exact. Sleep, like passion, essentially involves a bodily change that prevents a definite kind of cognition. It consists in a sort of chain or bond that has to be loosened (cf. λύεται, *Ethica Nicomachea*, VII

3,1147b6). But here the help from the parallelism seems to end. For sleep, the bond or blocking condition is located in the functional failure of a definite Aristotelian sense faculty, the *sensus communis* (*De Somno et Vigilia*, 2,455b8—12), a faculty intermediate between external sensations and the imagination.[16] The purpose of sleep is the natural and necessary preservation of animals (b13—28). Its physical cause is 'a sort of concentration, or natural recoil, of the hot matter inwards' (*De Somno et Vigilia*, 3,457b1—2; 458a25—28). None of these three specific explanations will apply in case of weakness of will. The directions in which the detailed accounts should be sought are thereby indicated. But the accounts themselves are not provided in the Aristotelian writings.[17]

IV

The analysis of the passage in question, then, against the general background of Aristotelian ethics, seems to offer a satisfactory enough instantiation of the way that ethics is related to medicine and to the changing nature of man. Ethics regards medicine as an art whose purpose is bodily health ([5], 338a26—30). Bodily health is an integral constituent of a complete life span, and a complete life span is a requirement (*Ethica Nicomachea*, I 7,1098a18—20; 9,1100a4—5) of the human happiness that constitutes the goal of Aristotelian ethics. Accordingly medicine comes in global fashion under the direction of ethics, and is an aid in attaining the supreme goal for which ethics strives (*Ethica Nicomachea*, I 1097a17—24). The extent to which it is to be pursued in the community, and the qualifications required in the persons who are to take it up, fall under the supervision of ethics (*Ethica Nicomachea*, I 2,1094b1—6). At the same time medicine is recognized as a science with its own distinctive method, which accordingly cannot be dictated by any other science no matter how superior.

From these Aristotelian tenets some corollaries pertinent to today's setting may be readily drawn. In general, ethics requires that the practice of medicine be directed to and subordinated to the general human good. This means that the government should promote it and subsidize it to the extent necessary for the welfare of the citizens, and should enforce rules regarding the qualifications of those permitted to practice it.[18] Under the norms of distributive justice and commutative justice, ethics requires that medical practitioners respect all the rights of the patients and render the services to which they are obligated, receiving in return appropriate remuneration for their services. At the same time, outside interference in questions that are to be decided solely from a medical viewpoint would run counter to the Aristotelian conception of method in the sciences.

Further, both ethics and medicine deal with man, a composite of soul and matter. The composite is an essentially changeable nature, changeable through both moral persuasion and physiological alteration. Moral persuasion is effective only up to a point, namely, as long as a man's moral habituation is able to function. When through drunkenness, or mental disease, or overwhelming passion it no longer has actual influence, the physical and psychic factors alone direct a man's action. The situation has to be handled on the physiological and psychological plane. As it is the medical practitioner who puts this type of knowledge into practice, the ready corollary to be drawn is that medicine can here tender essential service to ethical conduct. There is no need to labor this point today. Cures for alcoholism, the prescription of tranquilizers, and the use of other therapeutic aids for persons who want to follow their better moral judgment, testify to it abundantly.

Today nobody will want to accept the Aristotelian picture in its entirety. The advance in mathematical and experimental science on the one hand, and on the other the different outlooks in modern philosophies and in the Judeo–Christian and Moslem tradition, have drastically changed the ambient in which ethical thinking takes place. The habitat is no longer the closely-knit culture of the Greek city-state. But the insights of the Aristotelian ethics range far beyond the social and physical limits in which they were engendered. To regard them as irrelevant because ancient would be to misunderstand their nature. Their origins lie deep in the innermost recesses of human personality itself. They have in consequence proved capable of fecundating each new ambient as it arises. They may still be made one's own with enthusiasm and with profit.

The *Nicomachean Ethics*, in fact, continues to fascinate students today as few ancient documents can. Its method, because so deeply human, is always very much alive. It is surprisingly capable of adaptation to modern problems, and, as an American philosopher has remarked, it can be applied 'to *any* cultural heritage.'[19] Precisely because of this sensitive universality and vital openness to each new situation, the Aristotelian writings cannot be expected to provide ready-made answers to particular problems in ethics. To look in their pages for cut and dried solutions to modern questions would be to misinterpret fatally the nature of the thinking they develop. They focus on human life, life that keeps changing with man. But because they spring so genuinely from actual human motivation and conduct, they range as wide as human activity itself.

Accordingly, the Aristotelian writings are not geared towards doing a reader's thinking for him in ethical problems. Rather, they inspire and guide him towards penetration into the actual moral situations facing him in real

life, towards analyzing them into their components and following them
through to the problem's solution. They are never meant to serve as a
substitute for personal reflection and hard intellectual work of one's own.
What they teach the reader is the much more difficult and more important art of
doing his own thinking through each new set of circumstances in an incessantly
changing human life. It is in this way that they continue to have relevance and
importance for current ethical thinking.

Pontifical Institute of Mediaeval Studies,
Toronto, Canada

NOTES

[1] Later in the period of the Greek commentators the anonymous scholiast, in
Commentaria in Aristotelem graeca, XX ([19], p. 422.9–24) likened the case to a
physiological explanation of a drunken grammarian's inability to do his professional
work, since rising vapors caused by his condition cloud his mind. Only when the vapors
are dispersed is he able to pursue his science. On the scanty information about dates and
capacities of this scholiast, see H. Paul F. Mercken [27].

In the middle ages Aquinas [3] was content to observe that the body is changed
(*transmutatur*) by passions such as lust or anger. This physical transformation has to go
if there is to be a return to a sound mentality. Other than that, Aquinas just noted that
the explanation does not belong to ethics but has to be learned from the physiologists,
that is, from those engaged in the study of nature.

In modern times, C. L. Michelet [28] reproduced the Greek scholiast's short
commentary to serve as explanation. Sir Alexander Grant [24] referred to Sextus
Empiricus ([42], VII, 129–130) for the Heraclitean notion of sleep, translating *agnoia* not
as 'ignorance' but as 'oblivion.' John Alexander Stewart, in his invaluable *Notes on the
Nicomachean Ethics* [34], mentioned Grant's reference to Sextus, recalled the account
of sleep and waking in *De Somno et Vigilia* (see infra, n. 15), and suggested that the
Greek scholiast's statements on drunkenness imply a recollection of that Aristotelian
passage. John Burnet [6] noted that the problem is being dismissed by Aristotle from
ethical treatment, but that 'to us, of course, it is just the fundamental question.' Burnet
referred to *De Somno et Vigilio* for the explanation, and to the case of drunkenness in
the pseudo-Aristotelian *Problemata* (III 13, 873a1), and to Aristotle's understanding of
pleasure. Harold H. Joachim [22] interpreted the *agnoia* as not 'absence of knowledge,'
since that could not be morally condemned, but as 'error.' Jules Tricot in his translation
[35] refers to *De Somno et Vigilia* just for 'indications' of an explanation. William F. R.
Hardie [18] mentions it in similar fashion. Olof Gigon [15] sees intent to distinguish
ethical treatment from physiological research through reference to the special literature
on drunkenness and sleep. René Antoine Gauthier and Jean Yves Jolif [14] likewise
regard the passage as 'une fin de non recevoir: la question posée relève d'une discipline
qui n'est pas la nôtre,' but they refer only to the Greek scholiast's account, which they
regard as probably taken from the Aristotelian explanation of sleep.

On the other hand Franz Dirlmeier [10] maintains that Aristotle certainly does not cite
De Somno et Vigilia, and that he is hardly thinking of Heraclitus but rather of
researchers like Diogenes of Apollonia. Muirhead (1900), Marshall (1909), Weldon
(1930), Plebe (1957), Warrington (1963), Günther Bien (1972) and others give no
special attention to the passage.

A survey of the commentators, accordingly, does not yield any firm information on the physiological processes by which the weak-willed person is restored for Aristotle to moral integrity. Regarding the transmitted text itself, however, there is no special difficulty. It has no variants important enough to demand attention. On the question about the authenticity of the chapter in which it occurs, see Walsh [36]. The passage may be accepted today without hesitation as authentic. But the notion 'physiologist' has to be taken in a much wider sense than in its current use. It had a different background (infra, n. 5). A number of English translations merely retain the Greek term. Aquinas (supra) used the term but offered an explanation that would be immediately apparent to his readers, namely, a person versed in the Aristotelian study of nature. Similarly William Wilkinson [37] gave the Latin translation 'qui de natura rerum disputant.' The notion would include what today comes under the competence of the psychologist. The 'physiologist,' remarks the Greek scholiast ([19], p. 422.13—14) in regard to the present passage, has expert knowledge about what part of the *soul* and which of its faculties are being affected.

² In this way it exercises the highest authority and functions as 'the most architectonic' discipline (*Ethica Nicomachea*, I 2, 1094a26—27). In the middle ages Abelard [1] could apply to the others the metaphor of 'waiting-women' in relation to ethics, a metaphor taken from the Judeo—Christian tradition from Philo on to describe the relation of all the others to Scriptural knowledge.

³ On the exercise of verbal therapy in ancient Greece, see Pedro Laín Entralgo [17]. Actually, Laín Entralgo (pp. 241—242) acknowledges this type of therapy 'never came to have real existence' in the Hippocratic tradition, the kind of medicine that Aristotle would regard as 'scientific.'

⁴ Συμφυῆναι (*Ethica Nicomachea*, VII 3, 1147a22). Cf. Plato (*Statesman*, 258DE), where the knowledge of carpentry and crafts in general is regarded as 'inborn' (σύμφυτον), as though existent in the craftman's activities, in contrast to theoretical sciences like arithmetic, which are not embedded in activities of that kind. Werner Jaeger [21] remarks: 'Aristotle would not recognize as valid our modern objection that it (ethics) is indeed a science, but only insofar as it is theory.' Aristotle means it to be a science insofar as it is practical. It is the sovereign science 'that employs all the others as its tools' (p. 55).

⁵ See Laín Entralgo ([11], pp. 139—148). Cf. pp. 39—42). The natural philosophy of the Presocratics ranged globally through areas that today are assigned to psychology as well as to the various natural and life sciences.

⁶ In this regard Laín Entralgo ([11], p. 148) quotes the Hippocratic work *On Places in Man*, ed. Littré VI, 278: 'The *physis* of the body is the principle (*archê*) of the *logos* in medicine.' The *archê*, in a context like this, meant the starting point from which the entire scientific treatment (*logos*) proceeded.

⁷ 'I also hold that clear knowledge about natural science can be acquired from medicine and from no other source, and that one can attain this knowledge when medicine itself has been properly comprehended, but till then it is quite impossible.' *On Ancient Medicine*, XX; trans. William H. S. Jones. Cf. Jones ([25], pp. 42—43).

⁸ On the etymology, which allows both meanings, see Hjalmar Frisk [12]. There are a number of penetrating studies on the history and development of the notion, e.g., Lovejoy [26] and Holwerda [20].

⁹ Aristotle (*Physica*, II 1, 192b8—193b21). Cf. I 7, 190b29—191a12; Δ4, 1014b16—1015a19.

¹⁰ See 'form, in virtue of which individuality is directly attributed' (*De Anima*, II 1, 412a8—9; trans. W. S. Hett). Cf. *Metaphysica*, Z 3, 1029a28—30. On the natural teleology implicit in the Aristotelian vital form, see the 'Prologue aristotélicien' in Gilson [16].

¹¹ The notion of soul as a physical part of the whole man is peculiarly Aristotelian, and is something that Western tradition has found very difficult to grasp. The dominant

conception has been either dualistic, reaching its extreme in Descartes and satirized by Ryle as the ghost in the machine, or Neoplatonic, in which body in general was regarded as being in soul [30].

[12] In this regard the Aristotelian contrast of soul and body as agents becomes much more clearly articulated in Aquinas, who had to think deeply against the Christian background of flesh warring against spirit. A discussion on the topic may be found in my article [29].

[13] This point is tellingly made by Alberto Galli [13].

[14] For Aristotle, choice (*proairesis*) is the source or first principle (*arche* – cf. supra, n. 6) of practical science (*Metaphysica*, E 1, 1025a22–24) and of moral conduct itself (*Ethica Nicomachea*, VI 2, 1139a31). Against this Aristotelian background Aquinas [2] is able to regard moral philosophy as dealing with an order set up by human reason in voluntary actions.

[15] The Latin title, used in the Oxford translation, is *De Somno et Vigilia*. It is often referred to today as *De Somno*. It is commonly accepted as genuine, and there is no serious reason to doubt its authenticity. The reasons in its favor are solid, and the only modern rejection of it along with the other *Parva Naturalia* is based on Zürcher's unacceptable chronology of the Aristotelian writings. On the topic see Paul Siwek [33].

[16] For the historical background of the *sensus communis* in this Aristotelian meaning of the phrase, see John Isaac Beare [4].

[17] The Pseudo-Aristotelian *Problemata*, XXVII, 1–7, 947b12–950a16, discusses the physiological accompaniments of fear, courage, temperance, intemperance, self-restraint and its lack, but not the therapeutic manipulation of them to restore moral equilibrium. W. H. S. Jones ([23], I, xiii–xix) notes the tendency of the Hippocratic writers to describe the course of the symptoms rather than to mention the cures applied. One does not find the precise physiological account desired here.

[18] For a discussion of the way professional medical conduct was maintained in ancient Greek times, see Jones ([24], pp. 32–37).

[19] See Randall [31].

The concluding paragraphs of this paper have been somewhat revised in the interests of focus upon points brought out in the commentary and in the subsequent discussion from the floor. I appreciate Professor Spicker's remarks and concerns, am in substantial agreement with them, and regard them as furnishing a valued complement to the points dealt with in my paper. The differences seem to be only in the nuancing. For instance, Professor Spicker draws attention to the 'tacit premise' that 'the end of medicine is not only health but the improvement of individual moral conduct' (p. 148). This is implicitly Aristotelian, as long as the 'not only . . . but' is correctly understood to mean for Aristotle that the form of a material thing contains its own orientation to something more ultimate. Like 'honor and pleasure and intelligence and every excellence' (*Ethica Nicomachea*, I 7, 1097b2), health is sought for its own sake *and* for happiness. There is no question here of two things that 'are added up together' (b17). In any non-ultimate end such as 'health' (*Metaphysica*, α 2, 994a9) the ultimate end is always being sought, according to the characteristic Aristotelian teleology (a8–10; b9–16). Medicine thereby concentrates on health only, but in so doing and *without added* orientation has as its purpose human happiness. No 'additional obligation' (p. 148) is thereby imposed. To say that medicine's 'ultimate purpose . . . cannot be anything other than the *health* of the patient' is true for Aristotle only with the understanding that health itself is meant by its very nature for happiness.

The physician's task, then, is to bring about the health of the patient. With that health, the patient works out his own happiness. It is hard to see how any 'paternalism' is involved, either on the part of ethics or on the part of medicine. The sovereign authority of ethics over the practice of medicine is in the Aristotelian view no more paternalistic than the right of expropriation in regard to the private property owner. In either case the sovereign authority bears on full-fledged citizens, not on minors, and is exercised only for the common good, not for lesser interests. On the other hand the power of medical intervention to affect moral judgment (p. 150) does not justify medical *hubris* or usurpation of moral sovereignty any more than does the medical power to damage or destroy life physically by means of poisons. In neither case is 'paternalistic' authority exercised over minors, but wrongly assumed moral sovereignty over human life. The right of each patient to do his own thinking and work out his own happiness has to be safeguarded. The physician contributes towards this by promoting health. Could a man who had been rendered physically or psychically incapable of thinking for himself in face of governmental programming and engineering be considered by any stretch a healthy person? For Aristotle the proper function of a man is to lead a self-sufficient life in which the man's intelligence is dominant (*Ethica Nicomachea*, 17, 1098a1–17; X 7, 1177a12–1178a8). At least in the Aristotelian setting a bodily condition in which this function is rendered impossible can hardly be considered human health, the goal of the physician's art.

BIBLIOGRAPHY

1. Abelard, *Dialogus inter Philos., Jud. et Christ.*, ed. Rudolf Thomas, nos. 1265–1305.
2. Aquinas, *In I Eth. Nic.*, lect. 1, Spiazzi nos. 1–2.
3. Aquinas, *In VII Eth.*, lect. 3, Spiazzi no. 1351.
4. Beare, J. I.: 1906, *Greek Theories of Elementary Cognition from Alcmaeon to Aristotle*, Clarendon Press, Oxford, pp. 250–301.
5. Bonitz, *Index Aristotelicus*.
6. Burnet, J.: 1900, *The Ethics of Aristotle*, Methuen, London, p. 304.
7. Democritus, *Fragments*.
8. Diels, H.: 1964, *Die Fragmente der Vorsokratiker*, 11th ed., rev. by W. Kranz, 3 vols., Weidmann, Berlin.
9. Diogenes Laertius, *The Lives of Eminent Philosophers*.
10. Dirlmeier, F.: 1967, *Nikomachische Ethik*, Akademie-Verlag, Berlin, p. 482.
11. Entralgo, P. L.: 1970, *The Therapy of the Word in Classical Antiquity*, trans. by L. J. Rather and J. M. Sharp, Yale Univ. Press, New Haven.
12. Frisk, H.: 1970, *Griech. Etym.*, 1052–1054.
13. Galli, A.: 1074, 'Morale della legge e morale della spontaneità secondo S. Tommaso', in Pontificia Accademia di San Tommaso d'Aquino (ed.), *San Tommaso e il pensiero moderno*, Città Nuova Editrice, Rome, p. 110.
14. Gauthier, R., and Jolif, J.: 1970, *L'Ethique à Nicomaque*, 2nd ed., Beatrice-Nauwelaerts, Louvain and Paris, II, 614.
15. Gigon, O.: 1967, *Die Nikomachische Ethik*, 2nd ed., Artemis Verlag, Zürich and Stuttgart, p. 347.
16. Gilson, E.: 1971, *D'Aristote à Darwin et retour*, J. Vrin, Paris, pp. 11–31. London, II, 207.
17. Grant, A.: 1885, *The Ethics of Aristotle*, 4th ed., Longmans, Green, and Co., London, II, 207.
18. Hardie, W. F.: 1968, *Aristotle's Ethical Theory*, Clarendon Press, Oxford, pp. 286–287.
19. Heylbut, G. (ed.): *Commentaria in Aristotelem Graeca*, XX.
20. Holwerda, D.: 1955, *Commentatio de Vocis quae est* ΦΥΣΙΣ *Vi atque Uso*, J. B. Wolters, Groningen.
21. Jaegar, W.: 1957, 'Aristotle's Use of Medicine as Model of Method in his Ethics', *Journal of Hellenic Studies* 77, 61.

22. Joachim, H. H.: 1951, *The Nicomachean Ethics*, ed. by D. A. Rees, Clarendon Press, Oxford, p. 226 (cf. p. 228).
23. Jones, W. H. S. (trans.): 1923, *Hippocrates*, Loeb Classical Library, Harvard Univ. Press, Cambridge.
24. Jones, W. H. S.: 1946, *Philosophy and Medicine in Ancient Greece*, Johns Hopkins Press, Baltimore.
25. Liddell, H. G. and Scott, R.: 1940, *A Greek–English Lexicon*, 9th ed., rev. by H. S. Jones and R. McKenzie, Clarendon Press, Oxford
26. Lovejoy, A. O.: 1909, 'The Meaning of Φύσις in the Greek Physiologers', *Philosophical Review* 18, 369–383.
27. Mercken, H. P.: 1973, *The Greek Commentators on the Nicomachean Ethics of Aristotle*, E. J. Brill, Leiden, I, 28.
28. Michelet, C. L.: 1949, *Arist. Eth. Nicom.*, 2nd ed., Schlesinger, Berlin, II, 228.
29. Owens, J.: 1974, 'Soul as Agent in Aquinas', *The New Scholasticism* 48, 45–64.
30. Plotinus, *Enneads*, IV, 3, 8.47–9.38.
31. Randall, J. H., Jr.: 1960, *Aristotle*, Columbia Univ. Press, New York, p. 248.
32. Sextus Empiricus, *Adversus Mathematicos*.
33. Siwek, P.: 1963, *Aristotelis Parva Naturalia*, Desclée, Rome, pp. x–xii.
34. Stewart, J. A.: 1892, *Notes on the Nicomachean Ethics*, Clarendon Press, Oxford, II, 160–161.
35. Tricot, J.: 1959, *Ethique à Nicomaque*, J. Vrin, Paris, p. 335, n. 1.
36. Walsh, J. J.: 1963, *Aristotle's Conception of Moral Weakness*, Columbia Univ. Press, New York and London, pp. 183–188.
37. Wilkinson, W.: 1803, *Arist. Eth. Nicom.*, 2nd ed., Clarendon Press, Oxford, p. 314.

STUART F. SPICKER

MEDICINE'S INFLUENCE ON ETHICS:
REFLECTIONS ON THE PUTATIVE MORAL ROLE
OF MEDICINE

Father Owens' presentation of the way that medicine is related to ethics, staked against the formidable background of the *Corpus Aristotelicum* is – unlike that of almost all extant writings on contemporary issues in medical ethics – from its very inception an extremely original one. In addition to his reminder that for Aristotle physiological knowledge of the human body can illuminate factors at work in ethical conduct – medicine being able thereby to 'render essential service to ethical conduct' ([9], p. 137) – he is and remains concerned with the changing nature of man. For Professor Owens as for Aristotle the composite of body and soul 'is an essentially changeable nature' ([9], p. 137) and the very condition, perhaps, of the possibility of moral ignorance which itself takes place in the composite. Apparently following Aristotle, Professor Owens expressly denies that the essential nature of a particular person, his or her soul, is susceptible to any kind of change whatsoever, whether we attend to the earliest embryonic stage or the penultimate stage just prior to death, and he leaves aside (rightly I think) questions of eschatology. Thus his reflections, though in some places preliminary – like his tacit attack on contemporary existentialism and its view of the human condition – and in others recapitulative – like his thesis that man's essential nature is permanent and not made by or changed by man ([9], p. 133) are never simply programmatic or historical.

It would be malapropos and evidence of medical misjudgment, therefore, if not (even less politely) importunate to insist that Professor Owens, like a descendent of Jupiter, induces the birth from his head of a fully-formed and updated medical ethics of Nicomachus, the physician of Stagira, as the latest Minerva springing forth, fully panoplied and embossed with the Caduceus, as Asklepios. More modestly, as philosopher (I almost said 'The Philosopher,' for we have all been influenced since 1951 by his monumental work, *The Doctrine of Being in the Aristotelian 'Metaphysics'* [8]) steeped in the profound Aristotelian tradition, Professor Owens has offered us a response to the inverted question which Professor R. M. Hare pursues [4]: not 'Can

S. F. Spicker and H. T. Engelhardt, Jr. (eds.), Philosophical Medical Ethics: Its Nature and Significance, 143–151. All Rights Reserved. Copyright © 1977 by D. Reidel Publishing Company, Dordrecht-Holland.

ethics or moral philosophy (and hence the moral philosopher) be of help to those who must cope with the myriad of issues in medicine which have a moral dimension?' but rather, 'Can medicine be of some help to ethics?'

This Symposium on 'Philosophical Medical Ethics: Its Nature and Significance' was, from the very beginning, organized on the premise that ethics has definite bearing on medicine and that philosophers, theologians, and others have something to contribute in dialogue with physicians and other health professionals and practitioners. But it is equally important, especially in the opening hours of the Symposium, not to fail to consider the bearing medicine might have on the foundations of ethics especially since for 'The Philosopher' this was the more appropriate concern, as Professor Owens has already indicated.

Before raising a few questions for Professor Owens to consider and before taking the liberty, as commentator, of drawing a few implications of his thesis for medicine, it might be useful to remind ourselves of some of the important parallels that obtain between the *method* of the physician and that of the moral philosopher. I am not thinking here of the simile of the midwife, as Plato portrays Socrates, wherein the philosopher is forever delivering the plethora of *a priori* or innate ideas which under the Platonic bedcovers are forever present but in need of gentle delivery prior to the actual birth, in which simile the philosopher is like a physician; nor am I thinking of the parallel that exists between the Greek ideal, the ethical life, and, as Werner Jaeger concludes in *Paideia*, 'the ideal of Health' ([5], III, p. 45). I am not even thinking of the fact that for the Greeks ethics, like medicine, is a practical discipline not a theoretical science, though, of course, they are sciences in the properly understood sense of *scientia*. Rather I am thinking of the method employed in medicine and in ethical inquiry as reveals itself in the *Corpus Aristotelicum*. That is, the praxis of the physician and that of the ethical philosopher 'always deals with individual situations and with practical actions' ([6], p. 54). Whereas medicine is always aimed at health, ethics aims at the human good, the highest object for Aristotle. We recall that for him what we call good exists not as a universal, that is the same for all, but in as many forms as there are forms of activity. Medicine aims not at *health as such* but at the health of each and every particular person. So just as one will not be a better physician having contemplated the idea of health itself, so no philosopher who inquires into specific ethical dilemmas will profit much from contemplating the supreme and universal good, the good itself. The physician is interested in the health of this or that patient, the particular, since he or she is trained, as physician, to care for, heal, and perhaps cure individual patients. The physician seeks the good in the individual case and can ill afford to transcend the differences which offer themselves in empirical, practical experience. So too, the moral philosopher seeks the good in the individual case, and hence he often generates a series of cases which hopefully elicit intuitive suggestions in order that he may peruse a variety of subtle cases which exist along a continuum between the more polarized, extreme cases. He does so even if the cases are construed by means of various thought experiments and the fancy of the philosopher's imagination. Some philosophers even consider actual cases today and make skilled use and analyses of these as well. In short, medicine and ethics are quite similar in method. As Aristotle remarked in *Nicomachean Ethics*: ' . . . matters concerned with conduct and questions of what is good for us have no fixity, any more than matters of health. The general account being of this nature, the account of particular cases is yet more lacking in exactness; for they do not fall under any art or precept, but the agents themselves must in each case consider what is appropriate to the occasion, as happens also in the art of medicine or of navigation' ([1], II, 2, 1104a3—10). Medicine and ethics are in this sense similar sciences. Decisions to be made by clinicians are appropriately compared to those made by the good man as well as the captain of a ship on the high sea. Medicine, ethics, and navigation deal with the particular situation, and medical ethics, as Hans Jonas had adroitly stressed, is necessarily casuistical, since its method requires that one deal directly with the individual situation that modifies the general *logos*. We should expect not precision or exactness in medicine any more than we should expect it in ethics; neither should we take the method of the mathematician as our paradigm model. For not much is stable or open to fixity in matters of ethics or in matters of health. Furthermore, in medicine as in ethics there are really no absolutely binding general rules or theories of right practice. All one can do is be very explicit regarding the special circumstances of the situation. At this juncture we must revert to the more fundamental Aristotelian position which appears in Book II of the *Nicomachean Ethics* in which it is argued that men naturally have the capability of developing the moral virtues which may be brought to completion by habit ([1], II, 1103a14—26). The growth of man's moral qualities is construed on the analogy with excess or defect of exercise, food or drink, and strength and health. Sir David Ross points to this parallel as the germ of the doctrine of the mean ([10], p. 189). It is in Book II that Aristotle introduces in a preliminary way his conception of the mean [*to meson*] and the extremes of excess and defect ([1], II, 1104a10—27). He tells us that by the mean he does not intend the absolute mean of the thing itself but the mean relative to ourselves as determined by reason [*logos*] or as an intelligent man, a man of foresight [*ho phronimos*] would determine it ([1], II, 1107al—2). In his attempt to follow the mean as method, the man of practical wisdom (the physician as well, I would argue, as the philosopher) develops habits of making choices that are relative to, and proportional to, the time, the place, the individual, the resources in the situation, etc. He creates habits which enable him to adapt natural impulses to appropriate ends. And such habits had of necessity to become ingrained or 'imbedded' in his character by appropriate training and education. Since it is impossible, according to Aristotle, for any man or group of persons to construct general rules, moral laws for example, that will encompass all human situations, conduct is not determined in any particular situation by *nous* or intellectual insight but by *phronesis* or practical wisdom, the perfect excellence of practical *nous*. The man of foresight, then, arrives at right action by means of 'moral deliberation.' If one asks how one can become like the man of practical wisdom and discover the relative mean in all situations, we are told, at first, that 'we must act according to the right rule, right reason.' Here Aristotle remarks that this is 'a common principle and must be assumed' ([1], II, 1103b33—34). One method of determining the relative mean in human situations is to trust the mature wisdom embodied in our teachers, and that same advice is offered for the physician apprentice. But the same question haunts the reader: How does the man of practical wisdom, *ho phronimos*, discover the relative mean in life's multifarious situations? What kind of person is he? The first suggestion offered by Aristotle is certainly unsatisfactory, namely, *mimesis* or imitation. Even Aristotle himself is dissatisfied with his answer. I let him recapitulate:

Since we have previously said that one ought to choose that which is intermediate, not the excess or the defect, and that the intermediate is determined by the dictates of 'right reason' [the right rule], let us discuss the nature of these dictates. In all the states of character we have mentioned, as in all other matters, there is a mark to which the man who has 'reason' [the rule] looks and heightens or relaxes his activity accordingly, that is, there is a certain standard which determines the mean states which we say are intermediate between excess and defect, being in accordance with 'right reason' [the right rule]. But such a statement, though true is by no means clear; for not only here but in all other pursuits which are objects of knowledge it is indeed true to say that we must not exert ourselves nor relax our efforts too much nor too little, but to an intermediate extent and as 'right reason' [the right rule] dictates; but if a man had only this knowledge he would be none the wiser — e.g., we should not know what sort of medicines to apply to our body if some one were to say 'all those which the medical art prescribes, and which agree with the practice of one who possesses the art.' Hence it is necessary with regard to the states of the soul also not only that this true statement should be made, but also that it should be determined what is 'right reason' [right rule] and what is the standard that fixes it. ([1], VI 1138b18—34)

It is not my intention to try to offer a solution to the question posed by the competence of the man of practical wisdom, who is able time after time, like a good clinician and a good man, to know what the mean or right proportion is. Aristotle's position comes full circle: The *phronimos* or physician who not only possesses practical wisdom but acts upon it has 'right reason,' which is 'right' because it accords with practical wisdom, and hence the *phronimos* is able to locate the mean wherein virtue lies. There is only one clue that even begins to suggest a solution, and it may be well if we think of the clinician here as the *phronimos*. The *phronimos* is said to apprehend and apply *logos*, *orthos logos*, right reason, the right rule. He deals with particulars, things human, human patients: for what is done and to whom it is done are always particulars. Moreover, *phronesis* is essentially practical and chiefly concerned with the particular. And particulars are intuitively apprehended by a kind of 'perception' [*aisthesis*]. Consider Aristotle's remark in Book VI of *Nicomachean Ethics:*

That practical wisdom is not scientific knowledge is evident; for it is, as has been said, concerned with the ultimate particular fact, since the thing to be done is of this nature . . . . And practical wisdom is concerned with the ultimate particular, which is the object not of scientific knowledge, but of perception – not the perception of qualities peculiar to one sense but a perception akin to that by which we perceive that the particular figure before us is a triangle . . . . ([1], VI, 1142a23–30. Cf. 1143a35–b14).

Hence the kind of perception which is possessed and exercised by the *phronimos* is not perception proper, i.e., an act of one or more of the senses. The objects of the sense are certain definite qualities. Nor is the perception of the *phronimos* that which apprehends objects of more than one special sense, e.g., the common sensibles, e.g., motion, figure, and number. Rather the kind of perception here in question and at work in medicine is an immediate apprehension exemplified in the perceiving that 'the particular figure before us is a triangle.' Thus to say that the *phronimos* 'sees' the mean can only mean that he apprehends it immediately. And yet the perception of the *phronimos* or *iatros* is distinct from that of the geometrician or theoretician, respectively. Aristotle gave no special name for the immediate apprehension of the appropriate means which the *phronimos* possesses. All we are told is that in practical deliberations the *phronimos* is said to have 'perception' [*aisthesis*] which enables him to apprehend immediately or intuitively the ultimate particulars.

With these preliminary remarks, parts of which were designed to draw a few implications of Professor Owens' thesis for medicine, let me bring out two questions which his paper raises quite straightforwardly but which require a brief recapitulation of the argument generated first by the Greeks:

(1) The supreme goal of an ethical life is the life of contemplation and theoretical speculation — that is, happiness;

(2) Health is a necessary condition or at least 'an integral constituent of a complete life span' ([9], p. 15), in which a person can fulfill his or her destiny in the sense of realizing the final or 'supreme goal' of life;

(3) The end of medicine is bodily health. (St. Thomas reminds us that health is the form of the body.)

Ergo: 'Medicine comes . . . under the direction of ethics' ([9], p. 136), since its end is to preserve life directed towards its fulfillment.

What is most interesting about this argument is that it includes a tacit premise, namely, that the end of medicine is not only health but the improvement of individual moral conduct through improvement of the individual's moral judgment. That is, the end of medicine is also to make men better in the moral sense in which case the agent, i.e., the patient, acts ideally as he or she ought to act. This may have been Aristotle's view, but, indeed, it is not sustained as an additional obligation on the part of physicians. The Spanish physician, Pedro Laín Entralgo, whose works are now becoming well known to audiences like this one, argues that the end of medicine is health; it is not moral goodness or what he calls 'felicity,' that is, happiness. I offer his remarks:

No minute or subtle reflection is necessary to make us aware that, in the case which has been selected as our norm or model, the *proper* end of the medical relation is the health of the sick man. The immediate purpose of this relation – the purposes which must always be present if the doctor proceeds as a doctor – are the formulation of a diagnosis and the prescription of treatment; its ultimate purpose, however, cannot be anything other than the *health* of the patient. This apparently obvious statement must be energetically underlined, because contemporary medicine, inebriated at times by the incipient and fascinating success of its techniques for modifying human nature – techniques which are pharmacological, physiotherapeutic, surgical, psychotherapeutic, social, etc. – has come to the point of thinking that the purpose of the doctor as such may be, beyond purely physical health, the *moral goodness* of man (making men good) or the *felicity* of the human condition (making men happy) .... [B]ut this illusion I reject wholeheartedly; even more, I consider it a grave aberration of the mind. The proper function of the doctor as such is not to make men good or happy, but healthy. As a doctor, he can and ought to go no farther than this ([3], p. 262).[1]

Hence Professor Owens' interesting explication of the Hellenic tradition should compel our reflection, especially those whose calling is medicine. I raise, then, my first question: Is there a moral obligation on the part of physicians, and perhaps other health practitioners, to practice their art (and science) toward the end of making patients better in the moral sense? Recall Professor Owens' argument that since the composite, body and soul, is essentially changeable through physiological alteration and moral suasion ([9], p. 137), the physician should be directed, in curing his patient's alcoholism or mental illness, to effect a change in the patient's moral judgment, since that judgment may have been negatively affected by the abandonment by the 'correctly habituated man' of his 'lifelong habituation' ([9], pp. 133–134). Where once was, let us presume, an agent in possession of moral knowledge as 'imbedded' in his habituation, now overcome by illness, the patient can no longer make correct moral judgments. Here one is reminded of Michel de Montaigne's essay, 'Apology for Raymond Sebond,' in which he says, 'When Cleomenes, son of Anaxandridas, was sick his friends reproached him for having new and unaccustomed humors and fancies: "I should think so," he said, "for I am not the same man that I am when in health. Since I am different, my opinions [read 'moral judgment'] and fancies are also different"' ([7], p. 424). With illness, then, it may be that moral habituation goes and then, as Professor Owens suggests, 'so goes moral knowledge.' Presumably, morally wrong acts are rooted in moral ignorance and hence, to put it positively, a person who has moral knowledge can never act wrongfully — at least this is the Greek thesis.

A second question flows from another argument:

(1) Moral ignorance would be eliminated wherever possible, since it is a condition open to alteration by cultural forces, physical and psychic conditions, environment, etc. That is, our 'second natures' are open to alteration. Recall that in Book II of *Nicomachean Ethics* Aristotle maintains that the moral virtues derive from habit, are acquired powers of 'second natures,' and do not arise by nature ([1], II, 1103a14–26). Our habituation enables us to live and choose according to the principle of the mean, since there can never be a final set of moral rules for all human conduct.

(2) Biomedical and biobehavioral interventions — psychopharmacology, psychosurgery, behavioral modification and engineering, and other therapeutic techniques — are efficacious ways, under certain conditions, of restoring a person's habituated conduct.

Ergo: Physiology, that is, medicine, holds the key to improving human conduct on the part of patients. Professor Owens reminds us that Aristotle could not accept part of the thesis of Democritus which has it that 'wisdom rids the soul of passions,' since wisdom is generally powerless to rid the soul of a given passion. But if physiology can in principle rid the soul of passion, say by drugs and ethyl alcohol or, as in Aristotle's day, wine ([2], III, 871a–876a30), then should we not conclude (as we might and as Professor Owens would have it) that it is morally permissible for medical science to modify human behavior and therefore human conduct by affecting moral judgment ([11], pp. 222–261). This does generate the second question which, of course, is the kind of question persons at this Symposium are prone to raise: To what extent, if any, is medical intervention paternalistic? Given the strong impetus today of the patients' rights movement and various documents like the American Hospital Association's Hospital 'Patient's Bill of Rights'[2] which have been well circulated and frequently adopted throughout the nation, is it not counterproductive to further introduce restrictions on the patient's agency in the total enterprise of medical decision making? Is not the 'Hellenic view,' as I shall call it, a return to greater medical paternalism in advocating medical interventions which have as their intent the alteration of the patient's conduct, moral goodness, and perhaps happiness? Is it not *hubris* of the worst sort to advocate that medical practitioners attempt to effect directly their patient's conduct, moral judgment, and happiness through medical interventions whose end Laín Entralgo argues, is the health of the patient. To be sure, goodness and happiness are not necessary consequences of health, what Laín Entralgo calls a 'psychosomatic habit of the individual nature' ([3], p. 263). The concern I voice here has to do with human freedom; the patient is now making his or her own liberty of central importance in the physician/patient relationship. For Laín Entralgo and others the achievement of goodness and happiness 'ought not and cannot be the object of the doctor but the particular enterprise of the person himself, since he is the titular and the administrator of his own liberty' ([3], p. 263).

Notwithstanding some reservations which I have regarding the main thrust of Professor Owens' paper, I think we are fortunate indeed to be the benefactors of his years of dedication to the *Corpus Aristotelicum*, which also results in his philosophical acumen, which today has served to remind us that medicine has been viewed as the guardian of personal moral life along with its other obligation to secure health for the patient; he suggests that empirical conditions and physiological matters of fact can be importantly relevant in coping with the fragility of our moral judgment. He has accomplished this not by subsuming his work under the rubric of metaethics or modern moralizing but through the glass of a traditional yet visionary normative ethics grounded in the most authentic Aristotelian tradition. Modern views to the contrary notwithstanding, we would do well to recall that Aristotle, in preparing his ethical treatises, was concerned with the practical guidance of human action, which led him to remark, with some care, that he was inquiring 'not in order to know what virtue is, but in order to become good, since otherwise his inquiry would have been of no use ...' ([1], II, 1103b26–28). Quite in that spirit 'The Spanish Physician' writes: 'A healthy person may be good or morally bad, very happy or miserable, and will be the one or the other according to the peculiar character of the world which he inhabits, the use he makes of his liberty, and in the end the favorable or unfavorable sign that presides over his fortune' ([3], p. 263).

University of Connecticut School of Medicine,
Farmington, Connecticut

NOTES

[1] The original Spanish edition (1964) appeared in *La relación medico–enferme*, Madrid, Ediciones de Revista de Occidente, pp. 235–258.
[2] Cf. 'Statement on a Patient's Bill of Rights,' Board of Trustees, American Hospital Association, November 17, 1972.

BIBLIOGRAPHY

1. Aristotle: *Ethica Nicomachea*. Trans. by W. D. Ross.
2. Aristotle: 'Problems Concerned with the Drinking of Wine and Drunkenness', *Problemata*, Book III. Trans. by E. S. Forster.
3 Entralgo, P. L.: 1957, 'The Doctor–Patient Relationship in the General Framework of Interhuman Relationships', in *Contemporary Spanish Philosophy: An Anthology*, University of Indiana Press, Notre Dame, Indiana, pp. 250–277.
4. Hare, R. M.: 1976, 'Medical Ethics: Can the Moral Philosopher Help?', this volume, pp. 49–61.
5. Jaeger, W.: 1945, *Paideia: The Ideals of Greek Culture*, trans. by G. Highet, III, Basil Blackwell, Oxford.
6. Jaeger, W.: 1957, 'Aristotle's Use of Medicine as Model of Method in His Ethics', *The Journal of Hellenic Studies*, 77 (Part 1), 54–61.
7. Montaigne, M.: 1948, *The Complete Works of Montaigne*, Stanford University Press, Stanford, California, pp. 318–457.
8. Owens, J.: 1951, *The Doctrine of Being in the Aristotelian 'Metaphysics'*, Pontifical Institute of Mediaeval Studies, Toronto, Canada.
9. Owens, J.: 1976, 'Aristotelian Ethics, Medicine and the Changing Nature of Man', this volume, pp. 127–142.
10. Ross, W. D.: 1959, *Aristotle*, Meridian Books, New York.
11. Tracy, T. J.: 1969, *Physiological Theory and the Doctrine of the Mean in Plato and Aristotle*, Mouton & Co., The Hague.

SECTION V

METAPHYSICS AND MEDICAL ETHICS

BERNARD TOWERS

ETHICS IN EVOLUTION

My first task is to clarify my deliberately ambiguous title. When I was invited
to contribute to this symposium, and was required to provide a title, I was
not at all sure from precisely which point of view I would want to address the
subject of 'Metaphysics and Medical Ethics' from the requested standpoint
of 'coming into being and passing away.' So I chose a title that would
maximize my options, knowing that in so doing I would be in the mainstream
of an evolutionary process which has led to the emergence of man, and
through him to the emergence of metaphysical analysis of the ethics of
human behavior. I shall be arguing for an ethical pluralism, and for a
tolerance of novelty such as is inherent in the evolutionary process at least
until or unless the novelty proves itself to be non-viable.

In the interval between the invention of the ambiguous title and the
composition of the paper, I decided at least what *not* to write about. First,
then, I shall *not* be attempting a history of the evolution of ethics in the
written record — if indeed it would be proper to speak of an 'evolution' over
a period of time which, however long it may seem in relation to our
individual life-spans, is nevertheless truly infinitesimal on the time scale of
biological and pre-biological evolution. If the history of ethics and ethical
theory is not my theme, nor is the evolution of ethical insights as they might
occur in the development of children through adolescence to adults. Such a
study would take us into areas of psychology and psycho-analysis which I
must forego in the interests of the theme essayed by Thomas Henry Huxley,
and his grandson Julian, in their two Romanes lectures, delivered at an
interval of half a century: the first under the title 'Evolution and Ethics,'
given in 1893, the second delivered as 'Evolutionary Ethics' in 1943 [6].
The problem is fundamental and truly agonizing: we now know that our
world is a world in evolution, a world in process, and are just beginning to
understand how that process operates. In this new setting the question of
ethics, as indeed of meaning in the deepest sense, appears in sharpest relief: in
the light of modern insights, is there any kind of meaning, pattern, order, a
right and a wrong to be discerned in nature, or is it the case as was thought
after the dawn of the new scientific philosophy in the seventeenth century,

*S. F. Spicker and H. T. Engelhardt, Jr. (eds.), Philosophical Medical Ethics: Its Nature
and Significance, 155—168. All Rights Reserved. Copyright © 1977 by D. Reidel Publishing
Company, Dordrecht-Holland.*

that ' 'tis all in pieces, all coherence gone'? [4] I shall argue that such is *not* the case, but it is evident that this has in fact been the conclusion of many recent thinkers, and of vast numbers of people who have followed the 'received opinion'. The loneliness and sadness of this bleak conclusion is well indicated by Francis Bacon, the contemporary artist who has done so much to express on canvas the modern existential *Angst*. He says 'I think that man now realizes he is an accident, that he is a completely futile being, that he has to play out the game without reason' [17].[1] Such a conclusion, which strikes, of course, at the very heart, not merely of our own deliberations at this symposium, but at intellectual enquiry *tout court*, is the inescapable result of, (a) nineteenth-century acceptance of Tennyson's conclusion that nature is 'red in tooth and claw' [20], (b) misunderstanding of the true meaning of 'the survival of the fittest' (conceived of in terms simply of the physical prowess and aggressive tendencies of individual biological organisms[2]) and (c) the naive assumption of the twentieth-century that, because genetic mutations and recombinations (which represent the ultimate pool from which nature selects the 'fit') are events based for the most part on chance, there can be no order or logic, no reason or significance to be discerned in the natural phenomenon called evolution. Given this kind of mind-set or *Zeitgeist* it is hardly surprising that typical reactions of those not engaged in the study itself are either (1) to accept such ignorant analyses and to portray the resulting horror through one's own medium (as do some painters, poets, novelists and playwrights), or (2) to create a psychological state wherein a superficial or 'notional' assent can be given to the idea that the natural world constitutes an evolutionary process, but wherein real assent (which implies acceptance of all the implications of the theory for human beings, both as individuals and as a species) is withheld or denied. Teilhard de Chardin, in one of his penetrating insights into the contemporary ethos says, 'What makes and classifies a "modern" man (and a whole host of our contemporaries is not yet "modern" in this sense) is having become capable of seeing in terms not of space and time alone but also of duration, or — and it comes to the same thing — of biological space-time; and above all having become incapable of seeing anything otherwise — anything — *not even himself*' [19].

Modern philosophers have tended to ignore the issue, ever since the publication of G. E. Moore's strictures on ethical naturalism in his *Principia Ethica*. Two who have not are Anthony Quinton, with his 1965 paper on 'Ethics and the Theory of Evolution' [16], and Antony Flew, whose book entitled *Evolutionary Ethics* [5] was published in 1967. Neither seems to me to be 'modern' in Teilhard's sense of the term. Both certainly give 'notional' assent (which implies more than 'pays lip-service') to the reality of the evolutionary process, and Quinton develops an effective concept of 'appetitive utterances' to counter the argument of the anti-naturalists that it is *never* legitimate to derive an *ought* from an *is*. It is worth noting, at this interface symposium of philosophy and medicine, that Quinton cites health as a 'good' to strive for and draws on the factual data of the science of pathology as a necessary practical guide towards achieving that good.[3] By analogy, knowledge of biological evolution will give us clues as to what it is right to pursue and what it is right to avoid, provided only that we can determine what it is to be 'healthy' in an evolutionary sense. This is the topic I wish to pursue in this paper. But I want to emphasize at the outset that, just as there are many different but perfectly valid regimens in the pursuit of health, so there are many valid options in the pursuit of that *increasing complexity* which is the hallmark of the evolutionary process. There is not necessarily only one option which is ethically 'right', and the theory challenges ethicists to develop a normative ethic within an inescapably pluralist system.[4] The point is that, in order to be 'healthy' in an evolutionary sense we must learn to act in concordance with, and not contrary to, the process of natural evolution. In the same way, following Aristotle and Quinton, in order to be 'healthy' here and now we must act in concord with the rules of biology, of physiology and pathology. Such rules, whether in the biology of the here and now, or in evolutionary biology, are inescapably pluralist in nature. They are not, on that account, merely opportunistic or relativistic in practice. An openness to change and to 'modification by descent' is an essential element of the 'fitness' that predisposes to 'survival' in evolution.

Quinton, as we said, gives notional assent to the theory of evolution. He urges, but fails himself to give, real assent in the sense of pursuing its implications. The theme, of course, is too big and complex for a single paper. The direction of Quinton's thought is clear, however, from the concluding paragraph to his paper ([16], p. 130). 'The great virtue of the evolutionary moralists is that they are adept in a style of practical thinking which is of a scope appropriate to the problems of our time and set an example which should be more widely followed. Critics often complain about the triviality of contemporary moral philosophy. Their protest is just enough in outline but misplaced in detail. It is not so much that we should turn from the rights and wrongs of returning borrowed books by post to those of suicide but rather that we should enlarge our perspective to take in the problems of society as a whole and not those of such an artificial, transitory and fundamentally unimportant group as that of the two parties to an obligation.' The difficulty with the science of evolutionary biology, is that it is hard to get a feel for it, hard to acquire a genuine experience. And yet, as seems often to be the case in the philosophy of science, or in reflection on science, no amount of armchair theorizing about experience, no matter how astute and empathetic it might be, can substitute for the reality of the experience itself. In the field of medical ethics, particularly, this seems to me to be true, especially when one considers the problems, as a developmental biologist is bound to do, as components of the evolutionary process.

Quinton, then, makes the attempt, at least, to be 'modern' in Teilhard's sense. Flew hardly tries, and it is not surprising (except to the extent that it is typical of his prose style) that he justifies his neglect of Teilhard (whose writings Julian Huxley introduced to the English-speaking world) in the following words: 'certainly, in a less conciliatory vein, the present writer cannot regret the consequence of having to ignore Teilhard de Chardin' ([5], p. 4). Astringent remarks such as this are, of course, characteristic of Flew's generation of 'bright young philosophers,' produced in such profusion by the Oxford school after the Second World War. His book contains its predictable quota of barbed arrows, most of which fall characteristically wide of the real target. To anyone suffering from intellectual myopia (and who was not, in Oxford philosophy, in the 1940's and 1950's?) the only visible targets are in very short range. So, for instance, at one point Flew castigates the 'special absurdity — over and above whatever general fallacy may be involved in any attempt to deduce normative conclusions from neutrally descriptive premises — in appealing to a premise of this sort as if, simultaneously, it could both express such a law of nature and constitute a reason for acting in one way rather than another'. Such withering scorn is then followed by a 'proof' that there can be no psychological law of self-preservation because a Raymond Chandler character on one occasion neither follows nor appeals to it ([5], p. 33). This is to engage in a kind of game, or in that intellectual slapstick comedy which represents the twentieth-century's *trahison des clercs*. However skillful might be the use of those sharp verbal weapons, dutifully honed in PPE in Oxford, or in almost any Graduate School of Philosophy in the United States, the whole exercise is rather futile if the important issues, the really powerful forces (such as Bacon's understanding [see p. 156 above] of the evolutionary roots of our present discontent) go unnoticed and therefore unexamined. There are times during the reading of *Evolutionary Ethics* when a biologist is likely to explode, 'for chrissake, stop playing with words!'

Flew's final section, it is true, is precisely on 'seeing in an evolutionary perspective.' But even here he either damns with faint praise or destroys the impact of his own conclusions with verbal quips or understatements such as: 'If once we do grant this [an evolutionary perspective] and – to adapt a phrase used by Mrs. Carlyle's husband – "gad! we'd better!", it has certain implications both for ethics and metaethics, in the weak but important sense of "implication" rather sketchily explained above' ([5], p. 59). Flew's careful statement had been that 'what and all that may be implicit, in the weak if not the strong sense, in the discovery that moral ideas and ideals have evolved, is that moral claims cannot possess any supernatural authority' ([5], p. 58). How careful and typically 'donnish' a sentence! I'm reminded of the quatrain on some other writers by the poet, Roy Campbell:

> 'You praise the firm restraint with which they write –
> I'm with you there, of course:
> They use the snaffle and the curb alright,
> But where's the bloody horse?' [2]

Flew, it is true, does seem to have a bit of a hankering for a horse – or at any rate a pony – but his hankering comes across as a kind of nostalgia for the lost beliefs and yearnings of innocent childhood. Thus he says, in his concluding paragraph: 'Some men have a longing "to see things as a whole", to find some deep, comprehensive, unifying perspective against which they may set their everyday lives. No philosopher can afford either to despise or not to share such yearnings; and the evolutionary vision possesses the certainly neither universal nor despicable merit of being based upon, and not incompatible with, any known facts' ([5], p. 60). Now if it were only a matter of a longing for such an 'oceanic feeling', if all those who give what I call real assent to the theory of evolution were motivated thus, it would take only one astute Freudian analyst to complete the destruction, initiated by the philosophers, of such poor misguided visionaries. They could safely be left, thereafter, to their quixotic phantasies. Their horses, you see, would only be rocking-horses. Their satisfaction would derive from being rocked in the cradle of mother nature, or lapped in an oceanic experience characteristic of that earlier microcosm, the womb. They could be safely ignored. 'Evolution? Yes, of course, I assent to that,' the philosophical ethicist might say. 'So what?' Can we really afford to take that line, in view of all recent evidence *de rerum natura* (concerning the nature of things)?

Reflecting on the general refusal to take seriously the theory of evolution and its ethical and other philosophical implications, Teilhard says, 'One might well become impatient or lose heart at the sight of so many minds (and not mediocre ones either) remaining today still closed to the idea of evolution, if the whole of history were not there to pledge to us that a truth once seen, even by a single mind, always ends up by imposing itself on the totality of human consciousness' ([19], p. 218). It will be appreciated that he speaks of a 'truth', and not of a 'popular opinion.' We must, then, try to distinguish between fact and fiction in this difficult field of enquiry.

T. H. Huxley was, I believe, expressing no more than an opinion (however 'popular' or 'unpopular' it may have been with different groups in the circumstances of the time), when he concluded his Romanes lecture with, 'Let us understand, once for all, that the ethical progress of society depends, not on imitating the cosmic process, still less in running away from it, but in combating it' [6].

Much the same thought was expressed by P. B. Medawar in 1959: in his Reith lectures on 'The Future of Man' he says: 'It is a profound truth — realized in the nineteenth-century by only a handful of astute biologists and by philosophers hardly at all (indeed, most of those who held any views on the matter held a contrary opinion) — a profound truth that nature does *not* know best; that genetical evolution, if we choose to look at it liverishly instead of with fatuous good humor, is a story of waste, makeshift, compromise and blunder' [11]. That was Medawar in 1959, the *enfant terrible* of science. In the intervening years his views have changed somewhat, as we shall see.

Much of the cultural history of the twentieth century to date seems to me to represent reflections on this stark thesis. Much of the mythology associated with the 'Naked Ape' and his so-called 'Territorial Imperative' ([3], pp. 1, 10) devolves upon a serious (and I mean *really* serious) misunderstanding and misinterpretation of the facts of biological evolution. That you and I are products of an evolutionary *process* is, to me, indisputable. Whether or not this means we are part of a process 'red in tooth and claw' (which, if we are to make 'ethical progress', we must 'combat', to use the senior Huxley's term) or whether or not it is the case that, as Julian Huxley suggested fifty years later, this contradiction 'can be resolved' in the light of a deeper understanding of the nature of the evolutionary process [6] — we here, philosophers, biologists, medical practitioners, are involved in thinking about the implications of looking at ourselves and the world in terms of process, of 'coming into being and passing away', instead of looking at ourselves and everything around us in terms of 'beings and entities'. We must consider ourselves, in other words, to be manifestations of 'patterns of order in process,' rather than as manifestations of independent, discrete individuals.

Because, to think the latter is to be 'idiot' in the later meanings of that admittedly dangerous word. Reality, in other words, cannot be understood by 'modern man' except in the light of the fact of ceaseless *change*.

I thought hard about how I could best convey, at this 'interface' meeting between practitioners of medicine and practicing philosophers, the significance of the modern biologist's approach to himself and the world around him. I want to try to convey to you what it feels like to be a biological scientist steeped in the evolutionary mode: I mean, how does it feel to reflect on the fundamental relationships between oneself and all that constitutes one's environment – you, individually and collectively, the room, the podium, the ambient air, the sky outside. What am I, to be talking and gesticulating amongst such riches? And having been amongst hundreds of thousands of other such riches during all the years of my life, molded and shaped (either directly or indirectly) by each one?

To be honest, I'm not altogether sure. The mystery of being remains just that, despite all one's probings and analyses. But there are, at least, some honest facts from which to start.

For instance, if I take a look at my hand, and ask, 'what is this thing, in relation to – in commerce with – its surrounds?' I can say that it is composed of millions of cells – microscopic objects – and of intra- and intercellular material, all of which are in some important sense linked with the fertilized ovum that contained the genetic information that contributed to the appearance of precisely me, rather than of someone else of different race, or sex, or color, or what have you. But that particular fertilized ovum, too, had a history, the full story of which leads one back not merely through thousands of years for recorded history, but through tens and maybe hundreds of thousands of years for the history of *Homo sapiens*, through millions of years for the history of the Hominids, tens of millions for mammals, hundreds of millions for land-vertebrates, and more than twice that for the vertebrates as a whole. It should be realized that, even with this time-span of some five hundred million years (compared with which the two and a half *thousand* that have elapsed since Hippocrates are as the twinkling of an eye) we are talking only of some 10–12% of the period since our own Earth was formed, and of only some 5% since that 'period of singular time', as the astronomers call it, when the universe began its present and continuing expansionist period – some ten thousand million years ago.

The hand which I see before me is a part of this process of evolution, of 'descent with modification'. The millions of cells, each of microscopic dimensions but 'enormous' in comparison with the size of their chemical constituents, have a direct lineage not merely throughout my own personal life-span, but way beyond, through the life-span of my family and race, and that of the whole human species, with all of the pre-human groups and elements of which we spoke above.

Even if we take the here-and-now of my hand 'in commerce with its surrounds', it is important to recognize that it engages in ceaseless interchange with all that constitutes its milieu: the chemical elements of which it is composed are in endless flux: some of the carbon that was previously a part of me, of my hand, is now exhaled through my respiratory system and in turn becomes a part of you — any one or all of you in this room. When we consider the chemical dynamics at work within the biosphere in its constant interchange with the inorganic system from which (or, rather, within which) the biosphere arose, we are forced to recognize that we are truly, and in the most literal sense, 'members one of another'. The statistical evidence suggests, in fact, that each one of us literally 'in-corporates' elements that once were in-corporated into most if not all pre-existing members of the species, and beyond into the mists of pre-antiquity.

George Wald, the Harvard biochemist and Nobel Laureate, emphasized this fact of the co-inherence of physical matter and human beings in the following dramatic way: 'It would be a poor thing to be an atom in a universe without physicists. And physicists are made of atoms. A physicist is the atom's way of knowing about atoms' [27].

It probably was always foolish and myopic for men and women to think of themselves as, first and foremost, individuals standing over against the rest of nature. It is essential that today we should recognize our true situation as a part — a culminating part, it is true — of a process which links us inextricably to our own environment, both present and past. If our future environment is to be something of our own choosing (which is the power our evolution has given us) then the most important question that faces us is to ask ourselves, 'how best can we maximize the opportunities, for the promotion of what is right and "good", that the present situation presents?'

The problem, so far as medical ethics — the choice of what is right and 'good' in current clinical situations — is concerned, was expressed most clearly by Hans Jonas, in 1973, in his paper on 'Technology and Responsibility: Reflections on the New Tasks of Ethics'. Jonas argues that advances in technological expertise have not only brought new ethical issues to our attention, but have actually changed the basis upon which we make ethical judgments. He says, 'For the very same movement which put us in possession of the powers that have now to be regulated by norms — the movement of modern knowledge called science – has by a necessary complementarity eroded the foundations from which norms could be derived; it has destroyed the very idea of norm as such . . . . . The very nature of an age which cries out for an ethical theory makes it suspiciously look like a fool's errand. Yet we have no choice in the matter but to try' [7].

Jonas, it seems to me, is too much impressed with the thunder of nineteenth century rationalists and reductionists, particularly as represented by their modern heirs such as Jacques Monod. The line of thought which they pursued and pursue leads inevitably to the nihilism, to which Jonas almost gives way, of which we spoke above.

Monod writes: 'Modern societies accepted the treasures and the power that science laid in their laps, but they have not accepted – they have scarcely even heard – its profounder message: the defining of a new and unique source of truth, and the demand for a thorough revision of ethical premises, for a total break with animist tradition, the definitive abandonment of the old covenant, the necessity of forging a new one. Armed with all the powers, enjoying all the riches they owe to science, our societies are still trying to live by and to teach systems of values blasted at the root by science itself' [15].

Monod writes as though he represents the outlook of all modern scientists. In fact, he represents that of a selection of scientists of a previous age. Hostile reaction to his book *Chance and Necessity* was not confined to non-scientists – indeed, many non-scientists seemed overwhelmed as much by the scientific eminence of this Nobel Laureate as by his writing skill and closely-structured logic (so close as to be blinkered). Criticism of the thesis was sharper from within the ranks of science itself, and some of the best of it has been gathered into a single volume with the title *Beyond Chance and Necessity* [9] – a title reminiscent of that important 1969 publication, *Beyond Reductionism* [8]. These two volumes and others demonstrate that there is a philosophical shift in modern science, away from old-fashioned materialism and reductionism, in much the same direction that philosophers of recent years have been freeing themselves of the shackles of logical positivism. It is of interest to note how P. B. Medawar has remained open to change: in 1959, as we have seen, he was as deliberately jaundiced as T. H. Huxley in his view of natural processes and their evident (to him at that time) lack of direction or significance. In January 1961, he published his notorious, acerbic attack on Teilhard de Chardin's views on the nature of the evolutionary process [12], and followed it with a wider onslaught in his Herbert Spencer lecture for 1963 [13].[5] One would have thought that Medawar would have been a natural ally of Monod, with his no-nonsense reductionism.

And yet, when Medawar interviewed Monod on the BBC in 1972 he hinted strongly (though they neither of them pursued the topic very far) that Monod, in developing his thesis, had failed to take account of Teilhards 'Law of Complexity-Consciousness' as the fundamental driving-force of evolution. As Medawar said on that occasion, 'In the process of evolution there is something gratuitous about the way living organisms seem ever to seek more and more complicated solutions to the problems of remaining alive' [14]. The point is of crucial importance: if mere 'survival of the fittest' were all that counted in evolution, then we should have to reckon the most successful species to be those that have survived the longest with the simplest biological organization. And yet the evolving world has unquestionably gone on producing more and more complex and interlocking organisms and systems of organisms in the gratuitous fashion suggested by the more mature Medawar. I do not want here to go into yet another exposition of Teilhard's Law of Increasing Complexity-Consciousness, but simply to draw your attention to a modern insight as profound as was Newton's discovery of the Force of Gravity.[6] Suffice it to say that any analysis of evolution that fails to take this postulated Law of Nature into account is *ipso facto* doing less than justice to the phenomena.

Where does this place us now, with regard to mankind's current explosive phase of technological evolution, and the ethical dilemmas to which that technology gives rise? All that I can hope to do, in the limited time at my disposal, is to alert you to the nature of the problem as I see it from the standpoint of what used to be called 'natural philosophy'. There is a vast amount remaining to be discovered and analysed about the process of evolution, that process concerning which 'a whole host of our contemporaries is not yet modern' (to use Teilhard's phrase again). Where are we to place mankind (especially in his recent expansionist phase) in the cosmic process? Must trends that we discern during the scientific era prolong themselves in an exponential way, or is it possible that the Law of Increasing Complexity-Consciousness, operating as it must through the fourth dimension of *time*, operates through cycles of *contracting and expanding time* (seen as a measure of change)? This would seem to be the way of it when we study the record of remote events ('remote', I mean, in geological, not in historical, time). Phases of explosive evolution, with wide divergence of often bizarre and always rapidly-progressing forms, crop up from time to time. And then there is a retrenchment, with a slowing of the rate of change and a gradual selection of those groups that prove themselves better 'fitted' to survive, and prove it by actually surviving. It is characteristic of the evolutionary process that with the achievement of each layer of increasing complexity in organization, the speed of change has itself increased. This is said to be one of the causes of our current distress: mankind has not yet had time to adjust to the vast technological changes that have come about in recent centuries. But we should recognize, in my view, that expansionist phases of the past have always been self-limiting, and that there is no reason to think that the present phase of evolution, now in the full swing of 'noogenesis' (i.e. development of what Teilhard termed the noosphere) will not shortly enter a natural phase of retrenchment. Indeed it seems to me to be already doing so. The Industrial Revolution has done its job, and shown us how to harness power and improve the material standard of living of increasing millions of people. There is no reason to think that, given goodwill (a big given!), honest politicians (even bigger!) and skilled diplomats, the present American standard of living (standard, at least, for all but the very poor) should not become the norm on a world-wide scale, As to what would happen then, with increasing comfort and leisure for untold numbers, various scenarios have been postulated. The one that seems to me to be the most probable is that sketched out by Gunther Stent in his book *The Coming of the Golden Age: A View of the End of Progress* [18]. Arguing from detailed analyses of the recent history of the biological sciences – and especially from his intimate knowledge of Monod's field of molecular biology – and from the history of art and music with their ever more frenetic exploitation of 'novelty,' he concludes that we are approaching (and in many instances have already reached) the limits of exploitation permitted during the expansionist phase of post-Renaissance civilization. With the end of the customary notion of 'progress' (seen as fundamentally expansionist) we shall enter a phase of inward-turning self-assessment, contemplation, and sheer enjoyment such as we see in some popular movements today. That will be, for Stent, the coming of 'The Golden Age.' In Teilhard's evolutionary scheme it will represent a visible manifestation of that process of *enroulement* ('infolding') which he always saw as more fundamental to the evolutionary process than the traditional *déroulement* ('unfolding') of nineteenth-century thinkers. Both phases are necessary, but unfolding is of itself meaningless unless it leads to an infolding where the more 'conscious' component of complexity-consciousness can manifest itself.

To this meeting of philosophers, biologists, and physicians, I speak essentially as one of the middle group. I want to encourage both the philosophers and the physicians among you to continue or if necessary to start to think in terms of biological evolution. Then, when we have become familiar with its modes, we should rethink our approaches to medical ethics in the light of the new insights which evolutionary thinking gives. This is the agenda. But first we must learn to work in an evolutionary setting. Just as a sculptor in wood must learn to work 'with the grain' of his material if his work is to be successful, or a sculptor in stone with a knowledge of the physical and chemical characteristics of *his* material, so must we learn to understand the nature of the psycho-biological characteristics of the process from which we have arisen, and of which we form a part, if we are to discern what is 'right' to do and what is 'right' to refrain from doing. Not everything that can be done, to and for our patients, ought to be done. The responsibility to decide belongs to us, and after us to our descendants, operating in the light of their subsequent experience of the consequences of the actions which we ourselves undertook.

Ethics deals with behavior. It seems to me that we are currently witnessing the development of a scientific study of the roots of human and animal behavior that could be as significant for future understanding as was the scientific study of human and animal morphology in the past two centuries, a study which formed the basis for the development of evolutionary theory in the nineteenth century. As yet the science of ethology is only in its infancy. As knowledge increases and deepens, I think we shall see the possibility for the development of that new ethical theory which, as Hans Jonas puts it, 'we have no choice . . . . but to try' [7] .

Center for the Health Sciences,
University of California at Los Angeles,
Los Angeles, California

NOTES

[1] It does not, of course, follow that the presence of accidental factors in evolution makes the process 'futile' or 'without reason,' any more than that the indeterminancy inherent in particle physics destroys the logic and rigor of classical physics.
[2] For the meaning of 'fitness' in evolution, see [25] .
[3] Cf. Owens (this symposium) on the similar significance which Aristotle attaches to physiology.
[4] Cf. MacIntyre and Pellegrino (this symposium).
[5] For a critique of Medawar's papers, see [21] .
[6] For further analysis, see [24] and [26] .

BIBLIOGRAPHY

1. Ardrey, R.: 1967, *The Territorial Imperative*, Collins, London.
2. Campbell, R.: 1949, 'On Some South African Novelists', in *Collected Poems*, Vol. 1, The Bodley Head, London, p. 198.
3. Desmond, M.: 1967, *The Naked Ape*, Cape, London.
4. Donne, J.: 1611, *An Anatomy of the World. The First Anniversary of the Death of Mistress Elizabeth Drury*.
5. Flew, A. G. N.: 1967, *Evolutionary Ethics*, Macmillan, London.
6. Huxley, T. H. and Huxley, J.: 1947, *Evolution and Ethics 1893–1943*, Pilot Press, London.
7. Jonas, H.: 1973, 'Technology and Responsibility: Reflections on the New Tasks of Ethics', *Social Research* 4, 31–54.
8. Koestler, A. and Smythies, J. R.: 1969, *Beyond Reductionism: New Perspectives in the Life Sciences*, Hutchinson, London.
9. Lewis, J. (ed.): 1974, *Beyond Chance and Necessity*, Garnstone Press, London.
10. Lewis, J. and Towers, B.: 1969, *Naked Ape or Homo Sapiens?*, Garnstone Press, London.
11. Medawar, P. B.: 1960, *The Future of Man. The Reith Lectures 1959*, Methuen. London.
12. Medawar, P. B.: 1961, 'Critical Notice of *The Phenomenon of Man*', *Mind* 70 N.S. No. 277, 99–106 (reprinted in Medawar, P. B.: 1967, *The Art of the Soluble*, Methuen, London).
13. Medawar, P. B.: 1963, 'Onwards from Spencer: Evolution and Evolutionism', *Encounter* 120, 35–43 (reprinted as 'Herbert Spencer and the Law of General Evolution' in *The Art of the Soluble*).
14. Medawar, P. B. and Monod, J.: 1972, 'The Ethic of Knowledge: Sir Peter Medawar in Conversation with Jacques Monod', *The Listener* 88, 136–139, BBC, London.
15. Monod, J.: 1971, *Chance and Necessity*, Knopf, New York. Vintage Books Edition, pp. 170–171.
16. Quinton, A. M.: 1965, 'Ethics and the Theory of Evolution', in I. T. Ramsey (ed.), *Biology and Personality: Frontier Problems in Science, Philosophy and Religion*, Barnes and Noble, New York.
17. Silvester, D.: 1975, *Interviews with Francis Bacon*, Thames and Hudson, London; Pantheon, New York, p. 28.
18. Stent, G. S.: 1969, *The Coming of the Golden Age: A View of the End of Progress*, Natural History Press, New York.
19. Teilhard de Chardin, P.: 1959, *The Phenomenon of Man*, Collins, London, p. 219.
20. Tennyson, A.: 1850, *In Memoriam*.
21. Towers, B.: 1965, 'Scientific Master versus Pioneer: Medawar and Teilhard', *The Listener* 73, 557–563, BBC, London (reprinted in [23]).
22. Towers, B.: 1967, 'Optimism and Pessimism in Contemporary Culture', *Pax Romana Journal* 2, 20–22 (reprinted in [23]).
23. Towers, B.: 1969, *Concerning Teilhard, and Other Writings on Science and Religion*, Collins, London.
24. Towers, B.: 1971, 'Evolutionary Trends and Human Potential', in *New Values: New Man. Proceedings of the 1970 International Future Research Conference*, Kodansha, Tokyo.
25. Towers, B.: 1971, 'The Scientific Revolution and the Unity of Man', in J. R. Nelson (ed.), *No Man Is Alien*, E. J. Brill, Leiden.

26. Towers, B.: 1973, 'Time and the Growth of Complexity', in G. O. Browning *et al.*
   (eds.), *Teilhard de Chardin: In Quest of the Perfection of Man*, Fairleigh Dickinson
   University Press, Cranbury, N.J.
27. Wald, G.: 1958, Introduction to new edition of Henderson, L. J.: 1913, *The Fitness
   of the Environment: An Inquiry into the Biological Significance of the Properties of
   Matter*, Beacon Press, Boston.

RODERICK M. CHISHOLM

COMING INTO BEING AND PASSING AWAY:
CAN THE METAPHYSICIAN HELP?

I. WHAT WE HAVE A RIGHT TO BELIEVE ABOUT OURSELVES

I assume that, in our theoretical thinking, we should be guided by those propositions we presuppose in our ordinary activity. They are propositions we have a right to believe. Or, somewhat more exactly, they are propositions which should be regarded as innocent, epistemically, until there is positive reason for thinking them guilty.

A list of such propositions would be very much like the list of propositions with which G. E. Moore began his celebrated essay, 'In Defence of Common Sense' ([7], pp. 32–59). The list I might make for myself may be suggested by the following: (1) I am now thinking such and such things and have such and such beliefs, feelings, and desires. I now see people, for example, and I don't see any unicorns. And I have thought such and such other things in the past and then had such and such other beliefs, feelings, and desires. (2) I now have a body of such and such a sort and I had a body of such and such a different sort in the past. And (3) I am now acting with the intention of bringing about such and such things — and I could instead have acted with the intention of bringing about such and such other things. In the past I have acted with the intention of bringing about such and such other things, and I could then have acted with the intention of bringing about such and such other things instead.

There is such a list that each of us might make. The items on the list are obvious and, one might think, so trivial as not to be worth mentioning at all. Yet some of those who now say that these things are trivially true may say, at the end, that strictly speaking they are false. But one can't have it both ways.

A sceptic may ask: 'Might it not be that I'm mistaken in suggesting there are these things we know about ourselves? Isn't it possible that I am deluded about these things?' Of course, it's *possible* that I am deluded about these things. It's *possible* that I will wake up in a few minutes and find myself in a hospital. But from the fact that it is thus theoretically possible that I am deluded it hardly follows that it is now reasonable for me to think that I am

S. F. Spicker and H. T. Engelhardt, Jr. (eds.), Philosophical Medical Ethics: Its Nature and Significance, 169–182. All Rights Reserved. Copyright © 1977 by D. Reidel Publishing Company, Dordrecht-Holland.

in fact deluded. Until you give me some very good positive reason to think the contrary, it is now reasonable for me to assume that I am in a room with other people and not suffering from hallucination or delusion.'

These are some obvious truths about myself, then, which it is now reasonable for me to accept. But these truths, if we take them at their face value, imply that I am an *ens per se*; that is to say, they imply that, in the strictest sense of the word 'is', there *is* a certain thing which is I.

Now some philosophers have held that the word 'I' is a logical construction, a mere *façon de parler*, like the expressions '5' and 'the average plumber.' One can *show* that '5' and 'the average plumber' are logical constructions. For one can take sentences in which these ostensible terms occur ('5 is 7 less 2' and 'the average plumber has 2.6 children') and translate them into other sentences no longer containing terms ostensibly referring to 5 and the average plumber. If I, too, am simply a logical construction, or *façon de parler*, then the various truths on the list that I have made could be reformulated without reference to me. They could be re-expressed in new sentences which contain no terms, such as the word 'I', which ostensibly designate me. The new sentences might contain terms designating what I now call my sensations, as Ernst Mach and Bertrand Russell once thought, or they might contain terms designating my body or certain parts of my body, as other philosophers have thought. But these various philosophers do not *know* that the word 'I' is thus a logical construction, a mere *façon de parler*. No one can take the sentences I have cited — the truisms about myself — and translate *them* without loss of meaning into sentences referring only to things other than me. If you think that I am mistaken about this, just consider the truth which I can now express by saying, 'I don't see any unicorns,' and try to put exactly what *that* says in sentences which don't refer to me.

Perhaps you will say on reflection: 'Well, I can't do it now, but maybe some day somebody will do it.' This would be like the sceptic we just considered. It is possible you can show I am a mere *façon de parler*. And it is possible that I am now lying in a hospital bed somewhere. But what have these mere possibilities got to do with what is going on in fact? They certainly do not mean that I *am* deluded with respect to the truisms that I began. No one has been able to show that these truths can be paraphrased as truths about some entity or entities other than myself. And therefore no one has been able to show that I am not an *ens per se*.

I say, then, that we have a right to assume that persons are *entia per se*, that there *are* persons, in the strict and philosophical sense of the expression 'there are.' You and I, in short, are real things and the terms that designate us are not linguistic fictions. But if there *are* persons, in the strictest sense of the expression 'there are,' then persons are such that either (i) they exist forever or (ii) they come into being but will not pass away or (iii) they will pass away but never come into being or (iv) each is such that it came into being and will pass away. I assume that the last of these four possibilities is the one that is most likely. You and I exist now but there was a time before which we did not exist and there will be a time after which we will no longer exist.

We should be clear, at the outset, about one very simple point. The concepts of *coming into being* and *passing away* are not merely physiological concepts. Consider the relation, for example, between the concepts of *passing away* and *dying* and assume (what, of course, is doubtful) that the latter concept is pretty clearly fixed. If by 'passing away,' we mean, as I do, *ceasing to be*, then if we say that the body dies we cannot say that it passes away – for the body continues to exist but in such a way that it is no longer alive. It may well be that, when the body dies, then the person whose body it is passes away – that the person ceases to be. But the two concepts are different. It is *logically* possible that, when the person's body dies, then the person does *not* cease to be. And it is also *logically* possible that the person ceases to be *before* his body dies. To admit this distinction is not to say that there is any likelihood that these possibilities are actual. The point is only that it is one thing to say that a person's body has died and it is another thing to say that the person has ceased to be, even if in fact the two events coincide.

And, similarly, the concept of *coming into being* is not the same as any physiological concept. Conceivably there is some physiological event which coincides uniformly with the coming into being of a person, but to say that this physiological event occurs is not the same as saying that a person comes into being.

The points I have just made are typically philosophical. I know they will bring forth two quite different reactions. One reaction will be: 'But why insist upon what is trivial and obvious?' And the other reaction will be: 'What you say is obviously false.' As long as there are people who react in the second way, and I know that there are such people, it is worthwhile to insist upon what is obvious, even if it is trivial. For, as Aristotle said, if you *deny* what is trivial, then there is no hope for your investigation.

Of course there may be philosophers or there may be people practicing medicine who do not think there are any persons. And this means, if they are consistent, that they don't believe with respect to themselves that they ever came into being or that they will ever pass away. For people who do really believe that, I have no message — except to urge them to think again.

II. ALTERATION

One of the ways in which a metaphysician can help a nonmetaphysician is to protect him from bad metaphysics.

People are sometimes led to think that nothing persists through any period of time and hence that all things are constantly ceasing to be and new things are constantly coming into being to replace them. This was the view of Heraclitus who said 'You cannot step into the same river twice.' (One of Heraclitus' followers, according to Aristotle, held that things are in such constant flux that you can't even step into the same river once.) If this view is true, then it would be incorrect to say that you and I have existed for any period of time. The things that bore our names at any given moment yesterday have since then ceased to be and you and I are no more the same people as those people of yesterday than we are identical with each other. This view is a disastrous beginning, if our aim is to understand coming into being and passing away.

Why would anyone think that such a thing is true? Respectable philosophers, I regret to say, have accepted this view. When philosophers don't simply pick their theories out of the air, they arrive at them in attempting to deal with philosophical puzzles. The kind of puzzle that has led philosophers to think that everything is in flux, in the sense in question, may be illustrated as follows.

You say to me: 'I see you have a new fence in your back yard.' I say: 'No, it's the same fence I've always had.' You say: 'But your fence is red; the fence you used to have was white.' I say: 'No, it's the *same* fence; I painted it, that's all.' And you say: 'But it *couldn't* be the same fence. If something A is identical with something B, then whatever is true of A is true of B. But if today's fence is identical with yesterday's, how can it be that the old one is red and the other is white?'

Very great philosophers, I'm afraid, have tripped up over that one. (Some have been led to conclude, not that everything is in flux, but that things be identical with each other even though they don't have all their properties in common.) What went wrong in the dialogue we have just imagined?

Consider the sentence: 'Today's fence is red and yesterday's fence was white.' One trouble with it is that the dates are in the wrong place. For what we know is not merely that there was something which was *yesterday's fence* and which was white. It is rather that there *is* something which is a fence and which was *white yesterday*. And it's not merely that there is a thing which is today's fence *and is red*. It's rather that there is a fence which is *red today*. The fence I have now and the fence I had yesterday have *all* their properties in common. I have had just one fence — one which is red today and which was white yesterday.

If you don't see the error that was involved in using the expressions 'today's fence' and 'yesterday's fence,' perhaps this analogy will help. Consider someone who reasons as follows: 'Mr. Jones, the husband, is very meek and submissive. Yet Mr. Jones, the father, is extremely authoritative and overbearing. But one and the same thing can't be meek and submissive and *also* authoritative and overbearing. Therefore there are two Mr. Jones's — Mr. Jones, the husband, and Mr. Jones, the father.'

Saying what went wrong in this case is like explaining a joke. But perhaps we should risk it. It's not that Mr. Jones the husband has properties that are different from those that Mr. Jones the father has. It's rather that Mr. Jones is such that he is meek and submissive toward his wife and overbearing and authoritative toward his children!

All this is to spell out, once again, what ought to be obvious. But let us keep the moral in mind: The fact that a thing has *altered* in a certain way does not imply that the thing has ceased to be and that some new thing has come into being.

III. COMING INTO BEING AND PASSING AWAY SECUNDUM QUID

We are assuming, then, that persons — you and I — are real things, *entia realia*. And we are also assuming that they come into being and pass away. But this means that the coming into being and the passing away of persons is also the real thing. That is to say, it's not a pseudo kind of coming into being and passing away; it's not that kind of merely apparent coming into being and passing away that some of the scholastics called coming into being and passing away *secundum quid*. Let us consider for a moment this pseudo kind of coming into being and passing away.

In his book *Generation and Corruption*, Aristotle considers a man who had a talent for music and who then lost this talent but continued to exist for some time thereafter. Aristotle described this fact by saying: 'The musical man passed away and an unmusical man came to be, but the man persists as identically the same.' ([1], I, [4], 319b.) One is inclined to ask: 'Why on earth did Aristotle express himself *that* way? After all he was just talking about a certain alteration. Why didn't he say that a man *ceased to be musical*, instead of saying that a musical man *ceased to be*?'

It should be noted that we, too, sometimes talk that way. That is to say, we sometimes use such expressions as 'coming into being' and 'passing away' to describe what is in fact the mere alteration of a persisting subject. Thus you may ask me: 'How is our old friend Jones?' And I may reply by saying: 'The Jones you knew doesn't exist any more. He's just dull and bitter now.' A reporter once wrote, after visiting one of our great comedians in a nursing home in California: 'Alas, the great comedian is no more.' But the man – the man who had been a comedian – persisted for some time after that.

It was a result of Aristotle's way of talking ('the musical man ceased to be'), that medieval philosophers – St. Thomas, for example – came to distinguish between (1) coming into being and passing away *per se* and (2) coming into being and passing away *per accidens* or *secundum quid*.

We have coming into being *per accidens*, or *secundum quid*, when a thing alters in some way or other – when there is something which so changes that it first has a certain property and subsequently has a certain other property instead. This is what happens if a musical man is said to cease to be and an unmusical man to come into being when in fact one and the same man persists through the change.

Let us consider some other examples.

IV. SOME ADDITIONAL EXAMPLES

It is sometimes said that, when one becomes aware of a feeling or of a sensation, then the feeling or sensation is something that comes into being *ex nihilo*. When British and American philosophers, in the first third of the present century, were concerned about the status of what they called appearances or sense-data, they took very seriously the possibility that these are things that come into being, *ex nihilo*, when the appropriate physiological and psychological conditions obtain.[1] But isn't the fact of the matter that, when a feeling or sensation is thus said to 'come into being,' what actually happens is that the person or subject is simply altered in a certain way? In making me feel sad, for example, what you do is, not to cause a feeling of sadness to come into being *ex nihilo*, but to cause me to have a certain property – that of feeling in a certain way. And analogously for making me aware of an 'appearance' for 'sense-datum.' What you do is simply to cause me to sense in a certain way. But if this is true, then the so-called coming into being and passing away of feelings and sensations is simply coming into being and passing away *per accidens* or *secundum quid* – and not coming into being and passing away *per se*.

Let us consider another type of case. One might say: 'If I turn the light on over our heads, I will make a *shadow* come into being out of nothing. And if I then turn the light out again, I will cause the shadow to go out of existence – without leaving any traces behind. And so isn't this genuine coming into being and passing away – coming into being and passing away *per se*?'

I think the answer is no. But it is instructive to consider the case somewhat further. What we conveniently describe as a shadow coming into being and passing away can also be described, somewhat less conveniently, as an alteration in what we might call the shadowed object, or the shadowed objects. When I create a shadow on the floor, what I do is merely cause a certain part of the floor to be darker, to reflect less illumination than it had before. And when I make the shadow cease to be – to disappear without remainder – all that I do is to cause the relevant parts of the shadowed object to reflect light once again. So we don't have a coming into being and passing away *per se* of shadows. All we have is a coming into being and passing away *per accidens* or *secundum quid* – a mere alteration in the shadowed object.

Let us note that a shadow is a paradigm case of what some medieval philosophers called an *ens per alio* – and what we might call an 'ontological parasite.' *Entia per alio* were thought of as things that got all their being, so to speak, from *other* things. Thus a shadow has no being of its own. Anything we seem to be able to say about it is something that really is a truth-just about some shadowed object or other. The shadow is entirely parasitical upon its object. And this is really to say that there aren't such things as shadows.

Whatever thus comes into being or passes away *secundum quid* is not a real thing: it is an ontological parasite, at best a mere *façon de parler*.

V. THINGS THAT BECOME OTHER THINGS

Sometimes we say that a certain thing x *became* a certain other thing y. And we take our statement to imply that the first thing x then ceased to be and the second thing y then came into being. In such a case, we are speaking of coming into being and passing away *secundum quid*: *x* and *y* are ontological parasites and not *entia per se*. This may be seen as follows.

If the first thing became the second thing, then we may say:

(1)   There exists a *z* such that *z* once was *x* and *z* now is *y*.

Suppose now we add

(2)   *x* has now ceased to be and *y* hadn't yet come into being when *z* was *x*.

If we take 'coming into being' and 'passing away' literally and thus mean coming into being and passing away *per se*, then our two statements will imply

(3)   There exists a *z* such that (i) *z* was once identical with *x*, (ii) *z* is now identical with *y*, and (iii) *x* but not *y* no longer exists.

But (3) is absurd. Therefore, if (1) and (2) are true, they must be taken to refer to coming into being and passing away *secundum quid*. The fact of the matter was simply that *z* was altered in a certain way.

If at a certain time, a thing literally *becomes identical* with something it hadn't been identical with before, then the thing came into being at that time and it wasn't identical with anything before.[2]

VI. ELANGUESCENCE

Reflection upon the coming into being and passing away of sensations, feelings, and shadows may bring to mind a monstrous hypothesis proposed by Kant in the *Critique of Pure Reason*. Different things, he said, may have different *degrees of reality*. It is possible, he thought, for the degree of reality of a thing to increase or to decrease in a continuous manner. And so, he said, a thing 'may be changed into nothing, not indeed by dissolution, but by gradual loss (*remissio*) of its powers, and so, if I may be permitted the use of the term, by elanguescence.'[3]

Kant is to be taken literally here. He was clear that existence is not a predicate. Yet he thought that some things could have *more* existence than others. It is as though he thought that there is a path between being and nonbeing, so that one day you may set out from nonbeing and head in the direction toward being with the result that the farther you go in that direction the more being you will have. But surely there is *no* mean between being and nonbeing. If something *is* on a certain path, then that something *is*.

Or if it *isn't* yet, then it cannot be on the path between being and nonbeing.[4]

Of course things may be more or less endowed. But things cannot be more or less endowed with respect to being. What is poorly endowed *is* poorly endowed and therefore *is*.

One might object: 'Consider an intense pain that becomes less and less intense and finally fades away. Doesn't it become less and less real and thus gradually cease to be?' The objection would ignore the point we have just made about ceasing to be *secundum quid*. When we say that the pain gradually faded away, we are talking about the alteration of a person: we are speaking about the way in which a person felt or the way he experienced something. Thus one might say, similarly, that the feeling of sadness faded away and finally ceased to be altogether. But the fact of the matter is only this: a person felt less and less sad until he finally reached the point where he didn't feel sad at all. And we should remind ourselves, moreover, that even if we do reify pains and feelings of sadness, we have no ground whatever for saying that the feeling that is less intense is *less real* than the feeling that is more intense.

'But if one thing has more properties than another isn't it more real than the other?' *No* thing has any more or any less properties than does any other thing. Every property and every thing is such that either the thing has that property or the thing had the negation of that property. If you can play the viola and I cannot, you do not have *more properties* thereby than I do. To be sure, you have the property of being someone who can play the viola and I don't have *that* property. But I have the property of being someone who cannot play the viola and *you* do not have that property.

VII. THE COMING INTO BEING AND PASSING AWAY
OF PERSONS

If persons are real things, or *entia per se*, then the coming into being and passing away of persons is *not* a matter merely of something or other being *altered* in a certain way. When my body dies, then it is altered in a certain way. And if it happens to be the case that I then cease to be, as it well may be, then my ceasing to be is *not* just the fact that my body has been altered in a certain way. And when I came into being, this may well have been at the time of a certain alteration of the foetus, or of a certain alteration of matter that was going to become a part of the foetus. But whatever alteration that may have been, that alteration was not the same event as my coming into being. For our assumptions imply that persons are *entia per se* and not *entia per alio* — not ontological parasites like shadows.

What does all this have to do with the facts of biology and physiology, with the questions about when human life begins and ends? Not very much, I am afraid. What I have said so far won't help anyone in dealing with *those* questions. But if you begin at the point at which I have begun, you will want to put the question first the other way around. What do the facts of biology and physiology, the things we know about the beginning and ending of human life, tell us about the coming into being and passing away of persons? Here, too, I am afraid, the answer is, not very much — or not very much as far as anyone can possibly know. But there may be some relevant points that the metaphysician can make.

The United States Supreme Court decreed, in the case of *Roe v. Wade*, in 1973, that the foetus prior to a certain stage of development is not a 'person in the whole sense.' Possibly the ruling presupposes Kant's absurd hypothesis about degrees of reality. Then it would be telling us that, in its foetal stage, the person is somewhere between being and not being ('On the one hand, he doesn't really exist, and on the other hand, he doesn't really not exist'). But it would be more charitable not to assume that the court was presupposing bad metaphysics. And it is more likely that the court meant only that becoming a human being is a gradual process: the foetus is on the way to becoming a human being but, at its early stages at any rate, hasn't got there yet. One could take a similar view about the process of ceasing to be a human being. The one who is moribund is gradually ceasing to be a human being; in the early stages of his illness he is still a human being, but in the later stages not.

This view has recently been set forth by Lawrence C. Becker in *Philosophy and Public Affairs* [2]. It may be summarized in the two theses, 'Entry into the class of human beings is a process' and 'Exit from the class of human beings is a process' [2]. The expression 'human being' is certainly a proper term of biology and physiology; one cannot quarrel with these theses on terminological grounds. But I am not at all convinced that this gradualistic theory, even if it is true, will help us very much in dealing with the philosophical and ethical questions which are involved in the coming into being and passing away of those things that may thus gradually become or cease to be human.

To see that these theses may not help very much, let us consider the consequence of assuming that they are true. We may do this by relating them to what we have already said.

Consider just the process of becoming a human being. (As Professor Becker makes clear, much of what we can say about the process of becoming a human being can also be said, *mutatis mutandis*, about the process of ceasing to be a human being.) Let us consider this thesis, that entrance into the class of human beings is a gradual process and take it together with what we have already assumed. Thus we have:

(1)   I am one of the members of the class of human beings;

(2)   There was a time at which I did not exist;

(3)   Entrance into the class of human beings is a gradual process.

Let us now consider our three premises together. I am as certain as I am of anything that the first of these premises is true. And I do not think that there are many of us who would challenge the second. The third premise is the statement of the biological hypothesis we are now considering.

Our premises quite clearly have these two consequences:

(4)   There was a time at which I was not one of the members of the class of human beings.

(5)   My entrance into the class of human beings was a gradual process.

The second of these consequences — 'My entrance into the class of human beings was a gradual process' — may suggest the process of entering a room. If we consider a man who is entering a room, we may say that his entrance is gradual in this sense: it begins with the entrance of the front part of one of his feet and this is followed by the entrance of more and more parts of his body. And then, when he gets them all in, he has entered the room. But perhaps a more accurate figure would be that of a sober man who becomes drunk: his entry into the class of the people who are drunk might be thought to be gradual.

But now consider this further consequence:

(6)   There was a time at which I existed but had not yet entered the class of human beings.

If I went through the process of *becoming* a human being, as (5) tells us, then I was not *already* a human being when I started to go through this process.

What (6) tells us can be rephrased this way:

(7)   My coming into being antedated my entry into the class of human beings.

Consider Aristotle's conception of the musical man once again. Aristotle might have said: 'A musical man came into being but the man himself had existed long before.' And then he could have said that the man's coming into being antedated his entrance into the class of musicians. For the man can become more and more musical without thereby coming into being, just as a man can become more and more drunk without thereby coming into being. And, analogously, one could say that I came to be more and more human but without thereby coming into being. In each case, the thing that went through the process of gradual entrance is assumed to have antedated that process.

This is a consequence, then, if we take what is obvious and combine it with the thesis that 'entrance into the class of human beings is a process.'

If entrance into the class of human beings is a process, then my coming into being antedated my entrance into the class of human beings. This means that that event which is my coming into being is not the *same* as that event which is my entrance into the class of human beings. There was a time, before I entered the class of human beings, when I existed. And so, if someone at that time could have caused me to cease to be, my ceasing to be as well as my coming into being would have antedated my entrance into the class of human beings.

And if in the future someone causes me gradually to leave the class of human beings, then, while he is doing this, while I am gradually leaving the class of human beings, I will be there to make the exit, and the man will not yet have caused me to cease to be. When I am half way out of the room *I am* somewhere, partly in the room, partly outside, and partly in the doorway. Perhaps, once you have gotten me all the way out of the class of human beings, then you will have caused me to cease to be. But I suppose no one knows.

Would it help if we replaced the concept of *entrance* by the pair of concepts, *full* and *partial* entrance? Then we could distinguish between *full* and *partial* entrance into the class of human beings. And we could also do this in the case of entering a room. As soon as I get a part of my body in the room, then, however small the part may be, I have partially entered the room. And it is not until I have all the parts of my body in the room that I can say that I have fully entered the room. But I do not think this will help. For if we replace 'entrance' by the two concepts 'full entrance' and 'partial entrance,' then we have to give up the process theory. One has only to reflect just a little to see that both partial and full entrance can only be instantaneous.[5]

I am certain, then, that this much is true; if I am a real thing and not just a *façon de parler*, then neither my coming into being nor my passing away is a gradual process – however gradual may be my entrance into and my exit from the class of human beings.

If now we give the biologist and physiologist the term 'human,' perhaps we have a right to use the term 'person' for the sort of thing that you and I are. Suppose now we define *a person* in terms of what it *could* become. We might say, for example, that a person is a thing which is such that it is physically possible (it is not contrary to the laws of nature) that there is a time at which that thing consciously thinks.[6]

If we thus define a person – as that which is such that it is physically possible that there is a time at which it consciously thinks – then we cannot say that anything gradually becomes a person or gradually ceases to be a person. For if a thing has the property of being such that it is not contrary to the laws of nature that there is a time at which it consciously thinks, then it has that property from the moment it comes into being until the moment it passes away.[7] And so the questions we thought we escaped with our gradualistic concept of being a human may arise once again with the concept of a person.

VIII. THE MORAL OF THE STORY

If all of this is right, as it seems to me to be, then no one could have known just when it was that I came into being. And no one will know just when it is that I will pass away. Or perhaps the latter point should be put more cautiously: the present state of our knowledge is such that, if I have the misfortune to be one of those people who, as Lucretius put it, 'leave the light dying piecemeal,' then no one will know just when it is that I will pass away.

Hence it *may* be, for all anyone knows, that by terminating my mother's pregnancy at a certain very early stage, one could have caused *me* then to cease to be. (But it may also be that I did not come into being until after that stage.) And it *may* be, for all anyone knows, that, by disconnecting a life-sustaining device at a very late state in my gradual exit from the class of human beings, you will *then* cause me to cease to be. (But it may also be that I already ceased to be, sometime before that.)

Analogous things may be said about you and about everyone else.

And so where does this leave us with respect to the moral problems that are involved in causing someone to cease to be? Surely it is right sometimes to terminate a pregnancy or to disconnect a life-sustaining device. Doubtless such acts always call for an excuse.[8] But let's not pretend that, when we perform them, probably we are not causing anyone to cease to be. Let's have the courage to face the moral facts of the matter: occasionally it *is* right for one person to annihilate another.

Brown University, Providence, Rhode Island

NOTES

[1] See, for example, the discussion of 'Causation and Creation,' in [4], pp. 535ff.

[2] Aristotle attempts to circumvent this conclusion with his doctrine of prime matter and substantial change. I cannot believe that Aristotle was successful. But I think it is clear that, if one does wish to circumvent this conclusion, then one must appeal to a concept that is very much like that of prime matter.

[3] See the 'Refutation of Mendelssohn's Proof of the Permanence of the Soul' in [6], p. 373; B414. Compare also Kant's discussion of the 'degrees of reality' in the 'Anticipation of Perception,' B207 ff.

[4] Compare the criticism of Kant's doctrine in [3], pp. 92–97.

[5] We can, of course, retain proposition [6] above – i.e., 'There was a time at which I existed but had not yet entered the class of human beings' – if we replace 'entered' by 'fully entered.' What if we replace it by 'partially entered'? For all we know, the result might be a proposition that is false. It may be that, from the time I *did* come into being, whenever that was, I already had one foot in the door, so to speak, and was *part way* into the class of human beings.

[6] The moral philosopher might insist upon defining a person as a thing having *rights* of a certain sort. If now we should give *him* the term 'person', then we might appropriate the term 'self' and consider our definition as a definition of *a self*.

[7] And so we are saying more than that persons are things that are 'potentially thinkers.' For if we take 'potential' in its ordinary sense, then we may say that our potentialities are variable and dependent on our circumstances at any particular time. But our potentialities in this sense of the term are a function of what it is physically possible for us to be – a function of what the laws of nature do not preclude us from being. And physical possibilities, in this latter sense, are invariable. I have attempted to distinguish these various senses of possibility in more detail elsewhere ([5], Chap. 2).

[8] Can part of the excuse be that the persons involved aren't then humans in the complete sense? This moral question falls outside the scope of the present paper.

BIBLIOGRAPHY

1. Aristotle: *Generation and Corruption*.
2. Becker, L. C.: 1975, 'Human Being: The Boundaries of the Concept', *Philosophy and Public Affairs* 4, 334–359.
3. Brentano, F.: 1968, *Kategorienlehre*, Felix Meiner, Hamburg.
4. Broad, C. D.: 1923, *Scientific Thought*, Kegan Paul, Trench, Trubner, London.
5. Chisholm, R. M.: 1977, *Person and Object: A Metaphysical Study*, Open Court Pub. Co., La Salle, Ill., and George Allen and Unwin, London.
6. Kant, I.: 1933, *The Critique of Pure Reason*, trans. by N. K. Smith, Macmillan, London.
7. Moore, G. E.: 1959, *Philosophical Papers*, George Allen and Unwin, London.

H. TRISTRAM ENGELHARDT, JR.

SOME PERSONS ARE HUMANS, SOME HUMANS ARE PERSONS, AND THE WORLD IS WHAT WE PERSONS MAKE OF IT

(A commentary on the papers of Bernard Towers and Roderick Chisholm)

Both the position of Professor Towers and that of Professor Chisholm have importance for questions in medical ethics. Their concerns dovetail at the concept of a person. The ethical significance of abortion and the ethical significance of declaring a person dead are both informed by questions about when persons begin and when they cease to be. Person is an important category to understand because it is through those things which are persons that a moral community exists. By moral community I have in mind both the seat of values and the seat of rights and duties. As long as there are persons, nature can have value, even if all else in nature is treated in a reductive fashion and is regarded as without enduring purposes. And even if one holds that there are no natural or intrinsic goals in nature which would enable one to judge some actions to be natural or unnatural, one can still judge certain interventions to be immoral insofar as they bear improperly against other persons — that is, insofar as they violate their rights. If evolution should be seen as without a final goal, it would, *pace* Towers, still not follow from that that human values have lost their sense and place.

Bernard Towers raises issues concerning medical ethics which turn on our view of nature, especially nature seen in terms of evolution. He sees himself as giving an answer to the artist Bacon's pessimistic statement that 'I think that man now realizes that he is an accident, that he is a completely futile being, that he has to play out the game without reason.' Bacon, as quoted, seems to presuppose that if man is an accident, it follows that he is a futile being whose life is without purpose or goal. Moreover, his statement implies that in the absence of an ability to read from nature norms for ethical conduct, we are left in the arms of a nihilism. Towers wishes to find such norms in evolution.

S. F. Spicker and H. T. Engelhardt, Jr. (eds.), Philosophical Medical Ethics: Its Nature and Significance, 183–194. All Rights Reserved. Copyright © 1977 *by D. Reidel Publishing Company, Dordrecht-Holland.*

Towers suggests that we 'rethink our approaches to medical ethics in the light of the new insights which evolutionary thinking gives' ([8], p. 166). To this he adds the alluring remark that we must 'learn to understand the nature of the psychobiological characteristics of the process from which we have arisen, and of which we form a part, if we are to discern what is "right" to do and what is "right" to refrain from doing' ([8], p. 166). Professor Towers appears to be arguing either (A) that one should treat nature as normative for human conduct, or (B) that a better understanding of nature (seen through an evolutionary perspective as dynamic) would help persons to know what is likely to be conducive to (i.e., 'right' for) their purposes. '(A)' presupposes that (1) nature has intrinsic goals and purposes; (2) those goals and purposes are not only important for our moral considerations, but binding on our conduct; and (3) we can come to know what those goals and purposes are.

Professor Towers thus raises a set of basic issues: (1) Does nature, in particular evolution, have a goal or purpose, and (2) Can one read from nature or from the direction of evolution rules for moral conduct? One should recognize that these questions are core to traditional medical ethical issues such as the morality of contraception, sterilization, artificial insemination, as well as modern issues such as in vitro fertilization and gestation. The argument against such procedures has been in the main that they are immoral in being unnatural. Saint Thomas Aquinas, for example, argued against such practices as contraception on the grounds that they violated natural law, holding that 'to the natural law belongs everything to which a man is inclined according to his nature. . . . In this sense, certain special sins are said to be contrary to nature: e.g., contrary to sexual intercourse, which is natural to all animals, is unisexual lust, which has received the special name of the unnatural crime' ([2], I–II, Q. 94, Art. 3, p. 776). Aquinas could make these arguments because he held that nature was structured and ordered around final causes, intrinsic nisus to the pursuit of goals. He held, for example, that 'natural bodies are moved and worked towards an end, although they have no knowledge of an end, from the fact that always or nearly always that which is best happens to them, nor would they be made otherwise if they were made by art . . . . This must be traced back to God mediately or immediately' ([1], p. 114). Finally, Aquinas held not only that there are goals intrinsic to nature, and that they are good because they were made by God, but also that we as humans can know them and should conform to them. Saint Thomas thus argued, 'Human reason is not, of itself, the rule of things. But the principles impressed on it by nature are the general rules and measures of all things relating to human conduct, of which natural reason is the rule and measure, although it is not the measure of things that are from nature' ([2], I–II, Q. 91, Art. 4, p. 752). It is from arguments such as these that Aquinas concluded that contraception, sterilization, masturbation, and even having intercourse with the woman in unusual position were unnatural and therefore immoral ([2], II–II, Q. 154, Art. 11). What is important is that arguments such as these move from the way nature is to the way humans ought to conduct themselves. They represent a general attempt to find a norm for human conduct outside human reason – namely, in nature.

Arguments which attempt to find norms in evolution are often similar to Saint Thomas'. They substitute for an Aristotelian–Thomistic, static, normative view of nature a dynamic movement towards an inferred goal of nature, such as Teilhard de Chardin's Omega point, or some particular value such as the survival of our species, or a feeling of moral conviction based on the proposition that all moral sentiments are the result of evolution. But, in the absence of convincing theological premises (e.g., 'God established certain patterns in nature as normative for human conduct'), it becomes impossible to derive fundamental human obligations from the way nature is. One may simply ask why the direction of nature should be normative. This objection, even after a theological premise is supplied, remains until one secures a premise that 'one ought to do what God requires because God's will expresses our moral obligations.'

Fundamental moral obligations cannot be derived from goals most persons might have interest in, such as survival of the species, unless such interest can be shown to be integral to the very notion of obligation. Consider: though we may have interest in our species surviving, on what basis could ensuring survival be a fundamental moral duty? We may have the duty not to injure members of future generations, should there be future generations, but to whom do we have the obligation to ensure that there will be future generations? Surely not to merely possible future persons if they would not ever exist to be bearers of rights and duties (i.e., in the event that we decide not to procreate them). On the other hand, it does follow that, insofar as there shall be future persons, we have obligations to act in a way that will not fail to consider them as moral agents. But our interests, whatever they are, in the long-range survival of the human species, are not such as to constitute fundamental moral obligations, as long as we are going to mean by obligation to persons something other than our interests in them and the goods they might serve. For example, if one discovered that, by instituting a general tyranny of the form outlined in Orwell's *1984*, one could increase the survival of the human species by another million years. the reaction should simply be that the pursuit of any value should not be at the expense of using persons as means merely. Respect for persons is the logical condition for talking about moral obligations beyond concern for personal or communal interests.

The role of obligations to persons holds also with regard to what goals or inclinations we might find to be 'endorsed' as the products of evolution. Though moral sentiments may have been generated by evolution, one can still ask why they should be binding on our conduct, why they would be obligatory rather than simply imposed upon us. Yet very sensitive thinkers have sought the ground of morality in evolution. John Fiske, for example, asked, 'Are the principles of right living really connected with the intimate constitution of the universe?' ([6], p. 276). He then gave the following answer: 'Now science began to return a decisively affirmative answer to such questions as these, when it began, with Mr. Spencer, to explain moral beliefs and moral sentiments as products of evolution. For clearly, when you say of a moral belief or a moral sentiment that it is a product of evolution, you imply that it is something which the universe through untold ages has been laboring to bring forth, and you ascribe to it a value proportionate to the enormous effort that it cost to produce it' ([6], pp. 276–277). In short, if certain inclinations are products of the process of evolution, they achieve, according to Fiske and others like him, a moral status.

Can such an argument really hold? What if it turned out that humans in general were beastly and aggressive animals with a native interest and ability in waging war and that such inclinations were the product of evolution? That premise, combined with the fact that most species die out in the long run, and the thesis that the cosmos as a whole will either stagnate in entropy or collapse into a black hole eradicating any history of the past, suggests that if one wished to make moral inference from the general tendencies of nature, it would be good (i.e., in accord with the general tendencies of nature) to end in a flamboyant and ruthless *Götterdämmerung*. That, however, is a conclusion we would not likely accept, because accepting it would cause us to lose the distinction between obligations and interests, between the duties we owe persons as a condition of there being a moral law and the goods we have interest in (e.g., ending the world in accord with nature's tendencies). That is, it is a conclusion we *should* not accept insofar as the sense of obligations we have to persons turns on our respecting their integrity as moral agents, rather than on the pursuit of our interests. Whatever is immoral or moral will depend primarily upon its consequence for the persons who inhabit this cosmos. It is to them that we owe our fundamental obligations.

What is natural for us (i.e., proper to us as moral agents) is to act rationally with regard to our interests, within the bounds of respect for persons. For example, contraception, sterilization, artificial insemination by a donor, etc., are moral or immoral, depending on their consequences for persons; it is to persons that our strict moral obligations are due. We have obligations regarding nature, including human nature, but these are obligations to persons. We should decide concerning what is moral and immoral in medical practice on the basis of what conforms to a reasonable discharge of our duties to other persons. We may be inspired by a vision of evolution. As Darwin rightly stated, 'There is grandeur in this view of life.' Evolution may offer an inspiring, engaging, and awesome spectre for the reflective mind, even if it cannot directly determine the nature of our moral obligations. But in the end, nature, as Sir Peter Medawar stated, and as he is quoted by Professor Towers, 'does not know best,' or to put it more precisely (and in accord with George Wald, quoted by Professor Towers), apart from persons, nature does not know anything. Evolution and human nature place constraints upon what we as persons can do. Still, we as persons can, and properly should, attempt to set aside those constraints that impede our actions as moral agents. Being free, we as persons transcend even the limitations of evolution in being able to reflect upon those limitations and to judge them as being good or bad.

On the other hand, in being products of evolution and denizens of a universe in process, we ignore the evolutionary and processual character of our existence at our own peril. Understanding evolution should indeed contribute to the better discharge of our duties and obligations as indicated in account '(B)', mentioned above. As Professor Towers correctly argues, we will best find our way through the cosmos if we attend to its dynamic character and to the character of evolution on our planet. Evolution and process define our context so that our ethics are ethics in an ambience structured by evolutionary change. Ethics are ethics in evolution, not in that they are drawn from evolution, but in that they should be acted upon in consideration of evolution, the character of the coming to be and passing away of the world in which we discharge our obligations.

Not only does the world come to be and pass away, but so do we, and this brings us to Professor Chisholm's paper. Professor Chisholm advances some very interesting arguments with regard to the coming to be and passing away of persons, issues he sees (and I believe correctly) to be of importance for moral questions surrounding the practices of abortion and the turning off of respirators on the brain-dead. He addresses these issues through a consideration of the meaning of coming to be a human and ceasing to be a human. In particular he sees an irresolvable moral ambiguity attendant to practices such as abortion because, so he argues, we become human through a gradual process. But this argument turns on propositions such as 'My coming into being antedated my entry into the class of human beings' ([3], p. 179). Such language is, I will hold, ill-fitted to the facts of the matter and leads to a suggestion that one had been an entity temporally prior to being either a human or a person. It would be better to say that 'my being as a human antedated my entry into the class of persons.' One must, though, tread carefully with such statements, for not only are the concepts 'human' and 'persons' ambiguous, but so also is the use of 'my' and 'I'. Consider, for example, the statement, 'Thirty-five years ago I was only a twinkle in my father's eye.' From that it does not follow that I really mean, or should mean, that I was once a twinkle, or really ever existed in someone's eye. Or consider the statement, 'You had better keep your promises to me after I am dead.' Who will I be when I am dead for you to keep your promises to? Surely the statement can have meaning and sense without an appeal to a belief in ghosts or shades.

To draw the distinctions needed to account for our coming to be and passing away, one must attend to the distinction between persons and humans a bit more insistently than does Professor Chisholm. Thus I am persuaded that it would be better to rephrase his sentence, 'Entrance into the class of human beings is a process' ([3], p.179), in words suggesting not that one was an entity of some sort prior to being human, but indicating instead that one was human prior to being a person. The statement would read: 'Our entrance into the class of persons [rather than humans] is a process.' 'Human' identifies membership in a particular genus *Homo*, or, more precisely, the species *Homo sapiens*. Human nature in this sense is that set of biological and psychological idiosyncrasies and characteristics which defines us as a particular species, in contrast to other animals, including perhaps rational animals which may exist on planets circling distant stars. But 'person' in a strict sense identifies the class of moral agents — that is, rational free agents including not only rational animals, humans, and Martians, but angels, devils, and gods as well. Given this distinction between humans and persons, and the proper rewordings, one can avoid what I take to be a strange conclusion: that I existed prior to becoming a human.

There are, moreover, important distinctions to be recognized among the uses of 'I' and 'me.' When I was a fetus, 'I' was in a different sense than 'I' am now, or than 'I' will be when 'I' am dead. Moreover, if minds and brains are bound together in the ways in which experience suggests they are, there is a difference in kind between the meaning of 'I' in the statements, 'I was once a fetus,' and 'I was once asleep.' When I was a fetus, no one knew who I would be. There was not yet a person to know. But when I am asleep, there is a person to have known, and to know again, and the perduring, developed embodiment of a person to be known while I am asleep. 'Person' with reference to the fetus indicates only an expectation; 'person' with reference to the sleeping individual indicates an entity with a personal past, and a continued embodiment of that personal existence. Whatever one might want to say of potentiality, there must be a difference in kind between the potentiality of the fetus to become a person and the potentialities of a person to awaken.[1]

Moreover, there is a difference between being a human and being a person. Professor Chisholm appears to use 'human' to identify membership in the species *Homo sapiens* (with which I would agree), and 'person' to identify the class of actual and potential selves (with which I disagree) ([3], p. 181). I contest his definition of person because he includes under 'person' those objects which have the potentiality of acquiring the abilities of a person, not simply those that show themselves to be persons in the sense of moral agents. In that fashion he would, I think, be caused to hold that zygotes are persons. I do not believe that is how we use the concept 'person,' nor does it accord with the meaning of 'person' as the object of moral respect, as an end in itself ([4; 5]). In particular, there is a difference between present and future states — potential persons, potential kings and potential presidents do not have the rights or significance of actual persons, kings or presidents.

Further, we do in fact distinguish in our language between humans and persons. There is a rich medieval literature which discusses those persons who may be angels. It includes discussions of those persons held to be in God, as well as of Jesus, who is held (by some) to have had both a human and divine nature. Distinctions between humans and persons remain of importance to medicine, for they bear clearly and centrally on the morality of abortion, the treatment of brain-dead but otherwise alive human individuals, the practice of fetal experimentation, the production of zygotes in vitro, as well as the employment of forms of birth control such as intrauterine devices which may act by preventing the implantation of living human zygotes. To be more insistent, I do not believe that our ordinary language, or our consideration of issues such as abortion and the definition of death, or the attitudes we have toward zygotes, human gametes, and cells in human cell cultures, can make sense without distinguishing the concepts 'person' and 'human'. 'Human' and 'person' are neither identical nor equivalent terms. For example, consider these locutions:

'Venus is a lovely person, but she surely is not human.'

'These cells in culture are human, those others are porcine.'

'This is a human fetus and that is a canine fetus.'

'The pilots of UFO's are surely not humans, but since they are rational agents we will have to treat them as persons.'

'The angel Gabriel is unlike any person you have ever met.'

What then do we mean by persons? In the strict sense of the term in the sense of moral agents to whom we owe respect as an element of the existence of a moral law, we must mean rational free agents. If we shall mean by persons those entities respect for whom is integral to a concept of obligation based on respect for the moral law, we can, as Kant argued, only mean self-legislative wills.[2] Or to put it another way, it is wrong (where 'wrong' means violating the very sense of an obligation of mutual self-respect among moral agents) to treat persons, ends in themselves, as means merely, because they are self-legislative wills. And only such entities (rational, self-conscious, self-legislative wills) are persons in this central and definitive sense, for only such entities can clearly and immediately, in virtue of a concept of moral law, be said to be the bearers of both rights and duties.

Now, not all humans are persons in this strict sense of being self-conscious, rational agents. I was a human long before I was a rational free agent. And though I was a potential person before I was an actual person (i.e., fetuses have none of the abilities, much less the accomplishments, of persons), insofar as I was a potential person, it follows that I was not yet an actual person, and was without whatever rights are peculiar to actual persons. Moreover, should I sometimes in the future be brain-dead but otherwise alive, it would be the case that, though 'I' would still be a living human in the sense that most of the functions of the body which embodied me would still be intact (e.g., 'I' would, perhaps, still be cross-fertile with other members of my species), 'I' would no longer be a person.

I will not rehearse all the issues at stake here except to indicate that we use the word 'person' in various ways. IBM is a person, I am a person, a one-week-old infant is a person. In none of these senses of 'person,' though, does 'person' mean the same thing. IBM is treated as if it were a person, as a unitary bearer of rights and duties which can be held responsible for its actions in ways similar to the way that you and I can; but in whatever way corporations and nations are persons, they are not persons in the sense that we are, as self-conscious free and rational agents. A one-week-old infant is not a person in the strict sense either. An infant is worthy of neither blame nor praise, like us who are self-legislative moral agents. But, out of various considerations of love, care, sympathy, and interest, not to mention expectation of the time in which the infant will be a free moral agent, we invest it with rights, though at this point we can require no duties. We thus create instead a social sense of person. Children, at least small infants, are persons within the fabric of the social role, 'child.' In contrast, the mother–fetus relationship is neither necessarily a social one, as is the mother–child relationship, nor one embedded in as broad and deep a spectrum of feelings and concerns. There is, moreover, no compelling set of interests (e.g., a need to expand the population) to outbalance the rights of the woman, a person strictly, and to compel us to regard the fetus as if it were a person strictly. Allowing unrestricted access to early abortions appears to be a requisite of the respect for the person of women; it provides sufficient time for a woman to act freely prior to the intrusion of social interests. Furthermore, abortions have a general utility as a means of population control, of avoiding the birth of deformed infants, not to mention the risks of pregnancy itself.

We are, in short, left with a distinction between persons and humans (and between strict and social senses of persons). This distinction can help us in understanding the significance of the coming to be and passing away of human persons — namely, that they are humans *simpliciter* before they are persons, and often human *simpliciter* after they have ceased to be persons (i.e., when brain-dead but otherwise alive). It also can free us from the gratuitous puzzle of what it was that entered into the class of humans in ' (7) My coming into being antedated my entry into the class of human beings' ([3], p. 179). It is humans that enter into the class of persons, and humans start at the moment of their conception.

The puzzle of who or what I was prior to entering into the class of humans can be escaped by simply attending to the language of the argument. The implication that I existed prior to my entrance into the class of human beings (e.g., '(6) There was a time at which I existed but had not yet entered the class of human beings', [3], p. 179) can be avoided by rewording (2); as it now stands, 'There was a time at which I did not exist' ([3], p. 179). When combined with (3), 'Entrance into the class of human beings is a gradual process,' there is the implication that I existed before I was a human being: '(4) There was a time at which I was not one of the members of the class of human beings' ([3], p. 179). But if (2) is rendered 'There was a time when the sentence "I [Professor Chisholm] exist" was false,' the mystery of a prehuman existence is lost, and usual distinctions are regained. A rewording of (4) would be, then, 'There was a time at which "Professor Chisholm is a human being" was not true of any entity.' The rewording of (2) and (4) does, I take it, better capture the intent of Professor Chisholm, who does not wish to begin with an assertion of a prehuman existence. When this is combined with the rewording of (3), i.e., by providing an explicit recognition of the distinction between humans and persons, our protection against the puzzle of prehuman existence is even more secure.

As to the question of processes and gradual change, Professor Chisholm's critique of Kant is too severe. Kant's argument must be read in terms of his general epistemology. Kant is not arguing that existence comes in degrees, but that there are degrees of intensity of the sensation that is part of any consciousness of the self as an object of inner sense. This does not conflict with Kant's other reflections that 'existence' is not a predicate. On the other hand, I would agree that persons are *entia per se* — but I would hold that to be the case only of persons as moral agents, persons strictly, not entities who are persons in virtue of a social role. The former are what they are in virtue of being self-conscious and self-legislative; persons are *entia per se* in the very special sense of being what they are in virtue of their own self-reference. And there seem to be good reasons to hold that the coming to be and passing away of persons is not a gradual process — one is either capable of self-consciousness or not. Such existence, though, is in and through physical circumstances which come into existence and pass away through processes.

One needs, as well, to make distinctions between the meaning of sentences such as 'He became a human at the moment of conception,' and 'He is a better example of a human than he used to be,' or 'He became a person in the strict sense whenever he became self-reflective.' and 'He is much more of a real person than he used to be.' There is a difference between becoming a human or a person, and becoming more truly human or more truly a person. Anything that is a human or a person, *is* a human or a person. But such humans or persons may be more or less deficient examples of humans or persons, and, with regard to a notion of the complete human or person, they can become more or less a human or a person.

Aside from these conceptual refinements, there is a further point to be made regarding how easily we can know whether an entity is a person. I do not think that identifying persons should be thought to be a mysterious or arcane endeavor. It should be straightforward, and turn, as Professor Chisholm suggests, on common sense considerations. One has little difficulty in deciding what the meaning of 'person' is, even in statements like 'UFO pilots are really persons,' or 'Chimpanzees and porpoises are really persons.' But one has good grounds to be puzzled by statements such as 'My palm tree is a lovely person,' or 'Some bacteria are great persons.' One should be able to know that fetuses or brain-dead humans are not persons by the same criteria used in deciding whether chimpanzees or palm trees or bacteria are persons: their behavior. One does not judge blindly when one says that a brain-dead person is dead, or that fetuses are not persons. In the absence of good information to the contrary, things should be taken to be as they appear — and that which lacks the physical perquisites of a person is not a person because minds exist in and through brains, and a body that has lost its brain has lost its mind, and one that does not yet have a sufficient physical basis for self-consciousness has none of the wits about it that persons have. In short, I believe we have good grounds for holding that, in performing an abortion or terminating the life of a brain-dead but otherwise living human individual, we are not taking the life of a person, a moral agent to whom we owe unqualified respect. We are taking human life, but that is another matter.

We are left then with distinctions between humans and persons, and a realization of the evolutionary settings of our existence. This returns me to a point made by Professor Towers: we are historical beings whose circumstances are characterized by process and evolution. I close, then, by stressing the distinction between being a human and being a person and by acknowledging that the latter is for us inseparable from the former. We as persons are always humans. Moreover, on the availability of such distinctions turn issues core to medical ethics — e.g., giving meaning to clichés such as 'treat patients as persons.' By helping us make such distinctions, bioethics can help us as creatures of evolution to act responsibly in terms of our obligations as moral agents. Professors Chisholm and Towers have contributed to our understanding of bioethics by raising central issues that lie behind questions ranging from those of abortion and the definition of death to those concerning planning for the use of the world around us.

University of Texas Medical Branch,
Galveston, Texas

NOTES

[1] One would indeed need to elaborate a meaning of person which met the conditions of being (1) currently self-conscious, or (2) having been self-conscious and maintaining the perduring physical basis for the reawakening of that self-consciousness, in order to understand our obligations to sleeping persons as moral agents. When one says, 'Joe is asleep now, but he will be waking up soon,' one knows, or could have known, who it is

who is asleep, and regarding whom it would still make sense to say 'he is' – i.e., in his intact embodiment. On more careful analysis, it may turn out that the right that sleeping persons have to continue to live is similar to the right that the dead have to have us keep our promises to them – i.e., a claim that exists because they once were self-conscious beings. Moreover, persons are entities that exist over time and over gaps of time which they can unite under an 'I think.' The sleeping person exists in such gaps in self-consciousness, in and through his or her embodiment.

² As Kant put it: 'For it is just the fitness of his maxims to a universal legislation that indicates that he is an end in himself. It also follows that his dignity (his prerogative) over all merely natural beings entails that he must take his maxims from the point of view which regards himself, and hence also every other rational being, as legislative. (The rational beings are, on this account, called persons.) In this way, a world of rational beings (*mundus intelligibilis*) is possible as a realm of ends, because of the legislation belonging to all persons as members' [7].

BIBLIOGRAPHY

1. Aquinas, S. T.: *Summa Contra Gentiles*, Book 3, Chapter 64, in A. Pegis (ed.): 1945, *The Basic Writings of Saint Thomas Aquinas*, vol. 2, Random House, New York.
2. Aquinas, S. T.: *Summa Theologica*; translations from A. Pegis (ed.): 1945, *The Basic Writings of Saint Thomas Aquinas*, Vol. 2, Random House, New York.
3. Chisholm, R. M.: 'Coming Into Being and Passing Away: Can the Metaphysician Help?', this volume, pp. 169–182.
4. Engelhardt, H. T., Jr.: 1976, 'On the Bounds of Freedom: From the Treatment of Fetuses to Euthanasia', *Connecticut Medicine* 40, 51–54, 57.
5. Engelhardt, H. T., Jr.: 1974, 'The Ontology of Abortion', *Ethics* 84, 217–234.
6. Fiske, J.: 1902, *Evolution and Religion in Excursions of an Evolutionist*, in *The Miscellaneous Writings of John Fiske*, vol. 7, Houghton, Mifflin and Company, Boston.
7. Kant, Immanuel: [1785] 1959, *Foundations of the Metaphysics of Morals*, trans. Lewis White Beck, Bobbs-Merrill, New York, pp. 56–57; 1938: *Kants Werke, Akademie Textausgabe*, vol. 4, *Grundlegung zur Metaphysik der Sitten*, Walter de Gruyter, Berlin, pp. 438–39.
8. Towers, B.: 'Ethics in Evolution', this volume, pp. 155–168.

SECTION VI

MORAL AGENTS IN MEDICINE

ALASDAIR MACINTYRE

PATIENTS AS AGENTS

I want to enquire in this paper why most work in medical ethics is so relatively fruitless and why the experience of working at its problems is so often frustrating. It is, I believe, a common experience for doctors, nurses, and others to become very excited when discussion of these problems is first opened up and past silences are broken. There follows a short period of increasing clarity during which disagreements and divisions are formulated. And then nothing or almost nothing. Where everyone had hoped to move towards a constructive resolution of these disagreements, instead they find themselves merely restating them. In such a situation it is worth looking at some of the limitations which have been imposed on our discussions hitherto, even though imposed only by ourselves. They have, I believe, two sources: partly they arise from the common state of moral argument and moral discourse in our culture; and partly they arise from special features of medical institutions and practices. I shall examine each of these in turn and in so doing I shall make two suggestions. The first will be that we have failed to solve the problems of medical ethics, because we have presupposed an answer and a wrong answer to the question: *Whose* problems are the problems of medical ethics? The answer which we have taken for granted is that they are the problems of physicians, surgeons, nurses, medical administrators, and social workers. The answer which we ought to give is that they are the problems of *patients*. My second suggestion will be that we have misclassified the problems by considering separately on the one hand such problems as those of euthanasia, abortion, or the duty of a physician to tell his patients the truth, and on the other hand the problems which concern the place of the physician or surgeon in social life (usually understood as questions about the organization and distribution of health care). Almost all treatments of those problems, including my own, have at least implicitly suggested that the former problems are internal to the practice of medicine and distinct from the merely external political and social problems. I am going to suggest by contrast that a solution to the latter problems may be a precondition for a solution to the former.

S. F. Spicker and H. T. Engelhardt, Jr, (eds.), Philosophical Medical Ethics: Its Nature and Significance, 197–212. All Rights Reserved. Copyright © 1977 by D. Reidel Publishing Company, Dordrecht-Holland.

I

I have argued elsewhere that moral debates in this culture generally have a highly specific form. Disagreement on some particular issue leads back rather quickly to the assertion of two or more sets of incompatible premises. 'The United States ought never to have entered the Vietnamese conflict.' 'Why not?' 'Because all violence is wrong.' 'Because the development of modern weaponry precludes making the kind of distinction between combatants and non-combatants which must be made if a war is to be a just war.' 'Because the Vietnamese were fighting a war of National Liberation.' All three answers, which lead in this case to the same conclusion, lead us back not merely to different premises, but to premises which embody radically different concepts. The first has its ancestry in something like George Fox's interpretation of the Sermon on the Mount, the second in Aquinas' understanding of justice, the third in a version of Marxism which owes more to Fichte than it realizes. And if this is the case with these premises which on this one issue lead to the same conclusion, it is even more obviously the case with those which lead to an opposite conclusion. 'America was right to enter the Vietnamese conflict and merely mistaken in not using tactical nuclear weapons to win it.' 'Why?' 'Because it is only by showing a will to go to the nuclear brink that aggressors can be deterred and war averted.' 'Because America is the custodian of the Western tradition and must repel its Communist enemies whenever they appear.' The latter claim has a long ancestry in all the stages which descend from the Roman concept of the Roman *imperium*; the former goes back beyond Bismarck and Frederick the Great to Machiavelli.

What we are confronted with is the inheritance from a variety of sources of a variety of fragmentary moral views torn from the contexts in which they were originally at home. As a result in moral debate incommensurable premise confronts incommensurable premise. I borrow the term incommensurable from recent philosophy of science to signify that we have no neutral court of appeal or testing-place where these rival claims may be weighed against one common standard. We have no overriding criterion of an established and defensible kind.

Hence important moral arguments in our culture are systematically unsettleable. They become all too soon exercises in assertion and counter-assertion. But it is not simply the case that we lack the means to convince each other rationally. If two reasonable parties to such a moral debate cannot discover criteria, appeal to which will settle the matter impersonally for both, then neither party can be basing his own conviction on such an appeal. Confronted with the dilemma which creates the debate, each individual can only make explicitly or implicitly an arbitrary choice. Unreason and arbitrariness are internalized.

I am not arguing that *all* moral debates in our culture *must* be of this kind but only that *many* in fact *are*; but among these the debates which constitute the problems of medical ethics figure notably. On abortion incommensurable claims about the rights of individuals over their own bodies, about murder as the taking of innocent human life, or about the need to weigh consequences for individual happiness or for world population problems may all compete. On euthanasia we attempt to weigh incommensurable claims about the value of life, the rights of patients, the duty to use extraordinary rather than ordinary means to preserve life, the rightness or wrongness of suicide, and so on. The outcome is invariably an impasse of the kind I have just described, a confrontation of arbitrarinesses, which then leads on to the type of frustration to which I alluded at the very beginning of this paper. But we can at least see now that this frustration and this arbitrariness have nothing specific to do with the special character of the problems of medical ethics; they arise from the general character of moral problems in our culture, that state of confusion which we sometimes dignify with the name of moral pluralism.

II

A second key feature of our moral culture is the loss of any widespread understanding of or allegiance to a particular concept of authority. The word 'authority' is of course and has been applied in a variety of ways and I have no wish to preempt it exclusively. It has been used for example by both political scientists and sociologists primarily to characterize well-established forms of the exercise of political or organizational power; and those who use 'authority' in this sense have commonly given functionalist accounts. Someone has to issue executive instructions in any organization, they have argued; and in any stable organization there must be a well-defined role from which such instructions issue and means for ensuring that they are obeyed. But authority, as I am now concerned with it, is something quite other. Consider the kind of authority wielded by a judge acting in an Anglo—Saxon common law tradition or by a senior schoolteacher or professor in a well-established educational tradition. In each case there is a rule-governed form of practice in which judgments as to how best to understand particular cases or in some

cases how best to reformulate the rules in the light of particular cases are
entrusted to certain individuals in virtue of a recognition of their having a
certain kind of experience and a consequent capacity for judgment.
Judgment is not in any ordinary sense the exercise of a mechanical skill. It
often has to go beyond existing precedents and the present formulations of
generalizations. No set of methodological formulas can ever exhaustively
define what procedures are requisite in the exercise of judgment. Any precept
may at some later stage have to be radically reformulated or even laid aside.
Nonetheless a prerequisite for the carrying on and the growth of such a
tradition is a succession of authoritative voices, so that the wielding of
authority itself becomes something that is transmitted, that is taught and
learnt. Authority cannot exist without institutionalized respect; authority
cannot exist unless we are prepared on some occasions to accept its
judgments as superior to our own, even when our own differ. Authority can
of course be exercised inadequately like any other skill or capacity; and it is
often found irksome especially by the young. In this connection two points
especially must be noticed, The first is that because the exercise of authority
involves both the accumulation of experience and the inheritance and
transmission of a tradition it cannot be wielded by the young and it will
normally be exercised by the oldest members of a society who are still
competent. The second is that although the exercise of authority may be
defective, its continued existence is obviously imcompatible with continuous
rebellion against it or even too frequent questioning of it.

About authority understood in this way I am now going to make three
strong claims. The first concerns its ubiquity. I began from examples of the
practices of law and of education. But authority also plays a key part in the
practices of religion — where such very different exercises of authority as the
rabbinical and the papal both fall under the description which I have
given — and of natural science. What Paul Feyerabend's cogent analyses of
natural science — with their emphasis upon the inadequacy of all general
methodological rules and precepts — reveal, is the necessary place of judgment and authority in science.

Feyerabend has adduced very strong grounds for believing that for any set
of rules of method proposed as an adequate guide to the progress of scientific
enquiry, there is some situation in the history of science in which the use of
just that set would have led science astray. The progress of natural science
therefore has depended on a willingness of members of the scientific
community to go beyond any particular set of rules, no matter how well
established; and this willingness is perhaps most obviously demonstrated in

the ability of the community to move into areas where agreement within the community cannot yet be secured. The early history of quantum mechanics bears striking witness to this ability. Feyerabend at this point in the argument of course moves in a quite different direction from my own. Both of us see an important resemblance between the scientific community and the churches and between the history of science and church history. But Feyerabend is both anticlerical and an anarchist; he therefore wants to repudiate this aspect of tradition and authority in science, becoming in so doing the Emerson of the philosophy of science who substitutes for the slogan 'Every man his own Jesus,' 'Every man his own Galileo.' I draw the opposite conclusion in part because Feyerabend's position seems to entail an entirely subjectivist view of what constitutes progress in science: progress is what each of us is pleased to think it is; whereas the premise from which he and I both begin – that the progress of scientific enquiry would have been inhibited by the adoption of any specific set of methodological precepts as adequate – requires for its truth the adoption of an objectivist view of scientific progress. To put matters elliptically and allusively, it emerges that Lakatos can only have been in the right against Feyerabend, if he was in the wrong against Michael Polanyi; objectivity requires a type of community in which tradition has a due place.

Hence my second thesis moves from the ambiguity of authority to its necessity as an underpinning for the continuity of all those practices which enable rationality to survive and to flourish. At any given moment those engaged in such practices may have to move collectively on to relatively unknown ground; and the possibility of doing so derives from the bestowing of authority on certain persons and/or certain roles. Authority and tradition, thus, on the view that I am taking, supply necessary conditions for the exercise of rationality. This view runs clean counter both to conservatism on the one hand and to liberalism and radicalism on the other; for both of these set up a theoretical opposition between the notions of tradition and authority and those of abstract rationality. A Burke – and his heirs from the French Revolution to the present day – and a Condorcet – and his heirs – at least agree in this. I am delighted to incur the enmity of both.

My third strong claim is that the flourishing of traditions requires a high degree of moral consensus. For no tradition flourishes unless those engaged in its practice can have a high degree of confidence both in each other and in commonly accepted authority. The flourishing of any form of practice requires a shared vision of the goods internal to that practice, shared beliefs about the procedures necessary to achieve these goods and about the allocations of roles and rights within the practice necessary to sustain procedures and achieve goods, and shared acceptance of the constraints necessary if the practice is not to be subverted by the pull of those external goods which often derive from successful practice – power, money, and fame.

All authority, all tradition, all practice require rational criteria; and there are periods when this requirement is so urgent that it may obscure the essential place of authority and tradition in all rational practice. When this is carried to a certain point, authority, in the sense that I have described it, may become incomprehensible; and a quite different concept of authority is substituted, the concept of authority as an organizational necessity. Organizational necessity, on this view, requires that some people direct and others comply. Inequality of power is considered to be of the essence of authority and inequality of money and fame reflect the necessary ways of rewarding effective uses of power. An organization exists to serve certain extrinsic purposes; it may become, it usually does become, more than a means to an end. But its goods are all external to it. This is the crucial distinction between an organization and a practice.

All traditions, all practices, are of course borne by forms of social organization; and there is always some problem about the relationship between authority relative to the relevant form of practice and authority within the organization. But when the traditional authority of practice is lost sight of, all that remains is a notion of authority defined in terms of organizational hierarchy. Something very like this has happened in our own culture.

One presupposition of the constitutional debates which preceded and followed the founding of the Republic was that political institutions were rooted in a morally homogeneous culture, a culture that recognized a number of legitimate centers of authority, of which the state was only one. Churches, schools, and town meetings all expressed forms and traditions of communal practice. What our constitutional documents assert is a need to restrain and limit authority. The Presidency must not become monarchical; no church must usurp the authority of the state; authority must not be irrationally coercive: these are central concerns of the Founding Fathers. Hence the American constitution is a series of *negative* prescriptions whose character alters as the morally homogeneous culture is destroyed by the acids of individualism, of economic competitiveness, of ethnic and religious variety. In the myths of individualist political philosophy, original contracts between autonomous individuals were to provide a foundation for community; in American history to a great degree the reverse has happened. Complex forms of community, with recognized centers of authority, have been dissolved into collections of individuals whose relations are governed only by negative constraints (rights) and contract. Consider the American high school. Originally the school represented the traditions of humanistic literacy in the American community and the teacher was the authority who represented that tradition locally. In the small towns of the Ohio valley in the early nineteenth century the teacher was the link between a high culture whose centers were far away — Boston, Philadelphia, London, Rome — and children whose parents could not themselves be the bearers of that culture, but who knew nonetheless where culture was and who transmitted it. When William Dean Howells went from Ohio to Boston and to Venice he was precisely acknowledging the authority of this web of relationships. In which local American communities today is the role of high school teacher endowed with this kind of significance?

The fate of the high school teacher who becomes first a devalued professional and then a defensive trade unionist, who has himself been taught for fifty years that the content which he has to transmit is less important than the teaching of skills in human relationships and so has lost the only ground for his authority, is heightened by the superstitious belief in youth so rampant in America. It is important to suggest that we do not take the harsh view that we do of aging and the aged because the old are treated so badly. It is rather that we treat the old so badly because of the views that we take of aging and the aged. In a society where the role of tradition is recognized, the old have a corresponding role; take away tradition and the old become functionless and redundant people. Where tradition is recognized, the telling of stories by the old to the young about their own youth and about the inherited past is an indispensable part of the transmission of the culture. When tradition goes unrecognized, the stories of the old become boring anecdotes.

As with aging, so with death. The concept of a tradition is the concept of a relationship extending through generations in which each generation finds the significance of its activity a part of a history which transcends it. No generation can usurp the place of another, and therefore for each there is a time to die. Death is not to be fended off, it is at a certain point to be welcomed and embraced.

I am suggesting conceptual links between the notions of traditions, authority, aging, and dying. For the moment I want to point only to the way in which the concept of education is part of the same cluster of notions. For a culture that has so largely lost its grasp of the concept of tradition, which has to find the significance of the present in the present, aging and dying become threats and a refusal to recognize their occurrence a psychological necessity for many. So arises the fetishism of youth and a precise reversal of roles. The old are not to teach and to discipline, but to envy the young. The final degradation of the high school teacher is at hand.

The general form of an argument has now appeared. All rational practices require the recognition of authority. But the recognition of authority depends on a flourishing of traditions which in turn requires a high degree of moral consensus, and ability to settle moral difference. Yet in the first section of the paper I argued that what we have in our present culture is moral arbitrariness and pluralism. It follows that we ought to expect tradition and authority to have become eroded and this has indeed happened. It follows also that this decay of authority should be expected to lead on to a decline in the possibility of rational practice and I have used the example of the high school teacher in the local American community to suggest that these expectations may also be being realized all too fully. Now medicine too is a rational practice and, if my thesis is correct, medicine too requires the continuous recognition of authority. It therefore becomes necessary to ask what impact these general features of our moral culture have upon medicine and more particularly upon the problem of medical ethics. But before I embark on this enquiry I want to examine certain specific features of medical practice.

III

It is clear that traditionally physicians and surgeons have claimed a kind of authority that has a moral component. Consider the difference between a patient's relationship to his or her physician and the customer's relationship to a restaurant owner or a client's relationship to his lawyer. Nobody in a restaurant tells us what to eat and nobody tells us in which restaurant to eat; within the limits set by price, order, and decorum anyone may eat where or what he will, wisely or unwisely. A lawyer advises his client as to the legal facts and the consequences of taking one course of action rather than another; but it is the client who must make the choices and who is liable for any consequences of his choice. Both restaurant owner and lawyer act under certain constraints; the restaurant owner is required to maintain hygienic standards in his kitchen and the lawyer to observe certain norms of professional conduct. But the customer or client is autonomous and the entirely contractual nature of their relationships is clear. Not so with doctor and patient.

Let us begin with a traditional view of the patient, so admirably analyzed by Parsons, Freidson, and others. To be cast in the role of the sick person is thereby to be absolved to some degree from responsibility; to invite a doctor to treat you as a patient is in certain respects to invite him to take responsibility for you. How much and what kind of responsibility varies with the character of the injury or the disease. Whereas incapacity of a certain kind disqualifies me from being a customer in a restaurant (if I am too drunk or too poor, they throw me out) or a lawyer's client (once it is established that I lack either mental capacity or the appropriate standing in a case, no lawyer will even advise me), it is incapacity that qualifies me as a patient. There are of course cases — a gravely injured and unconscious victim of an automobile accident, a delirious and hallucinating sufferer from an overdose of certain drugs — where the patient *cannot* exercise responsibility any longer. But we ought to note that this is the type of case where we cease to ascribe responsibility, using our ordinary non-medical criteria such as those set out by Aristotle in the *Nicomachean Ethics*; what is significant is the relatively small difference between the way in which physicians assume responsibility for patients in these latter types of case (where everyone would agree that *someone* must assume responsibility) and their assumption of responsibility for and over patients who suffer from a variety of aches, pains, swellings, fevers, and bruises, but who are in no way incapacitated for the exercise of responsibility according to our ordinary non-medical criteria. Traditionally, the patient puts himself in the doctor's hands. The doctor generally in return does not advise the patient of a variety of possibilities and leave the patient to decide; he generally does not in fact reveal to the patient his own processes of thinking in the way that a lawyer often and characteristically does, suppressing particularly such words as 'if', 'perhaps', 'but', and 'probably'. Instead he *tells* the patient what is necessary. The characteristic tone of voice of a doctor speaking to a patient is very different from that of either a waiter to a customer or a lawyer to a client. It signals a relationship which although it has important contractual elements is more and other than contractual.

This assumption of responsibility has no necessary connection with the possession of the technical skills of the physician or surgeon. It is a matter of history how the two came to be conjoined. The authority of the doctor over the patient is not of course the only kind of authority exercised in medical practice; there is also the authority of the senior physician or surgeon over the junior, the authority of the master craftsman over both the journeyman and the apprentice. These two forms of authority also have no necessary connection, and that this is so is made clear by the way in which junior doctors are taught to assume responsibility over and for patients in precisely the way that their seniors do. Gradations of authority within the medical profession are *not* reflected in the type of authority exercised over the patient.

In our culture only this kind of medical authority does not appear to us as odd and singular as it is, because we are familiarized with it from early childhood; but when we do learn to notice it, its oddity is all the more obtrusive because it is so very nearly without parallel in the rest of our social experience. I therefore now ask the question: in what setting would this oddity disappear? What background of beliefs and practices is required to make the exercise and acceptance of this kind of medical authority an intelligible phenomenon?

Consider a culture where there is a clear and established view of the good for man and where there is a rational consensus on the hierarchy of human goods. The variety of human practices is normatively ordered in terms of the goods which are internal to them and for each practice there is a profession specifically entrusted with the pursuit of that good and with the cultivation of those virtues necessary to achieve it. So the good of national independence is entrusted to the military profession, along with the virtues of courage and strategic thinking. The goods of rational enquiry are entrusted to the learned professions, along with the virtues of intellectual honesty, self-criticism, and theoretical thinking. The good of health is entrusted to the medical profession with its concomitant virtues. There is a moral division of labor and each part of the society has to repose trust in the other. We all entrust our young men and ourselves when young to the military authorities, our children and ourselves when children to the educational authorities, and our sick and ourselves when sick to the medical authorities. The distribution of powers is justified by the relationship of professions, goods, and virtues.

There never of course has been a society which was other than a radically imperfect version of this pattern. But the existence of concurrence in something like this pattern is the presupposition of the traditional understanding of military, educational, and medical authority. I even grossly oversimplify in suggesting that in the European culture which was the predecessor of our own, a culture whose dates run roughly from 1600 to 1850 and whose Eastern outpost was Königsberg, its Western the Ohio valley, this pattern of social life dominated our practices; but it did at least provide the accepted standard by which the society criticized itself. It was the view of man and his powers and his goods which legitimated social criticism. It was this view which provided the Ideal Type, or one of the Ideal Types, in the light of which social reality was not only judged, but also interpreted. And it is this view which increasingly informs the life, at least of university-educated physicians, in that culture after 1700. The portraits of the nineteenth century doctor in George Eliot and Flaubert testify to its continuing influence.

Remove this background and a profession becomes something anomalous and not wholly intelligible — not quite a craftsman's guild, not quite a trade union of skilled workers, not quite anything. Its various characteristics have lost their connection with the principles which made of their variety a relatively unified whole. This is what has happened in our culture, so I am suggesting, to such professions as schoolteaching and medicine, and it at once makes their peculiar claims to authority implausible and unintelligible. The recognition of authority and the concept of a profession are inseparably linked.

IV

Consider now another facet of the traditional doctor—patient relationship. In more traditional communities the same doctor treated the same patient for the whole of, or at least long parts of, his life. He was present at both birth and death. He treated whole families and not just individuals. His own private life was transparent to his local community. His relationship to the clergy and to the schoolteacher of the same community was a clear one. All three linked the small and intimate details of local pain, ignorance, and sin to a larger social and cosmic realm. They were moral and metaphysical presences. Modern medical practice and its social circumstances have destroyed this visibility. The patient may not see the same doctor even during the same illness on any two successive occasions; different doctors attend to different members of the family and to different parts of the body. The technical division of labor in modern medicine is incompatible with and helped to destroy the moral division of labor in traditional society.

The modern patient therefore approaches the physician as stranger to stranger; and the very proper fear and suspicion that we have of strangers extends equally properly to our encounter with physicians. We do not and cannot know what to expect of them. This situation is met in medicine as elsewhere by supplying organizational guarantees. The impersonal standards and structures of a bureaucracy are intended to ensure that we can confront *any* individual who fills a given role with exactly the same expectations of exactly the same outcomes. The individual is trained to fulfill a function and so to be substitutable for any other individual with the same training.

What often goes unnoticed is that what appear to be the same professional and moral rules, embodied in the same verbal formulas, may radically change their impact and meaning when they are carried over from a context of traditional social authority embodied in persons to a bureaucratic context where the rules govern functions and not persons. Let me note two possible aspects of such a change.

The first concerns the interpretation of the rules. All rules require interpretation. Consider the traditional overriding importance of the medical profession: to preserve life by any necessary means. Now consider the military surgeon on the battlefield surrounded by gravely wounded soldiers. Does this imperative require him to devote every possible effort to each man in turn, no matter how long this takes in each case? OR to rush from man to man doing whatever may be most effective in the shortest possible time? The imperative demand to preserve life is by itself necessarily silent. So in handing over authority to the traditional family doctor, we conferred on him a personal right of interpretation in virtue of his moral status. But bureaucracy aspires to remove rules from contexts of interpretation as far as possible; for it wants to substitute uniformity of expectations and predictive reliability for trust in persons. The outcome is imposed interpretation. Such imposition may reflect either a strong consensus in the relevant bureaucratic population — in this case physicians, surgeons, nurses, medical administrators, and so on — or it may reflect a deep lack of consensus, not representing a common mind, but substituting for one.

The second change in the impact and meaning of rules concerns their *sanctions*. In the traditional structures authority always is, and always is known to be, fallible. But it may fail us in two ways. The very notion of judgment involves an area in which the possibility of error may arise; and occasional honest error is therefore never culpable and never a ground for doubting or dispensing with authority. The traditional physician's mistakes are not so much his or her own errors, as they are mistakes deriving from the very nature of his activity. What a traditional authority must not do, and a traditional physician must not do, is to abuse the trust reposed in him by, for example, experimenting on a patient with new drugs without having received the patient's consent. Intellectual error is tolerable within the context of a trust that has not been abused; it provides no ground for accusation of breach of contract precisely because the relationship of patient to physician is not merely or even primarily contractual.

But it is a salient fact of modern medicine that physician error does provide a ground for accusations of malpractice and it does so because the relationship between physician and patient has been reduced to a purely contractual one.

V

It may be thought that the conclusion to which I have been moving is that we ought to try and move towards an older and more traditional social world. But I shall leave that Utopian fantasy to the conservatives. If, as I have suggested, we stand among ruins, it is important to recognize that they are ruins. What would it be to recognize this in the realm of medical ethics?

A first prerequisite is to acknowledge that traditional medical authority cannot now be vindicated; and that to try to sustain or rebuild it is to engage in a dramatic charade. The social and intellectual context which conferred moral authority on the physician or surgeon has been too far destroyed. A second prerequisite is to recognize the nature of the condition which moral dissensus, moral pluralism, has imposed upon us.

The intellectual fathers of modern individualism envisaged an original state of nature in which isolated individuals who had not yet come together in political society existed in a condition where each man's self-preservation and self-defence were his own business. Some of them, and notably Hobbes, disowned the view that in speaking of such a state of nature they were making historical claims about the past; what, on Hobbes' own account, he described was the state into which we *would* fall if the bonds of political society were ever to be dissolved. It is not necessary to accept Hobbes' view either of individual human nature or of the bonds of society to hold that something like such a dissolution of community tending towards an individualistic state of nature has been at work in American society — and in many other advanced societies — for a very long time now. We are increasingly strangers to each other, reduced not so much to the condition of Hobbesian isolated individuals as to that of inhabitants of small communities at home or at work which survive as fragile islands of moral community in the larger chaos. It is a condition perhaps not unlike that of Benedictine monks in the Dark Ages or of small Roman communities surviving among the barbarian invasions. But they at least knew that they lived among catastrophe and disaster; whereas part of the character of our catastrophe and disaster arises precisely from the fact that its very occurrence goes so largely unrecognized.

What they had lost included both a community of established and shared beliefs *and* the material artifacts of culture. When the latter disappear it is easy to acknowledge the loss of the former two. But when the former disappear, while the latter still remain, it is much harder to recognize our condition.

Consider the examples, which I cited earlier, those of aging and dying. How we treat the aging and the dying and how we ourselves behave as we age and then die will depend in crucial part on what framework of beliefs we possess which enables us to identify aging and dying as particular kinds of social or cosmic events, possessing particular kinds of social or cosmic events, possessing particular kinds of significance or insignificance. Spinoza's 'The free man thinks of nothing less than of dying' cannot be understood except in terms of the whole argument of the *Ethics*; the Catholic Christian who places a skull on his mantelpiece presupposes a quite different set of metaphysical beliefs; and the lady with the blue rinse in Florida who behaves as if she were twenty, but who knows all too well that she is seventy-five, is as frenetic as she is because she does not know what kind of experiences she is undergoing.

Where a community of moral and metaphysical beliefs is lacking, trust between strangers becomes much more questionable than when we can safely assume such a community. Nobody can rely on anyone else's judgments on his or her behalf until he or she knows what the other person believes. It follows that nobody can accept the moral authority of another in virtue simply of his professional position. We are thrust back by our social condition into a form of moral autonomy.

Individualist moral philosophers have often portrayed autonomy as a central moral good. In the perspective in which I have been viewing the problems of ethics, it is rather a situation of last resort. But when we are in that situation truthfulness and integrity both demand that we allow nobody else to make our own decisions for us. At this point we have to remind ourselves that health, the preservation of life, and freedom from pain are goods which agents desire and seek for themselves, and that physicians, surgeons, nurses, and others are only brought on the scene in the first place because so often we are incompetent at securing our own health. What now we need to add to this is an understanding that there is no longer in our culture any moral authority to whom we can hand over judgment as to how these goods are to be related to each other, which is to have priority over which, and how they are related to other human goods. It follows that each patient has to be given the autonomy which will enable him or her to decide where he or she stands on such issues as euthanasia and abortion. We cannot expect any uniformity of choice on the part of patients, but at least no one will be imposing his choice on anyone else. What would the consequences of such a shift in the locus of decision-making be for doctors and for patients?

For doctors it is clear that there would be one centrally important consequence. They would no longer need to abide by one enforced moral code. It would be necessary of course to enforce on every practicing physician or surgeon and on every hospital or clinic that they publish the code held and practiced; and it would also be necessary to enforce the practice of the published code. Patients would then be able to choose to whom they would entrust their medical care with a clear understanding of the moral stances of everyone involved.

But what of the patient who is in no position to assume such a responsibility — the unconscious or delirious or mentally ill or retarded patient, for example? Here we ought to use the same procedures that we use elsewhere in our social life. We should establish means by which someone else — parent or child or designated friend — can assume responsibility in an emergency; we should make it at least easy and perhaps obligatory for all adults of sound mind to indicate what they want done to and for them if they cease to be able to exercise responsibility. We have to redefine the whole concept of the sick role in its relation to responsibility.

One obvious objection to this view is that it places a tremendous moral burden on every ordinary person; the problems of medical ethics become everyone's problems. But this of course is what they are anyway and to maintain the fiction that the medical profession can still defensibly claim moral authority in medical areas is to disguise our true condition, just because that authority is now a fiction. We have to invite patients to become active moral agents in an area where they have been passive; patients have to become agents.

A second objection might be phrased as follows: what you are advocating is surrendering to the confusions of the present. Clearly your earlier argument about the decline of the traditional authority of the high school teacher implied that that decline had had disastrous consequences and presumably ought to be resisted. Whereas you are now suggesting that a decline in the traditional authority of the physician ought to be a goal of policy. Surely this is grossly inconsistent.

The reply to this rejoinder is as follows: what makes the problems of medical ethics unresolvable in our culture is the lack of any shared background of beliefs which could provide a context for moral reasoning by providing a view of human nature and society. The morals and politics of pluralism try to provide out of the resources of the present a basis for both educational and medical practice — but those resources are too slender to make success possible. What is possible is to work with those with whom one does share sufficient beliefs to rescue and to recreate authority within communities that will break with the pluralist ethos. In education this means the creation and defense of high school and college curricula which do recognize tradition and authority of various kinds. In medicine it means working for a variety of new forms of medical community, each with its own shared moral allegiance. Within these the notion of authority could again begin to find context and content. But to ask precisely what forms it might take is to ask for a kind of vision of the future which the predicaments of the present will not allow us.

Boston University,
Boston, Massachusetts

EDMUND D. PELLEGRINO

MORAL AGENCY AND PROFESSIONAL ETHICS:
SOME NOTES ON TRANSFORMATION OF THE
PHYSICIAN–PATIENT ENCOUNTER

It is inevitable in a modern democracy which limits all absolute authority that all privileged groups should come under like scrutiny. What is surprising is that medicine and the other professions have only lately been called upon to submit their claims to moral authority to examination and justification.

At stake is the 2500-year-old image of the physician as a benign, authoritarian, authoritative, self-regulating member of an élite and noble corps endowed with special moral authority over the lives of those who seek his assistance. We cannot know what the new image will ultimately look like, nor whether patients will be better served by it. But the issue has been joined, and MacIntyre's essay lays bare the conceptual basis for today's most serious challenge to medicine.

My commentary will outline some of the further implications of the transfer of moral authority from physician to patients which MacIntyre argues by the *via negativa*. I shall argue for a similar conclusion by the *via positiva*, because I believe that a new foundation for professional medical ethics is required, one that is founded in the situation of being ill, and not in the socio-historical facts of medicine as a privileged profession.

MacIntyre's paper — and these comments — are in the domain of professional medical ethics, which should be distinguished at the outset from the more intensively cultivated domain of bioethics. Professional medical ethics deals with the normative questions inherent in the function of the physician *qua* physician — what his obligations are in that special relationship of the medical encounter, independent of the problem for which the patient seeks assistance. Bioethics concerns itself with the normative questions which inhere in the application of medical knowledge to specific problems like euthanasia, abortion, genetic and behavioral modification and the like. The first domain focuses on the interrelationships between persons, the second with the interaction between technological possibilities and human values. While they often overlap, these two domains are never precisely congruent.

S. F. Spicker and H. T. Engelhardt, Jr. (eds.), Philosophical Medical Ethics: Its Nature and Significance, 213–220. *All Rights Reserved. Copyright* © 1977 *by D. Reidel Publishing Company, Dordrecht-Holland.*

MacIntyre's line of argument is straightforward and cogent. The physician's traditional moral authority, and therefore his warrant for acting as moral agent for his patient, has been eroded by the compromise in our times of traditional concepts of authority and lack of moral consensus which could form the basis for settling moral differences. The patient must in consequence become his own moral agent and the physician must be far more explicit than ever before in the declaration of his own values, as well as permitting the patient to make his own moral choices about prolongation of life, rejection of treatment, abortion or selection of alternatives even in more ordinary clinical encounters.

The immediate effect of this line of argument is to open up a whole series of new questions which inevitably arise out of the confusion attending the dissolution of any idea firmly held by previous generations. Granting that criticisms of physicians and their authority are current themes in writers, cartoonists and polemicists from Martial through Bernard Shaw and Ivan Illich in our day, the majority of patients still expect physicians to act for them. What new partitioning of responsibilities and moral authority will emerge from the transference which MacIntyre espouses?

If physicians are expected to state their moral principles and their values, this means that increasingly patients must clarify their own. Is this asking too much? Some patients are educated and reflective enough to define what they believe in. But for some time to come, others will fail to see the implications of the moral choices in medical decisions. Is it the physician's responsibility to educate the patient morally as well as medically? Can he do so without compromising his own value system or imposing it upon his patient?

What is called for is something altogether salubrious in a democratic society: the determination by patients and physicians of what they hold to be inviolate and the ordering of each other's values in making medical decisions. But to be effective as moral agents, patients will need more education in moral reflection than is now very common. This is beginning to take place in colleges to some extent. But these issues will have to be broached in high schools, the public media, churches, and social groups if every patient is to exercise his medical options wisely.

If physicians must make their value systems known, so too will the institutions within which they work. For, once within an institutional frame the physician and his patient become part of a matrix of accountability which extends to the administration and the Board of Trustees. Institutional ethics is a region largely unexplored, but if patients are to act truly as moral agents, they must also know a hospital's position on the important moral issues. How can the obligations to enhance the patient's moral agency be defined institutionally and distributed among the functionaries? Is it not an institutional obligation to assure that the physicians who function within it do indeed allow the moral agency of each patient to be exercised? [9].

What residuum of obligations remains to physicians when patients do, in fact, become moral agents? For one thing, the physician will be expected to act in conformity with his declared values and guarantee those of his patient. But simply declaring values is not enough; the physician will still need a considerable measure of moral 'discretionary' space. The exigencies of clinical medicine are often — though certainly not always — such that on-the-spot decisions must be taken, as during an operation, a complicated diagnostic procedure, or emergencies. The careful declaration and calm exchange of views on moral choices which can occur in elective procedures is disturbed by emergencies, or when the patient is not conscious. Medicine is the science of particular cases and a large residuum of moral decisions must be made *ad hoc* — even when the general principles are clear and declared beforehand by physician and patient.

How much license will we permit physicians to do what traditional authority has customarily done — judge between rival claims or modify principles in exigent circumstances? Manifestly, the more urgent the situation the less requirement will there be for consulting patient or family. Where is the delicate balance drawn between assuming moral authority on the justification of an emergency and over-stepping the patient's moral agency? How does the patient keep the physician informed of changes in his own values? To what extent can a declaration made several years before bind in a clinical situation years later?

It is banal to say that moral choices are more often between two good things in conflict than between good and evil. What happens when two of a patient's moral values come into conflict? We can easily imagine the patient with an incurable illness who asks not to be kept alive but who also wants to be free of pain and suffering and also to have every chance of survival if it is at all possible. In such conflicts how can the physician be sure that the alternatives are really understood? Is he not expected to make some recommendation of how to relate one value to another? When surrogates make these decisions for patients, the physician must be sure the patient's interests are being represented — and there is no assurance they will be, even with a trusted surrogate.

What must not be overlooked is that physicians are also moral agents with values of their own. While they cannot morally impose their moral decisions on patients, neither can physicians be expected to subordinate their beliefs wholly to those of their patients. The medical encounter represents in fact the intersection of several value systems — those of the patient, of the physician, of the institution, and of society. Each system may make different demands. The physician who is morally opposed to abortion cannot perform one simply because his patients exercise moral agency in its favor, or because law, social mores, or hospital regulations permit.

To recognize the physician's moral agency, as well as the patient's, places the emphasis on the ethical ground between them which has all the unique dimensions of the I—Thou relationship Buber so perceptively outlines.[1] Clearly the several moral agencies must be reconciled in the ground between persons. Ideally, the decision should be taken mutually and belong to each of the parties involved, but not solely to any single party.

Where the several interacting moral agents cannot reconcile moral differences, one or the other must withdraw. Usually, it will be the physician who must decide whether he can continue to serve a particular patient when the patient's moral agency indicates some action the physician holds to be immoral. This is a difficult challenge to the ancient and long-held view of the physician as a noble, paternalistic, and authoritarian agent. Any new image of the physician must encompass these new features of the physician—patient encounter. A genuinely ethical relationship cannot exist without attention to the bilateral implications of the principle of moral agency and moral autonomy.

There are growing indications that the physician's technical authority may soon come under as critical an inquiry as his moral authority. To be sure, the majority of the public still regards the physician as a technical wonderworker, whose arcane language and knowledge preclude serious question. Physicians too, see their technical authority as unassailable, even if they might be convinced to yield some of their moral authority.

But how long will this immunity last? It is difficult to exercise intelligent moral agency without understanding the technical issues as well. How can a patient decide whether she wishes to run the risks of estrogen therapy or oral contraceptives without knowing a good deal about the risks? The moral issues in the case of Karen Ann Quinlan were inseparable, or even unintelligible without some grasp of the technical facts. The more his technical opinion is aired, the less secure will any individual physician be in making assertions.

The technical authority of the physician will assuredly be challenged as part of the growing skepticism about all expertise in modern society. There is considerable public suspicion that experts may be guided by a set of values or an ideology which preconditions the facts they gather, the way they arrange them, and the alternatives they offer to society. Recently, Kantrowitz suggested that the technical and value decisions of modern technology — like the use of the SST — be disengaged from each other. Professionals, in his view, should make technical recommendations which are then judged and set against human and social values by non-experts [5]. Those who feel, like Illich, that medicine is an ideology which may itself be the cause of ill health, are not insignificant in number [4].

Any reconstruction of the image of the physician in contemporary society will have to accommodate a new openness, therefore, about still another dimension of professional life heretofore taken for granted. Whether a sufficient number of members of society can be educated to exercise both moral and value judgments about the testimony of experts is highly problematic. What we shall need is a renaissance of the capacity of educated citizens to question critically, to reason dialectically, and to evaluate evidence outside their own expertise. In short, those attitudes of mind a liberal education can impart may once again become a premium for leadership in policy making. Philosophical inquiry will once again have to turn to concrete and immediate human issues.

Part of the effort will consist in the sort of clarifications which Professor Hare identified with moral discourse — the clarification of words and the meanings of ethical statements [3]. But it will be essential to go further. The public, the physician, and the patient must identify the bases of their pluralism and the presuppositions upon which they are founded before they can consider how they can be reconciled. If they are irreconcilable or incommensurable, how do we deal morally with the residual conflict?

Clearly, a host of new questions grows out of the thesis MacIntyre has propounded. I have adumbrated some of them — not to undermine that thesis, for I believe it to be sound. There is no other course in a democratic society. What these questions underscore instead is the residuum of moral obligations which still bind the physician, as well as the new obligations which confront him. The ages-old conception of what is normative in the medical encounter must obviously be profoundly altered as a consequence.

MacIntyre argues his case by the *via negativa* — showing how the physician's traditional moral authority is no longer tenable in the face of the general erosion of authority and the disappearance of moral consensus characteristic of our society. While his conclusion is unequivocal, MacIntyre gives the impression of regretting just a bit that things have turned out as they have.

I would like to suggest that the moral agency of patients is derivable by the *via positiva* as well. Its essence has always been buried in the very nature of the fact of illness, and the obligations which bind the physician grow out of that unique fact. What contemporary social and political philosophies impose as a necessity can be seen more positively as a new foundation for professional medical ethics — one perhaps more humanistically founded than traditional medical ethical codes have been.

MacIntyre asserts towards the end of his essay that physicians ' . . . no longer need to abide by one enforced moral code.' ([6], p. 211). All they need do is comply with the need to publish the code held and practiced. This may well be true for the specific choices subsumed under the rubric of bioethics, but it does not completely satisfy the need for a new and refurbished code of professional ethics. Even in a pluralistic moral climate, there is justification for a generally accepted code of ethics which will guide the behavior of physicians as physicians, regardless of the particular clinical situation being addressed. The patient exercises his moral agency, to be sure, by choosing the physician or hospital which most closely matches his own beliefs about how a given situation should be handled. But, there still remains the more general problem of the physician's ethical behavior in a unique personal relationship which can never be managed by prearrangement.

Some delineation of a more generally binding professional medical ethic seems warranted, even though a full development would be inappropriate in this commentary. As I have indicated elsewhere, I believe that the moral agency of patients and several other neglected features of traditional medical codes need to be acknowledged in new progressive codes [7]. My suggestion is that these neglected features are best derived from the impact of the fact of illness on the humanity of the patient [8].

Thus, being ill is in many ways a state of diminished humanity. The patient loses most of the freedoms which we regard as specifically human. His body is no longer the instrument of his will, and he cannot pursue the ends he has defined for his life. The patient is further impeded by pain, disability, or malaise. He has neither the knowledge nor the skill to repair the defect. He becomes dependent upon the power and good will of another person — the physician. The patient lacks the conditions for a free choice of what course he will take in coping with his difficulty. His concept of what is desirable and healthy is limited by the values the physician holds of what is good for him. Finally, the experience of illness shatters the patient's image of himself and his existence, and challenges his identity and his values.

In short, illness takes from us those things we cherish as most human —

our freedom to act in pursuit of aims we ourselves define; to make rational, free, and informed choices; and to do so from a position we have defined as our own. When the patient seeks out the physician, he is implicitly asking, at the least, to be restored to a more fully functional state. That state conforms to his vision of what is required to enjoy a human existence, one in which the freedoms lost in illness are once again operative.

If this is the case, the physician's obligation must be to assist the patient in the restoration of his damaged humanity. He does that by healing the body or easing its discomforts, of course. But he must also repair the defects in knowledge and freedom of the patient to determine the alternatives he wishes to elect and to retain his own values and his identity with them in so doing. The moral agency for which MacIntyre argues by the negative route can, therefore, be a positive obligation, regardless of the existence or non-existence of an accepted concept of authority or a consensus of values. Moral agency, I would argue, is owed the patient by virtue of the situation of being ill and the 'profession' the physician makes to heal the patient. This must include respect for the things most identified with the patient's image of himself and the values through which that image is expressed.

Charles Fried examines the fundamental concerns of the patient in personal medical care and arrives at a somewhat similar conclusion. He asserts that the patient has rights to lucidity, fidelity, autonomy, and humanity, the means by which the physician preserves the patient's life capacity [2].

These considerations — MacIntyre's insistence on the moral autonomy of the patient, Fried's on the patient's rights to preservation of life capacities for realization of a realistic life plan, and our own concentration on the damaged humanity of the sick person — all converge on the need for a revised, fresh, and updated code of professional medical ethics. The inquiry into what shall constitute such a code and from what philosophical basis it should be derived, is one of the most important tasks for medicine and society. MacIntyre's essay opens more widely a necessary and provocative avenue, the exploration of which should advance the discussion materially.

Yale University,
New Haven, Connecticut

NOTE

[1] 'What is peculiarly characteristic of the human world is above all that something takes place between one being and another the like of which can be found nowhere in nature' ([1], p. 203).

BIBLIOGRAPHY

1. Buber, Martin: 1965, *What Is Man?*, trans. by R. G. Smith, Macmillan, New York.
2. Fried, Charles: 1974, *Medical Experimentation: Personal Integrity and Social Policy*, North Holland/American Elsevier, pp. 98–104.
3. Hare, R. M.: 1976, 'Medical Ethics: Can the Moral Philosopher Help?', this volume, pp. 49–61.
4. Illich, Ivan: 1975, *Medical Nemesis: The Expropriation of Health*, Calder & Boyars, London.
5. Kantrowitz, Arthur: 1975, 'Controlling Technology Democratically', *American Scientist* **63**, 505–509.
6. MacIntyre, A.: 1976, 'Patients As Agents', this volume, pp. 197–212.
7. Pellegrino, E. D.: 1973, *Toward an Expanded Medical Ethics: The Hippocratic Ethic Revisited*, ed. by R. J. Bulger, MEDCOM Press, New York, pp. 133–147.
8. Pellegrino, E. D.: 1975, 'The Humanistic Base of Professional Ethics in Medicine', Jubilee Lecture, presented at Memorial University of Newfoundland, May 12, 1975.
9. Pellegrino, E. D.: 1976, 'Hospitals as Moral Agents: Some Notes on Institutional Ethics', Harvey Weiss Lecture, Presented at the Maryland–Delaware Hospital Association Meeting, January 7, 1976.

SECTION VII

Round Table Discussion

THE PHYSICIAN AS MORAL AGENT

OPENING REMARKS

STUART F. SPICKER

In the August, 1975, issue of *The Hastings Center Report* Daniel Callahan remarks that 1975 had been the year which witnessed a 'distinct backlash' in some quarters against bioethics. He cites four significant phenomena, the last of which is the most pervasive: 'There is a sense that much of what is labelled "ethics" represents a casual and irresponsible mischief-making, led by people with little understanding of research or practice' ([1], p. 18). Callahan's 'Scannings' makes its editorial impact by focusing on the hopefully illuminating and healthy tension that presently obtains between members of the scientific community and non-scientists, like philosophers, ethicists, lawyers, and historians. But the 'backlash' also emanates from and has representatives in the clinic, especially among those who practice the medical art, that is, by those who have 'endured the fire' — as Franz Ingelfinger, M.D.,[1] the distinguished editor of *The New England Journal of Medicine*, has put it ([3], p. 914). In the same editorial published in October, 1973, Dr. Ingelfinger remarks, somewhat caustically, that 'this is the heyday of the ethicist in medicine . . . . Yet his precepts are essentially the products of armchair exercise and remain abstract and idealistic until they have been tested in the laboratory of experience' ([3], p. 914). Dr. Ingelfinger is joined in his concern by Dr. Irvine H. Page, one of America's most distinguished physicians, who admits he is 'handicapped by a lack of training in ethics' ([5], p. 32) and who is, perhaps, as Ingelfinger suggests, 'not alone in his doubts about the intrusion of Big Ethics into medical research and practice' ([4], p. 44). Perhaps not a few practicing physicians believe that the umbrella of ethics has become too extensive in its coverage.

For this reason, the Symposium, Philosophical Medical Ethics, was, in part, convened. That is, it has become necessary to clarify, for example, the role of the physician as moral agent in society and to attempt to assuage some doubts and allay some worries on the part of these who are at the leading edge of the backlash. The Round Table Discussion which follows includes the views and reflections of two physicians and two philosophers, all of whom confront the question of the nature and extent of the role of the physician as moral agent. Franz Ingelfinger, for one, is firm in his belief that, for example, 'physicians who recommend or perform abortions must search their reasons and give them a moral basis. They must not,' he asserts, 'under any conditions, merely act as technicians who apply their skills, nor as me-too agents of a non-medical public policy of some sort' ([2], p. 727).

The following reflections by André Hellegers, Sissela Bok, Robert W. Daly, and Daniel Callahan are four perspectives upon the physician as moral agent. They differ in their focus and concern. They share, though, a common interest in coming to terms with the nature of the physician's dilemmas as a moral agent. The preceding discussions in this book have done much to outline moral quandaries in medicine from the patient's or subject's perspective – the patient's rights with regard to euthanasia, rights in the context of experimentation, criteria for determining the point of the death of patients, criteria for deciding when fetuses become persons. Other essays have touched on broad issues such as the way in which philosophical analysis can illuminate moral discourse concerning medicine, the need to see the patient as a moral agent, and reasons to appraise medical ethical issues within the context of our contemporary knowledge of evolution. Here, in closing this volume, we return to the physician's quandary – how is he or she to negotiate a way through the moral problems that medicine raises?

The Round Table Discussion returns to issues signaled in the opening brace of essays by Albert Jonsen and Louis Lasagna. Though the perspectives offered by the discussants are diverse, they indicate the issues that a contemporary professional code of medical ethics must address – conflicting commitments by the physician to patients, profession, nation, and mankind generally. Concepts such as health and disease are embedded in social and political concerns that reach beyond the interaction of any particular physician and patient. As a result, one is forced, as the essays of Professors MacIntyre and Pellegrino show, to appraisals of social and political questions. Medicine in its success is no longer a private issue but one that intrudes upon the commonwealth of all mankind. The physician as a moral agent is a social agent whose conduct must be assessed in terms that transcend but do not subvert the traditional physician–patient relationship. The tensions between patient–centered and society–centered medicine are displayed in the remarks that follow. They invite a reflective assessment of the changing role of the physician and of the goals and values we wish that role to sustain.

This assessment comes at a time in which a sound is correctly heard as a 'backlash in bioethics.' By December, 1975, however, Dr. Ingelfinger had himself interpreted the voice of the philosophers more correctly: Ethicists, he noted, 'do not claim to know the truth. But they do know the philosophical tenets that have shaped mankind's thinking about rightness and wrongness . . . . In spite of his fine character, Dr. Page's honest physician ([5], pp. 32–33) may not make the decisions he would make if he were acquainted with all the arguments and options . . . . The pace of modern medicine has brought the physician face to face with ethical issues that have moved from the theoretical to the practical arena' ([4], p. 43).

NOTE

[1] Dr. Ingelfinger, who was scheduled to participate in the Round Table Discussion, was, with regret, forced to withdraw from participation in the Symposium due to illness. We include some of his views to underscore the importance of the theme of the Round Table Discussion.

BIBLIOGRAPHY

1. Callahan, D.: 1975, 'Scannings: The Ethics Backlash,' *The Hastings Center Report* **5**, 18.
2. Ingelfinger, F. J.: 1971, 'Medical Obligations Imposed by Abortion,' *The New England Journal of Medicine* **284**, 727.
3. Ingelfinger, F. J.: 1973, 'Bedside Ethics and the Hopeless Case,' *The New England Journal of Medicine* **289**, 914.
4. Ingelfinger, F. J.: 1975, 'Ethics and High Blood Pressure,' *The New England Journal Medicine* **292**, 43–44.
5. Page, I. H.: 1974, 'Ethical Troubles: Who's Making the Rules?', *Modern Medicine* **42**, 32–33.

ANDRÉ E. HELLEGERS

In this brief presentation, I shall make a number of assertions about the physician as moral agent, which, if true, should lead us to think that we may be in for a radical change in the way ethics shall be done in the field of medicine in future. The assertions will involve both the changing content and context of medicine. The changes involve both changing medicine and changing morality.

Let me deal with morality first. I take it that there is agreement that in primitive Egyptian medicine, when supernatural powers were invoked in disease theory and the professions of clergyman and physician were often combined in one, there was no distinction between medicine, magic, and religion. The result was that, regardless of the soundness of ethical systems in force, there was at least a theoretical framework *in medicine itself*, which made it conducive to the physician's perception that he had to act as a moral agent. Let me suggest that it is a far cry from such a view of medicine to the Cartesian model in which the body could be seen as a machine, subject to the same laws of mechanistic causality as the rest of material reality.

Let me suggest, next, that a Cartesian model of medicine is not incompatible with the physician's being a moral agent, since it does not deny for man as a whole a transcendental destiny or a teleology. That, however, is a far cry from Monod's nonteleological model of man [2]. I do not assert, either, of course, that Monod's model denies the physician a role as moral agent; I simply assert that to act morally *qua* physician in Monod's model might require different action than in a model with room for a telos in man. And I would assert further that it makes a difference whether it is one's view that *man* has a radical *primacy* in the cosmos, or whether one takes the view of a René Dubos who sees man as needing to be in balance with a cosmos [1]. In fact, I would assert that it makes a radical difference whether one believes that there is a life hereafter and accepts the notion that there will be *a day of last judgment* or whether one does not. It makes a radical difference at least in one's perception of man's ultimate responsibility for future generations, say genetically.

Egyptian medicine, Cartesian medicine, Dubosian cosmological views of man, Monod's view, the existence or nonexistence of a God — none of these denies a moral role to the physician, but the *nature* of that moral role might differ with the philosophical view of man which one holds. At bottom is one's view of man.

Let me next briefly deal with some changes in medicine rather than in views about man. I would assert that there are presently in operation at least four notions of health or disease which might color the views which physicians have of themselves as moral agents.

The oldest view (model 1) would have it that disease is a process of inflammation or degeneration, which, if not corrected, may lead to further change and even death. It is an essentially somatic view of disease and probably best fits the model of the physician which the public has. In this model the physician is the 'saver of lives.'

With the development of epidemiology and biostatistics (or should we call it laboratory and mathematical medicine?), disease is a significant statistical deviation from an alleged bodily norm. In this model (model 2), there need be no complaints or symptoms, there need only be a numerical finding. The disease entities often go by names with the prefixes hyper- and hypo- and they assume a eu- or norm. This model perhaps resides more in Schools of Public Health than in Schools of Medicine. The model is not at loggerheads with the first one, except perhaps in the allocation of resources as between cure and prevention.

A third model of medicine could be called more functional than somatic or mathematical. It would see disease as an inability to function in society. Psychiatry notably belongs to this model of medicine. It is a dangerous model, for it begs the question whether the disease is of the patient or of the society. The perfectly normal Jewish nose in Nazi Germany, or the sagging breast or facial wrinkle in the United States, can become the proper concern for the physician in such a model.

A fourth model is the World Health Organization one, in which health is not the mere absence of disease, but the sense of total physical, mental and social well-being. If taken literally, it could ask of the physician that he prescribe a Cadillac for a patient who has a sense of inferiority from driving a Volkswagen.

Let me suggest that it is of some importance for our subject which model one believes the physician should follow. I suggest that the first two models would have the physician at least focus largely on the patient and that these two models are by and large, amenable to objective quantification. The last two models focus largely on society and are often not amenable to quantification since it is what the patient *senses* which is crucial. In such models, notions such as guilt, sloth, crime, and others become the proper province of the physician rather than of other functionaries, be they clergy, schoolteachers, or police.

If all human·acts and feelings are the result of biochemical phenomena, and if all body chemistry is the province of the physician, then such models make sense.

Accepting all four models simultaneously and seriously makes it the task of the physician to provide infinite life and infinite happiness without harm to others or to the cosmos, with 'the patient' defining whether he or she is diseased rather than the physician. It is, in my view, a dangerous notion. It is also a notion which can make it possible that the physician's role of the future can plausibly be seen as that of body engineer or body manipulator (including the mind with the body). It can make the *ability* to engineer its *warranty*.

It seems to me that a view of medical responsibility that is grounded in models three and four, rather than one and two, makes it quite plausible to change that first principle of former medical ethics: 'primum non nocere.' At least it could change the principle in its locus of application. It might become the physician's role to 'primum non nocere *societati*' rather than 'primum non nocere *patienti*.' Indeed, it could be a warranty for factually harming the patient for the good of society. The so-called 'cost—benefit analysis' would be focused not within the patient but would extend to society, with the patient becoming a means only and not an end also, to put it in Kantian terms. At the risk of gross oversimplification, the notion has elements of a communistic view of life, by which I simply mean to say that it has political as well as medical implications.

In case it is thought that my remarks today are very farfetched, I simply suggest that the debate is already fully upon us. I venture to say that one could find a near majority for the proposition that children who disrupt classes through their hyperactivity should be given drugs not to quiet them for *their* better learning, but for the better learning of the *other* children. The notion of castration as *therapy* rather than as *punishment* for certain sexual crimes is certainly not foreign to us. The notion of uppers and downers to titrate patients into compatibility with their surroundings is also widely practiced. The *patient* is to be treated, rather than the surroundings changed. So seen, abortion can be proper 'therapy' for a woman with an unjust wage.

I have not, in these remarks, made a choice as to which model of medicine *should* prevail. I have brought them up simply to raise the question of *where* the primary locus of a physician's concern might be when he or she is asked to act as moral agent. Is it with the patient or with society? The model of medicine which we have might govern the answer.

Let me here attempt one first, small, partial answer. Since, in models three and four, it is the *patient* who defines a disease, based on the subjectively perceived, rather than the *physician*, based on the objectively quantifiable, the notion of the physician as simple body engineer could place him or her in a position of denying that he or she is a moral agent at all. It could make the patient the sole moral agent in the medical enterprise. This approach is already widely used in abortion, in the prescription of drugs for mood control, in some forms of plastic surgery, and it is also central to the developing debate on euthanasia. It implies that if the physician *can* do, he *must* do, and it is sometimes compounded by a superficial notion of patient's *rights*. There are, I am quite sure, many people who hold that physicians or hospitals *must* do abortions, where no somatic disease is present, because the pregnant woman has *rights*, in the case of abortion called the right to *privacy*. I suggest simply that many people have not thought through the difference between 'abortion on request' and 'abortion on demand.' It is a paradox that many physicians will then perform the abortion on the precise moral grounds that, if *they* do not do it, the woman might exercise her right to privacy in private and abort herself.

What I am here suggesting is that if medicine moves from the individual somatic disease model to the social one, the physician is increasingly asked to render services which have no *moral* warranty in his knowledge *qua physician*, but in which he exercises his mechanical skills, and acts as moral agent, in response to a value perception which he holds *as just another member of the human race* who happens to be skillful at something. It seems to me that, so seen, medicine is increasingly prone not to be governed by an ethics of its *profession* but by the *personal* ethics of the physician, and, of course, of the patient.

For me this demands that we increasingly develop the possibility for physicians to dissent morally from what may, statistically, be 'standard *medical* practices.' Where a pluralism of values reigns, and where medical intervention is based on *value perceptions* rather than on *somatic needs*, in their classical sense described above in models one and two, the exigency of practicing medicine as a moral agent demands the possibility of a *plurality* of practices. I need not tell this audience how difficult it is to square this plurality of moral perceptions with the notion that, in law, malpractice can be determined by some such notion as 'community standards of medical practice.' But that is another matter.

For today I wish simply to reiterate what has been known for a long time. It is that how physicians practice medicine has long been affected by the philosophical perceptions of man which exist at the time they practice. I wish only to suggest today that there is developing, in addition, a tension about the proper *scope* of medicine which results from the notion that *social* diseases can be called *medical* solely because it became technically possible for physicians to intervene. It means that the physician is not only asked to know some medical ethics, but also some social ethics. And it is necessary for the public to realize that often what a physician does morally is not based at all on his moral insight as *a physician*, but is simply based on his own social perceptions.

Finally I need not, of course, stress the fact that there is nothing in premedical or medical education which *morally* qualifies the physician for his views and acts, any more than it qualifies any other human being. Indeed, to the extent that the physician, whether he be in training or in practice, is kept busy learning or practicing technical skills, he is precisely likely to lag behind in the moral discourse. The danger might then become that alleged ethical imperatives will be set by others than he, and that he will lose one of the greatest privileges of life, which is precisely to act as one's own moral agent.

BIBLIOGRAPHY

1.   Dubos, R.: 1970, *Reason Awake*, Columbia University Press, New York, pp. vii–xvii.
2. Monod, J.: 1971, *Chance and Necessity*, Random House, New York.

SISSELA BOK

The physician is a moral agent in several distinct senses of the word 'agent'. I propose to set these forth briefly, and to examine some perplexing ways in which they conflict.

(1) The most basic sense of the word 'agent' is that which implies freedom, competence, and power to act. It is in this sense that an agent is distinguished from a patient, or someone who undergoes some action. When we consider the role of physicians, they are clearly agents of this kind, both personally and as professionals, acting in reasonable competence and freedom. This is the sense of agenthood underlying Wesley's phrase:

He that is not free is not an Agent but a Patient [3].

Three other senses of the word 'agent' have to do with the relationship to others which agenthood usually comports:

(2) An agent is someone who acts *towards* another, with respect to that other. In this sense again, the physician is clearly an agent with respect to those he examines and treats.

(3) A stronger sense of the word 'agent' is causative. An agent is someone or something which produces an effect, as when the moon is an agent bringing about high tides. In this sense, once again, a physician can be an agent, for good or for ill, prescribing drugs so as to combat an infection, for example.

(4) One can be an agent in a fourth sense if one works *on behalf of* a person, or at the behest of that person, as does a literary or theatrical agent. In this sense once again (though perhaps not in a strictly legal interpretation), the physician can be seen as an agent. He acts on behalf of and at the request of patients, so as to free them from suffering and disease, aiming to render

them free to be agents on their behalf once again, and to help them shed the role of patient.

The noun 'patient' in itself has several meanings. As opposed to an agent in the first sense, a patient is someone who undergoes some action, who is acted upon. Second, a patient is someone who suffers or who is in a condition requiring attention of a medical nature. These two senses of the word 'patient' interact, so that the more intensely we accept or are subjected to the role of patienthood, the less able are we to be *agents* in any of the four senses described.

Doctors, then, are agents in four intertwined and at times conflicting senses. They are agents for themselves, with respect to their patients, upon their patients, and on the behalf of these patients. And all moral conflicts for physicians spring, I suggest, from conflicts between the imperatives of these different senses.

How far, for example, should a physician go in being an agent for himself, a medical entrepreneur? To what extent should help for society outweigh action on behalf of an individual patient in experimentation? When does the physician's causative agency fall short of, or exceed, what ought to be done on a patient's behalf? And what does it mean to act on behalf of a patient who refuses the treatment suggested?

I would like to turn, now, to a specific kind of conflict for physician and patient given this framework: the conflict which arises when physicians make decisions as agents on behalf of their patients which may be detrimental to the larger society — choices, moreover, for which these patients might themselves be blamed were they not excused by illness and suffering.

How far can physicians go in devoting a large quantity of scarce medical resources to a single patient? To what extent can such resources be expended on dying patients? How should one decide whether to use drugs to combat mild infections in patients when each use will increase the resistence against these drugs so that future sufferers from more serious afflictions will receive no help? Should physicians be concerned at all about the depletion of scarce resources so long as they do what they can on behalf of their patients?

The moral requirement that the individual at times place the common good before prudential thought for personal welfare is familiar. Many have shared Hobbes' vision of chaos and threats to common survival if all were to act merely on self-serving grounds.

The analogy often used is that of the commons [2]. If everyone sends cattle to graze in the commons, it will be overgrazed and killed. All have to exercise some restraint for the common good. But while such restraint may be possible on a village or family level, it may be that human beings are not now capable of exercising it on a national, much less global, level. We seem at present to be drifting towards an exhaustion, perhaps even an outright destruction of the global resources needed for survival. The inability to work together to conserve energy and to combat starvation threatens to bring us precisely to a Hobbesian state of nature. And the failure to restrain the development of lethal weapons and their sales for national prudential reasons carries yet more imminent threats.

The farther we come from the village level where benefits and harms can be clearly seen, moreover, the more difficult it is to have the imagination required to see the harm done to the commons by individual squandering or lack of forethought. Certain individuals benefit at the expense of an amorphous and distant social whole. And for each individual, the benefit may seem to vastly outweigh the harm thereby done to others, especially since the harm is not done to any one identifiable person.

In medicine as elsewhere, there is little global planning for the commons, and scant sacrifice for the common good. If there is to be restraint, some very hard social choices will have to be made. Professional organizations, governments, hospitals, and courts will have to be involved. But *must* we expect, also, that individual physicians exercise restraint in taking from the common pool of scarce resources for their patients? Or should we hold that physicians, when acting as agents on behalf of their patients, should reach out for every possible advantage for those patients, even at the expense of the common good? In other words, is there an obligation to act prudentially, not to say utterly selfishly, on behalf of others, even when it would be immoral to act thus merely for oneself?

The physician's task is altruistic: to serve others who are often ill, weakened, and in special need of support. Many have held, as a result, that physicians cannot be asked to exercise restraint for the sake of the common good. They have argued that to seek less than the best available help for a patient is a breach of faith with that patient [1]. This has been analogized to abandonment of a patient, an act which has been resisted both in law and in the codes of medical ethics.

This kind of reasoning can be advanced in defense of nearly limitless efforts on behalf of patients. In the words of a colleague at a recent seminar, it points to a credo of 'every man a Franco.'

But is it necessary to regard all consideration for the common good and for scarce resources by physicians as a breach of faith with patients? Must we choose between 'every man a Franco' and the abandonment of patients? I believe that a middle position can be defended. It is based on a more realistic look at that obligation, that promise, held to justify taking all available resources from the commons when a patient is thought to need them.

The way in which such a middle position can be established is the following. The doctor—patient relationship does represent a conscious under-taking of responsibility, a promise of a kind, and it does entail certain responsibilities. But not all promises can rightfully be made. In particular, a promise concerning what is not clearly at one's disposal cannot thus be made. I am reminded of the child who says to another:

> I promised Sara all your marbles. Now I must keep my promise by giving them to her.

In a world of great suffering and acute need, the exhaustion of the commons by those who rely on implicit promises to individual patients may depend upon promises which no one could have been free to make.

Having said this, I must now retreat a little on procedural grounds. For though in principle such questions should be of concern to physicians, the thought that they should weigh such factors in individual cases remains deeply troublesome in practice. Lines are hard to draw, and we would not want a society where patients live in fear that they might end up on the wrong side, from their point of view, of such a line.

What we *can* do, however, given our concern for the commons as well as our reluctance to have physicians weigh pro's and con's in each individual case, is to set forth much more clearly than has yet been done categories of cases where lines are *not* hard to draw, and where physicians should *not* be held back by thoughts of obligations from considering the common good. These are the categories of cases where there is already a conflict between the senses in which the physician is a moral agent — where the physician acts upon the patient, but not in a meaningful sense on that patient's behalf. These are the Francos, the permanently unconscious, and the patients subjected to treatment known not to be needed by them, for the sake of a lack of guidelines, or remuneration, or experimentation.

In all these cases, it is *already* not in the patient's best interests to undergo the treatment. When this treatment is not only unwanted or not needed, but a drain on scarce public resources, a cruel insult to the commons is joined with the injury to the patient. We could not be farther, at such times, from medicine as a truly altruistic practice.

Physicians should consider themselves justified, then, in not taking resources from the commons for patients who will be injured by them, or who cannot use them, or who refuse them outright. It is morally wrong to continue to give blood transfusions to an unconscious dying patient who cannot benefit therefrom. It is even more wrong to use blood transfusions in the unnecessary procedures to which unknowing patients are at times submitted. And it is wrong to force competent patients to accept treatment which they do not wish to receive. The current concern over the Karen Ann Quinlan case and the growing interest in signing Living Wills shows that people are coming to resist both the great suffering and the great squandering of resources which can come at the end of their lives.

Being an agent for others — even for those who are suffering — may therefore not remove us as far from ordinary moral judgment as has been thought. It may not point to ceaseless grasping for scarce resources in the name of being an agent for one's patients. Of course, our society must make greater efforts to remove the burden of choice from health professionals in difficult situations. And, of course, the public must come to protect genuine welfare by thinking of alternatives to letting hospitals and physicians cope alone with the care of the dying and the chronically ill. But physicians, as moral agents, can at times be responsible for protecting the medical commons, as well. Those common resources which are not at present fairly distributed or protected by public standards must be respected by all insofar as possible. There is no licence to squander them, even for seemingly altruistic purposes.

BIBLIOGRAPHY

1. Fried, C.: 1975, 'Rights and Health Care — Beyond Equity and Efficiency', *New England Journal of Medicine* **293**, 241–245.
2. Hiatt, H.: 1975, 'Protecting the Medical Commons: Who is Responsible?', *New England Journal of Medicine* **293**, 235–241.
3. Wesley: 1812, *Sermons*, xvii, 1.4Wks, ix, 224.

ROBERT W. DALY

The idea that physicians can be regarded as moral agents and so be blamed or praised for the morality of their actions is a cardinal tenet of philosophical medical ethics. This idea is grounded in a number of assumptions. Some of these assumptions are about moral agents. Some are about physicians. Four of these assumptions are as follows:

(1)   Like all human agents, physicians, by acting, make actual what is, in the absence of action, merely possible ([2], p. 134).

(2)   Like the actions of any class of agents, the actions of physicians entail the realization, or at least the attempt to realize in practice, one of a number of possible courses of action and the negation of other possible courses of action ([2], p. 190).

(3)   To praise or blame physicians for their actions from a moral point of view, is to criticize such actions as right or wrong (either prospectively or retrospectively) in the light of an awareness that the sort of freedom one has as a human agent depends in part on the intentions of other agents. To quote Professor John Macmurray on this point, 'The inter-relation of agents is a necessary matter of fact. But, it is also a necessary matter of intention' ([3], p. 119).

(4)   The actions of agents who are physicians are in general undertaken in order that the health of human beings be restored, maintained, or improved. As health is health *for* something, it is related in a complex fashion to the ways in which men desire to dispose of their freedom. But 'health' is neither a good which is itself an action nor is it just a state which is a result of what is done or omitted from doing. 'Good health,' which we say we enjoy and which has many forms, is to some greater or lesser extent a matter of good fortune. 'Bad health' which we suffer also has many forms and it is to some greater or lesser extent a matter of misfortune.

The good which physicians attempt to secure not only has many forms, but these dynamic states also depend for their presence on an indefinite and incomplete list of factors, only some of which prove to be the objects of our determination. Health being a good which bears a variable relationship to the powers of men to secure it, the paradigmatic actions of physicians – the performance of healing arts – are usually judged according to the excellence with which these arts are performed and not simply according to whether health is in fact restored, maintained, or improved.

The first three assumptions concern physicians as agents and are expressed in the language of moral philosophy. The fourth assumption is about agents who are physicians. This assumption restates the traditional wisdom of the West concerning the nature of health and of medical practice. My formal contribution to the work before us is to identify and to comment briefly on several *difficulties* which are encountered when one tries to connect assumption four with assumptions one through three. These difficulties are: (a) the lack of agreement among the peoples of the industrialized nation-states regarding the duties of physicians; (b) the problem of perceiving the difference between those moral problems which are intrinsic to modern medicine and those moral problems which are mirrored in medical relationships but which have their origin in some other corner of life; and, (c) the lack of a conceptual scheme for ordering the different sorts of moral knowledge which comprise philosophical medical ethics.

It is not my central purpose here to resolve these difficulties. Instead I intend to expose them to view and to show in principle why these difficulties require our attention if there is to be a discipline called philosophical medical ethics — or, more precisely, a philosophical discipline concerned in part with the morality of acts performed by physicians.

I. THE FIRST DIFFICULTY

As philosophical medical ethics is concerned with the acts of physicians at some level of generality, the first difficulty is to restrict the field of inquiry so that not every action of the physician falls within the purview of that discipline. What is needed is a list of the duties of the physician even if these duties are performed by others who, for good reasons, are not called physicians. But what are the duties of the physician? to poison the political enemies of the State in the interest of national security, or to insure international tranquility? to serve the State by policing the health of the populace? to build community and to be an instrument of social, economic, and political reform? to prolong 'life' — which may amount to nothing more than prolonging dying? 'to deliver immortality and limitless sexual powers to the public at no cost?' [4] to perform abortions and to kill beneficently when the radically infirmed agent desires to end his life? Is healing a person who is sick, injured, deformed, mad, or in pain still the first and distinctive duty of the physician? Is this art and ministry — the art and ministry of healing — still the key to understanding the duty to counsel, to consult, to teach, to inquire, to participate in medical organizations, to prevent infirmities, and to serve as a more or less adequate symbol of every man's wishes, dreams, hopes, and fears regarding health and infirmity, life and death?

The point of these questions is formal. Serious disagreements regarding the basic duties of the physician undermine the starting and finishing points of philosophical medical ethics. If the duties which the agent as physician ought to perform are in dispute, the subject matter of medical ethics cannot be clearly specified and the discipline called philosophical medical ethics will thereby be prone to exhibit a radical instability of form and content.

Current disputations regarding the office of 'physician' have, however, yielded one positive result. It is now recognized that, in consequence of his or her intentions, gifts, desires, inclinations, habits, and duties (however defined), the physician does act in relation to other moral agents. That in so acting, physicians also act as moral agents can no longer be denied — unless one wishes to deny altogether the possibility of human action, and, with this disavowal, defeat the very idea of morality.

II. THE SECOND DIFFICULTY

But if there were a common sense of what duties should in general comprise the office of one who is properly called a physician, and if there were agreements as to when these duties were rightly performed, not only with respect to prudence but with regard to moral rules and some principles of morality, and if various elites could be temperate and easily confine their enthusiasm for casuistry to its proper limits, there would still be moral struggles or conflicts of will among physicians and other agents. But these conflicts would occur between men and women of practical wisdom and those whose deliberations and actions were flawed by deceit, or by ignorance, or by dyscrasia, or by madness. In these circumstances, which are indicative of societies and civilizations more traditional than our own, one would find moral conflicts in the domain of medicine but relatively few moral problems — that is, moral problems of the sort which interest moral philosophers.

We do not, however, live in a primitive or a traditional society but in a society and civilization in which hopes for and expectations of redemption in *this* world are of the greatest consequence. The idea that dying is an aspect of living has, for example, been rejected. Health is now regarded by many as a commodity which can be fabricated or otherwise produced, packaged, and distributed by men, that is, by the workers and managers of the 'health care industry.' More generally, there is now extant among the peoples of the industrialized nations a yearning for a mode of being human which is free of all ills, suffering, and frustrations. Such hopes and expectations, which have grown steadily in the West since the 16th century, are coupled with the moral imperative to work unceasingly for such progress and with the countervailing injunction to eliminate from living, and from living well, every factor, sentiment, or consideration which does not have its place in some vision of passage to a millennium in which all peoples will live forever in perpetual contentment [1]. Fueled in its most recent designs by high octane cybernetics, the engines of ceaseless technological innovation continue to alter the material and the spiritual foundations of our institutions and lives on a weekly, if not a daily, schedule. It cannot be doubted that such imperatives and injunctions are characteristic of many of the moral conflicts which one finds among the *dramatis personae* of the domain of medicine.

The purpose of this side-trip into the historical and social sciences is to draw your attention to another difficulty in relating assumption four to assumptions one through three. It is a difficulty in perceiving the limits of philosophical medical ethics. In the course of time it may be possible to re-establish a working definition of what should and what should not constitute the duties of the physician. That is a matter of deciding what we want physicians to do. But are our moral sentiments, learning, and wisdom equal to the task of perceiving the difference between those moral conflicts and ethical problems which have their origin in the problems of health, and those moral conflicts which are *reflected* in medical relationships (because these relationships are human in every other way as well) but which have their origins in some other corner of life — for example, in one of the ubiquitous, largely implicit moral dilemmas of our age? Without daring to answer this question in an empirical way, I pass at once to a third difficulty which assumes that the answer to this question is in the affirmative.

III. THE THIRD DIFFICULTY

The third difficulty which one encounters in relating assumption four to assumptions one through three is not a problem of social construction or re-construction as is the first difficulty. Nor is it a problem of perception like the second difficulty. The third difficulty is an intellectual problem of a certain kind. It comes to our attention when we reflect on the ways in which agents who are physicians are in fact blamed for their conduct.

The physician is blamed when he uses the office of physician for some end which is clearly beyond the domain of medicine, e.g., to seduce the patient, or to use his relationship with the patient for the sole purpose of securing an economic advantage for himself. We also blame the physician when he practices medicine, but fails, in the process of practicing this art, to obey general moral rules. He does not keep his promises, or he verbally or physically abuses the patient and his family, thereby perpetrating a wrong.

Another type of blame comes about in consequence of incompetence in the practice of medicine — when the physician practices medicine, but does not practice it well. He may lack some trait which one expects a healer of infirmed persons to exhibit. For example, if the physician does not desire to help infirmed persons or is consistently impatient with them, he may properly incur censure. The physician may also be held at fault if he is too preoccupied with his own problems and cannot pay attention to the patient; if he is ignorant and lacks the sort of information he should have in order to perform the right service; or if he lacks essential skills and does not know how to perform some service (e.g., abdominal surgery, cardiac catheterization, psychoanalysis) correctly. The physician is also blamed for errors of judgment — errors regarding when and in relation to whom one should act, or in connection with which act should be performed, or with respect to judgments concerning the role of the patient's personality in shaping his infirmity. There is in addition a fourth kind of blame which can be laid at the feet of the physician. A physician may be well-trained and in general have good habits, but lack the wisdom to understand in what the nature of his goodness as a man and as a physician consists. He may lack the virtue of understanding his place as physician in the community of agents.

If one now examines the moral knowledge that is operative when physicians are blamed in these ways (and there are other ways besides), there appears to be more than one type of moral knowledge at work in the domain of medicine, for example, counsels regarding right action in different sorts of circumstances, canons of prudence, and principles of moral philosophy. The third set of difficulties in relating assumption four to assumptions one through three is this: What types of moral knowledge are operative in medicine, and how are these different types of moral knowledge to be fruitfully related to one another? I shall not attempt to resolve this difficulty. I simply want to observe that communication between and among philosophers and physicians cannot be sustained without an intellectual device for relating moral practice and moral theory in medicine.

The purpose of my remarks has been to expose three difficulties which one encounters in trying to relate some of the assumptions of philosophical medical ethics to one another. Philosophers and physicians engaged in the work of philosophical medical ethics need not cease their reflections on the substantive problems of medical ethics pending the answers to these questions. It is just that we will know more clearly the nature and significance of their reflections when the questions I have posed are answered as well as they can be.

BIBLIOGRAPHY

1. Geiger, T.: 1973, *The Fortunes of the West*, Indiana University Press, Bloomington, chapter 2.
2. Macmurray, J.: 1957, *The Self as Agent*, Faber and Faber, London.
3. Macmurray, J.: 1961, *Persons in Relation*, Faber and Faber, London.
4. Schwartz, H.: 1975, 'Let's Hear It for American Health Care', *Humanistic Approaches to Medicine*, Lecture Series, Upstate Medical Center, Syracuse, New York, November 19, 1975.

DANIEL CALLAHAN

Let me begin with some undeniable and uncontroversial propositions. First, the physician has moral obligations towards his patients, certainly those patients he voluntarily chooses to treat, and probably toward others as well. Second, the primary moral obligation he has toward his patients is that of promoting their medical welfare. Third, the welfare of his individual patients takes moral precedence over whatever other moral obligations he may have toward his profession or his society.

Those propositions, in summary form, represent what can be called the traditional ethics of the medical practitioner. As such, they seem to provide a reasonably clear and uncluttered set of principles for the making of decisions. The only problem with them is that, in actuality, they are no longer all that clear and they are increasingly being cluttered by the claims of other moral obligations. The most obvious kind of problem arises in the instance of the use of respirators to keep alive irreversibly comatose patients. Even if those patients are not 'dead' in terms of brain death criteria, and thus not legally dead, it is not at all evident just what it means to promote their medical welfare. A simple moral solution is to keep the respirator going – 'medical welfare' can be interpreted as being alive rather than being dead. Yet that such a simple moral solution is increasingly being disputed is obvious and needs no elaboration here.

An equally difficult complication is posed by the changing relationship between the physician and society. Physicians have for many decades now been regulated by various laws. Society long ago decided that it had some stake in the conduct of medicine and, in effect, said that the physician has obligations both toward his patient and toward the society. And that was seen as a reasonable enough assumption, even if it led to some muttering among physicians. Of late, however, it seems accurate to say that the public is making increasing incursions into the practice of medicine; the net of public participation and legislative regulation is being cast in a wider and wider arc. Whether one is sympathetic to their complaints or not, it is hard to dispute the claim of many physicians that their professional life is being burdened with a growing web of governmental regulation and bureaucracy.

The question I want to confront here is that of the moral right of a physician to ignore law and regulation when he believes them to be harmful to the medical interests and welfare of his individual patients. If one accepts the traditional proposition that the obligations a physician has to his patients take precedence over all other moral obligations, then it would seem to follow that a physician would have a positive duty to break those laws, or ignore those regulations, which in his judgment would jeopardize his patients.

A wonderfully candid statement of this position appeared recently in the journal *Medical Economics*. In an article entitled 'To Hell With All Those Laws – Let's Be Good Doctors!' Dr. Robert Ray McGee contended that 'as members of a dedicated profession' ([1], p. 99), the physician must run the legal risks of breaking the law, or being sued, or of doing that which is not sanctioned by statute if that is what is required to be a good physician. 'Do what your conscience dictates,' he writes, 'follow your best medical judgment, and take your chances. If you don't you'll be doing your patients a disservice. There's no way to practice good medicine if you let yourself get mired in the wonderland of tangled law that legislators and lawyers have erected around us' ([1], p. 92). As examples of what he means, he cites the turning off of respirators without court approval, the ignoring of informed consent requirements, the prescribing of a controlled drug by phone rather than in writing, and so on. In each case, he argues that the welfare of patients is promoted by ignoring what he calls 'legalistic nonsense' ([1], p. 92).

There are, to put it mildly, a few obvious objections against this stance. The tacit assumption is that physicians are above the law, that they have a higher morality to serve, and that laws and regulations reduce to mere 'legalisms.' Are all laws 'legalisms' or only those which happen to offend the physician? Would it be acceptable for the police to raid this physician's office without a search warrant to protect his patients from him, or to deny him access to a lawyer if he was arrested for breaking one of the laws he admits breaking? Or would he be prone to say that laws restraining the police from doing that which would deny him the protection of law are also just 'legalisms'? Or does he want to have it both ways — the law amounts to 'legalism' when it stands in the way of doing what he thinks best for his patients, but is good law when it allows him to do what he wants to do?

Dr. McGee, unfortunately, does not answer any of these questions. It is not clear that they even occurred to him. Yet all that may be put aside for the moment. Let us assume that this physician and others who share his view are otherwise law-abiding citizens, even citizens who believe in a rule of law. And let us assume further that they would not be pressed this far unless they felt in some strong manner that harm would result to their patients if they did not break the law on occasion. Can a case be made for their breaking the law? Or, to put the matter another way, are physicians moral agents only in relationship to their individual patients or are they moral agents in relationship to society as well?

Let me look at the latter question. Three points can be made. First, there is nothing in the tradition of medicine which says or implies that physicians are not citizens in the same sense that all other people are citizens. Thus there is every reason to believe that they, as beneficiaries of the rights and benefits of citizenship, have the same obligation toward legitimately enacted laws as all other citizens. Second, the same legal remedies are available to physicians as to other citizens. They can lobby to have laws changed and seek court relief if they feel they are being hampered in their work. Third, as physicians they are only allowed to practice in the first place by virtue of licensing and other governmental regulations. The purpose of these regulations is not only to protect the public from incompetent physicians but also to protect the physicians themselves from the presence in their midst of untrained, unqualified quacks. Again, then, they are beneficiaries of the law. It would be egregiously arbitrary to allow them to benefit from law when that is to their advantage and yet allow them to ignore law when it seems to them to be a disadvantage. In sum, the physician is a moral agent as citizen and has obligations toward society.

Second, there is no *a priori* reason why the physician should have the sole power of determining what is beneficial to patients. A distinction needs to be made here. When a physician is acting as physician toward an individual patient, his role is unique. The patient has put himself in the physician's hands and thus expects, as a matter of right, that the physician will do everything possible for his welfare. But there is no reason to believe that the patient has any right to demand that his physician should break the law if that is what his welfare requires. On the contrary, it would seem essential for the needed trust between physician and patient that the patient believe his physician will obey the laws regulating physicians – even if it might be recognized that, on occasion, the physician's acceptance of law might work to the patient's harm. Moreover, the laws about which physicians complain are normally laws put on the books to protect patients. In the nature of the case, laws are not written to deal with each and every idiosyncratic possibility – they are meant to protect patients as a class from a class of actions judged detrimental to their welfare. Inevitably, there can occur special situations where what is true in the generality of cases (i.e., protection of the patient) will not be true in specific situations (i.e., it is quite plausible that a full conveying of the truth to a patient may do that patient more harm than good). Yet this situation is hardly unique to medicine. Law, it has been said, is a blunt instrument, and it is well-recognized that its enforcement may do harm in some individual cases. But that is a necessary price for having laws in the first place. Hence, I would conclude physicians have no unilateral right whatever to break laws designed to protect the rights of patients even if, in individual circumstances, the physician judges that to do so would benefit the welfare of an individual patient. The fact that some patients may be willing to act in collusion with physicians to break the law hardly strengthens the moral case of the latter, no more than it would in any other circumstance where there is a collusion to break the law.

Third, it is well-recognized, even by physicians themselves, that the concept of 'medical judgment' is hardly fixed and objective. It is just what the term implies, a matter of 'judgment.' More than that, even supposedly 'medical' judgments will be suffused with moral values. The purpose of laws designed to protect the rights of patients is precisely to set limits to what may be done in the name of medical judgment; they say, in effect, that society has a stake in what legitimately constitutes such judgment. And since it is society which is the recipient of the possible benefits and harms of the practice of medicine, it is right and appropriate that it should be able to make judgments also.

Taking the above three considerations together, it seems impossible for a physician to claim that his moral duties toward his patients allow him a special license to break the law. Nonetheless, it is perfectly possible to imagine situations where the physician would find himself in an acute crisis of conscience – those situations in which his patient would indeed suffer harm if the law was obeyed. Is he really to allow that harm to come to pass out of respect for his duties as a citizen? Not necessarily. The saving grace of Dr. McGee's position is that, on the face of it, he is willing to be subject to the sanctions of the law — 'take your chances.' There are, I believe, a variety of conceivable circumstances, in medicine as in other areas, where morality would require that the law be broken. The problem, however, is how one is to recognize the possibility of such situations while, at the same time, not making a mockery of the very concept of law? In one way only: by an open and public admission that the law has been broken; society is then able to make its own decision about the legitimacy of his actions. Dr. McGee has done just that.

But even that solution, as clean and consistent as it may appear, has a major drawback. Take the case of informed consent. If a physician decides that full information might do the patient more harm than good, and then goes ahead with a hazardous procedure without getting the legally required consent, and then openly admits after the fact just what he has done, then society is in a position to judge his case; he can be made legally liable. Unfortunately, though, in the meantime his patient has been deprived, by the physician, of his rights, specifically the right to self-determination. Society may have recourse after the fact in punishing the physician for his failure to obey the law. Should the patient die, however, that patient has no recourse whatever. Wrong has been done him, the kind of wrong that cannot be repaired. If a physician can claim the right to do that kind of wrong in the name of conscience, then anything and everything can be equally well justified by the same principle. And that can only be called moral nihilism.

BIBLIOGRAPHY

1. McGee, R. R.: 1976, 'To Hell With All Those Laws — Let's Be Good Doctors', *Medical Economics* 53, 92ff.

H. TRISTRAM ENGELHARDT, JR.

CLOSING REFLECTIONS

This series of remarks leaves us with a charge to reassess the physician's role in terms of increased power and thus increased moral responsibility. The very impotence of pre-contemporary medicine saved it from the need of broad social and political accountability. The fact that medicine can now change the character of human life and enable a new life-style necessitates careful discussion and analysis of the values these realities carry with them. Medicine has enabled urban civilizations to exist without the recurrent fear of decimating plagues of contagious diseases. It has dramatically increased the life expectancy of infants and thus precipitated major crises such as the population explosion with its widespread demands for food and energy. The survival of individuals with chronic disease whose care is costly and who would in the past have died has forced us to consider how to allocate precious medical resources. This success has led to ever-rising expectations on the part of the public for miraculous means of diagnosis and treatment, which, if they were all pursued, would markedly diminish the resources to fund the amenities of the full, healthy life which such medical technologies might enable. Unbounded aspirations pursued under the aegis of seeking better health care cannot but have an impact upon the kinds of lives we can live and the types of societies we can fashion. The physician as a moral agent has become a social and political agent of under-recognized scope and power.

We are left, thus, with the problem of defining the physician's role in circumstances of increased power and increased societal interest in the effects of that power. The moral valence of that role will depend in part on our expectations from medicine and physicians. A careful attention to the meaning and role of values in medicine and the lines of responsibility among physicians, patients, citizens, and societies is an inescapable part of determining the physician's role — of deciding the division of responsibilities among physicians, patients, and society. Philosophical medical ethics has its warrant as a means to attain greater clarity in the midst of these pressing problems.

NOTES ON CONTRIBUTORS

Natalie Abrams, Ph.D., is Philosopher in Residence, New York University Medical Center — Bellevue Hospital, New York City.

Sissela Bok, Ph.D., is a Lecturer at Harvard University and in the Massachusetts Institute of Technology Program in Health and Technology, Cambridge, Massachusetts.

Chester R. Burns, M.D., Ph.D., is James Wade Rockwell Associate Professor of the History of Medicine, and Associate Director, The Institute for the Medical Humanities, and Associate Professor in the Department of Preventive Medicine and Community Health, The University of Texas Medical Branch at Galveston, Texas.

Daniel Callahan, Ph.D., is Director of the Institute of Society, Ethics and Life Sciences, Hastings-on-Hudson, New York.

Roderick M. Chisholm, Ph.D., is Professor of Philosophy and Romero Eltern Professor of Nature Theology, Brown University, Providence, Rhode Island.

Robert W. Daly, M.D., is Professor of Psychiatry, College of Medicine, State University of New York Upstate Medical Center, Syracuse, New York.

H. Tristram Engelhardt, Jr., Ph.D., M.D., is Associate Professor in The Institute for the Medical Humanities and the Department of Preventive Medicine and Community Health, The University of Texas Medical Branch at Galveston, Texas.

Richard M. Hare, M.A. (Oxon.), F.B.A., is White's Professor of Moral Philosophy, Oxford University, Oxford, England.

André E. Hellegers, M.D., is Director, Joseph and Rose Kennedy Institute for the Study of Human Reproduction and Bioethics, Georgetown University, Washington, D.C.

Albert R. Jonsen, Ph.D., is Associate Professor of Bioethics, School of Medicine, University of California at San Francisco.

Marvin Kohl, Ph.D., is Professor of Philosophy, State University College at Fredonia, New York.

Louis Lasagna, M.D., is Professor of Pharmacology and Toxicology and Professor of Medicine, University of Rochester School of Medicine and Dentistry, New York.

S. F. Spicker and H. T. Engelhardt, Jr. (eds.), Philosophical Medical Ethics: Its Nature and Significance, 247–248. All Rights Reserved. Copyright © 1977 by D. Reidel Publishing Company, Dordrecht-Holland.

Alasdair MacIntyre, M.A. (Oxon.), is University Professor of Philosophy and Political Science, Boston University, Massachusetts.

Robert U. Massey, M.D., is Dean, School of Medicine, The University of Connecticut Health Center, Farmington, Connecticut.

Sidney Morgenbesser, Ph.D., is Professor of Philosophy, Columbia University, New York, New York.

Rev. Joseph Owens, M.S.D., D. Litt., is a Senior Fellow in the Pontifical Institute of Mediaeval Studies, Toronto, Canada.

Edmund D. Pellegrino, M.D., is President, Yale-New Haven Medical Center, and Professor of Medicine, Yale University, New Haven, Connecticut.

James Rachels, Ph.D., is Associate Professor of Philosophy, University of Miami, Coral Gables, Florida.

Stuart F. Spicker, Ph.D., is Director of the Division of Humanistic Studies in Medicine and Associate Professor (Philosophy) in the Department of Community Medicine and Health Care, The University of Connecticut Health Center, Farmington, Connecticut.

Bernard Towers, M.B., Ch.B., is Professor of Pediatrics and Anatomy, Center for Health Sciences, University of California at Los Angeles.

John Troyer, Ph.D., is Assistant Professor of Philosophy, University of Connecticut, Storrs, Connecticut.

INDEX